GRINGA

A Contradictory Girlhood

Melissa Hart

SEAL PRESS

Gringa
A Contradictory Girlhood

Published by
Seal Press
A Member of the Perseus Books Group
1700 Fourth Street
Berkeley, California

Library of Congress Cataloging-in-Publication Data

Hart, Melissa, 1970-
  Gringa : a contradictory girlhood / by Melissa Hart.
     p. cm.
  ISBN 978-1-58005-294-8
  1. Hart, Melissa, 1970- 2. California--Biography. I. Title.
  CT275.H38672A3 2009
  612.8'25--dc22

                              2009007525

Cover design by Silverander
Interior design by Amber Pirker
Printed in the United States of America by Maple-Vail
Distributed by Publishers Group West

For my mother

CONTENTS

1 •

SALIDA

My love of Spanish began with a flash card depicting a disembodied ear. "*La oreja.*" I read the words printed on the back and flipped over the card to study the line drawing of a thick and fleshy lobe, a delicate swirling auricle.

"*La oreja*," I said to my mother across the wide table at the public library.

"The ear," she replied and reached up to touch her new gold studs.

In previous months, I'd finished my third-grade homework and accompanied her to lessons in cake decoration—squeezing glossy frosting curlicues from cloth bags topped with star-shaped metal tips—and sewing classes with their baffling array of straight pins and fragile dress patterns. "Too sedate," my mother concluded. "We need to expand our minds. Let's take Spanish."

"Why bother?" my father had demanded that Monday night before our first class. He stood in the doorway of our elegant oak and crystal home with Katie and Tim, my younger sister and brother, still chewing on their honeyed biscuits from dinner. "You want to study something useful? Learn Japanese."

"This is Southern California," my mother retorted. "Patricia Sanchez says in ten years everyone here will be speaking Spanish."

Patricia Sanchez was Tim's new bus driver. The year prior, George had manned the squat orange bus that my brother, born with Down syndrome, rode to school every day. Tall and bald, George announced his arrival by honking the classic "Shave and a Haircut." He always carried bubble gum in his pocket—the kind you unwrap for a comic strip to read while you chewed. He doled the gum out liberally to his students and their siblings. I loved George.

The first day of kindergarten for Tim, the bus rolled up to drop him off and the driver merely honked three perfunctory blasts. Tim tottered down the bus steps supported by a stranger in a navy-blue uniform—someone vaguely frightening with curly black hair allowed to keep its gray and a tanned and wrinkled face devoid of makeup.

"¿Esta un hombre?" I asked, tugging on my mother's sleeve as we walked down the rosebushed path to the street to retrieve my brother.

"It's not a man. She's a woman," my mother whispered, red-faced. "Her name is Patricia Sanchez, and she's fluent in Spanish."

But if Patricia Sanchez heard me questioning her gender, she gave no indication. "See ya, Timmy," she said in a deep, rasping voice. "Adios, Maggie." She climbed up into the driver's seat, navigated our cul-de-sac with ease, and took off with a jaunty wave.

"¡Adios!" my mother echoed.

"Maggie?" I whispered as I trailed her into the house. My mother was Margaret—always had been.

"What happened to George?" I demanded.

"He's got a different route this year." My mother beamed with a sudden, incomprehensible joy. "Patricia Sanchez is our driver now."

There were no Latinos, Chicanos, or Hispanics in our upper-class gated community. There were only people like us. My mother and I pretended allegiance to their Tupperware parties, to their Brownie troops, to their Sunday morning services at the Presbyterian church. But Monday nights at six, we leaped into her brown and white station wagon, cranked up her Joni Mitchell cassette, and burned rubber down Main Street toward the library.

"Spanish is the language of Miguel de Cervantes," my mother told me on the way to class, as she passed the Kmart and the Shell station with its long line of cars waiting for fuel. "*La lengua de Don Quixote.*"

My mind flashed on the gray sock puppet in Mr. Rogers's Neighborhood of Make-Believe. On television, Donkey Hodie lived in an amorphous location called "Someplace Else" after King Friday forbade him to build a windmill beside his castle. But Hodie spoke a braying sort of English, not Spanish.

His dialect ran to snorts and hee-haws. I frowned. Was this what we were going to learn at the library?

My mother paused at a four-way stop beside an oak tree. An enormous yellow ribbon encircled its trunk to commemorate the American hostages in Tehran. Her eyes went to the oak and clouded with sympathy. "*Palabras son libertades,*" she murmured.

I shook my head. "I don't get it."

"Words are freedom," she translated, and drove on to class.

Memory can be a royal pain in the ass. Why can I remember a sock puppet, along with my yellow-and-white-checked Holly Hobbie curtains from Sears and the batlike screeches of sword ferns scraping against my parents' picture window in the arid Santa Ana winds, but not recall my first Spanish teacher? The person responsible for *la oreja*, the instructor who offered me freedom in a packet of flash cards, remains elusive to me.

There were ten of us in that community Spanish class—me, seven middle-aged white people, my mother, and one eager Japanese woman. I have no idea why the others enrolled. Perhaps, like my mother, they'd fallen in love with the romance of the language, with its lyrical cadence and vivid nouns. The images on our thick pack of flash cards are burned into my brain: *la nariz* with its bulbous, comical nose; *la boca* depicting a seductively smiling mouth; *el pelo* showing a shorn lock of hair darker than my mother's teased blond updo, and even darker than my own brown ponytails.

After class, we quizzed each other as we waited in an hour-long line for gas at the station. "*¿El carro?*" she prompted me, rolling her *rs* expertly around her tongue.

"The car," I replied. "*¿El gas?*"

"The gas."

We sat patiently in the crowd of silent cars and shuffled through our flash cards until we'd mastered them all.

"*¿El arból?*" she asked as we passed the same oak tree on our route home. The ends of its yellow ribbon undulated wistfully in the hot Indian summer breeze.

"The tree," I replied. "*¿El padre?*"

"Your father."

In Spanish as in English, he was always "your father." My father. Not her husband.

"*Hola, padre*," I greeted my father as we walked in from class. "*¿Cómo está usted?*"

He sighed heavily, stood up from his enormous orange chair, and turned to head upstairs to his bedroom, where he'd sleep for six hours before dragging himself out of bed at 4:00 AM for his workday commute. Over his shoulder, he addressed me. "Speak English," he said.

Even my little sister, Katie, could say a few words in Spanish, thanks to television. Every afternoon, we dove into my father's chair to keep a date with *Sesame Street*. We giggled at the Ladybugs' Picnic, at the Claymation orange singing Bizet's *Carmen*, at the cartoon owl that hooted *"peligro"* at the rumble of a passing train or a piano falling out of a fifth-story window.

"*Peligro*," I repeated to Katie. "Danger."

Sometimes my mother prepared cheese, olive, and Ortega-chili-speckled triangles of tortilla for us on a TV tray. "Tortilla Flats," she called them, holding up her dog-eared Steinbeck paperback by the same name. But more and more often, she disappeared—summoned by three blasts from the school bus horn—and remained outside talking with Patricia Sanchez long after *Sesame Street* had ended.

I stopped accompanying my mom down the path to retrieve my brother. Instead, I remained in the chair. Unlike George, Patricia spoke little to me. "*¿Cuántos años tienes?*" she asked me once, and since we hadn't gotten to age in our Spanish classes, I attempted to answer with what I had learned.

"*¿La oreja?*"

With no bubble gum forthcoming, I shuffled back up the path to the house, my mother's laughter lilting behind me like the supple strings of Spanish guitars.

One afternoon, my father got home from work early. Katie and I were still stuck together in the chair like Siamese twins, gazing at the TV, when he strode into the kitchen. My mother marched in behind him. She said something I couldn't hear. My father replied in a loud, angry voice. "She's a bad influence. I want you to stop talking to her."

Katie turned up the volume on *Sesame Street*, but my father's words drowned out the puppet salsa band singing in a nightclub. I craned my neck to look at him over the top of the chair. He wore his three-piece brown suit and black tie, incongruous with my mother's cutoffs, bare feet, and inside-out green sweatshirt.

"I'm more than just a housewife and a breeder!" she snapped.

My father paused, digesting this information in silence. The blue-mustached maraca player on TV sang, "*Salida* is the way you go out."

"I've gotta get out of here. I feel like a Stepford wife!"

My father set down his briefcase with a thump of leather against linoleum. "Just what exactly are you proposing, Margaret?"

My mother cleared her throat. "I need a college degree. I can't live like this anymore."

Katie and I leaned forward in the orange chair to catch the lounge singer's words: "There are lots of Spanish words that you might know about / But there's only one best way to say which way is out / And that's *salida* . . . "

The rest of the lyrics vanished beneath my father's thundering reply. "I work nine hours a day, and I expect my goddamn dinner on the table when I get home—not some intellectual who's too busy socializing with a bull dyke to wash the dishes!"

A pan clattered onto the stove. Glass shattered. Rigid, Katie and I stared straight ahead as puppet musicians carried the egomaniacal lead singer out the nightclub's EXIT door.

The move happened quickly—my mother must have planned it for months. First, she found homes for our pets. I walked into our back yard one day to find the enormous rabbit pen empty, the chicken wire door wide open. I didn't mind the loss—the big gray mother bunny had once bitten a sizable chunk out of my thumb, perhaps in feminist protest against her own relentless breeding. But I missed our cat.

"Mommy, where's Stripe?" Katie asked after school one day. Our twenty-pound tabby possessed the disconcerting habit of thrashing his banded tail when eating or sleeping, and purring when someone—usually my brother—pissed him off by pulling his ragged ears. But I hadn't seen him in days.

My mother emerged from the bathroom in her pink velour robe, hair wrapped in a towel. "Stripe is gone," she said.

"Gone?" Katie and I traded a bewildered look. "Did you shake the Meow Mix box?" I demanded. "And do your cat whistle?"

Once, we had forgotten Stripe at my grandmother's house—just headed down south for the six-hour trip home without him. An hour went by before Tim hit his forehead with his hand and said, "That cat is gone." Katie and I began to cry, and my mother made my father turn the station wagon around and drive all the way back to Monterey for our cat.

But now, she merely shrugged off her towel. "Stripe found a new family."

Katie and I stared at her aghast—not because our pet had hightailed it to someone else's food dish, but because our mother was suddenly, inexplicably, a brunette.

"Mommy! Where is your hair?" Katie reached up to feel her own blond pigtails. Her pale brow furrowed in terror.

I gloated. For years, I'd been outnumbered—the dark horse, a brown sheep in a family of blonds. Now my mother's hair gleamed the same chestnut hue as my own.

She rubbed it with a towel. Wet, it hung to her shoulders. Without mascara and lipstick, she looked like our teenage baby sitter. "I needed a change," she said vaguely. "Believe it or not," she added, more to her reflection in the bathroom mirror than to us, "this is my natural color. I might even keep the gray when it shows up."

"¿Por qué?" I demanded. All the women in our neighborhood—the mothers of my friends—patronized Miss Clairol in varying shades of blond.

"Why not?" My mother turned on her blow dryer. When she didn't answer, I shuffled down the shag-carpeted hallway to the room I shared with Katie and lay on my bed. My stuffed Grover puppet reclined against the pillow sham. I picked him up and fastened his Velcro arms around my neck for comfort.

A little while later, three short blasts of a horn sounded in the street below. I longed for George and the simple pleasures of his bald head and bubble gum.

"Honey, it's time to go." My mother paused in the doorway, dressed in her cutoffs and a Wonder Woman T-shirt. Her face, like Lynda Carter's, glowed with excitement and the anticipation of adventure. "Your brother and sister are already in the car."

"Where're we going?"

"I'll tell you later." She handed me the pack of Spanish flash cards bound by a red rubber band. "We need to get a move on, pronto."

I followed her downstairs and outside. Our station wagon stood, motor running and doors open, in the driveway. Katie sat in the back seat. Tim gobbled graham crackers in the front. The short orange bus idled in front of our house, and Patricia Sanchez leaned against the station wagon in her blue uniform. She handed my mother a piece of paper inscribed with a crude map.

My mother gave her a quick hug. "*Hasta la vista. ¡Gracias!*" she added as Patricia climbed into her school bus and gunned the engine. She turned to me. "He'll be home soon. *¡Ándele!*"

"That means 'Hurry up,'" I told Katie as I got into the station wagon. My mother buckled Tim in and jogged around the back to lock the hatch. Four suitcases were crammed into the trunk, along with a box of books. I recognized *Don Quixote de La Mancha*.

My mother jumped into the car and flipped back the ends of her still-damp, newly brown hair. She backed the car out of the driveway without putting on her seat belt.

"Where're we going?" I repeated.

"Someplace else," she replied and sped down the street.

A few months earlier, we'd piled into the wagon to check out a brush fire raging in the foothills near our house. Now I looked up at the clear blue sky. I smelled no smoke—only exhaust as my mother blew through the four-way stop and raced to catch up to the bus. Coming up parallel to it, she thrust her left fist through the open window. "*¡La libertad!*" she cried.

I gazed at the yellow ribbon tied around the thick-trunked oak as we flew past it. Compassion for the hostages gripped my chest. We passed the school where my third-grade teacher had taught me to sing a song about the colors of the rainbow, the park where my Brownie troop had learned to track animal prints in the soft black dirt. Beside me, my sister applied blue eye shadow to the macabre Barbie head mounted on a pink pedestal. "We're going someplace else!" she sang out, plunging a foam-tipped wand into a tray of pink lipstick. "We've got to get gorgeous!"

I gripped the packet of flash cards. The line drawing of a woman's strong-featured face sat on top of the deck. "*La mujer,*" I whispered. The next flash card depicted a drawing for which I held a sort of terrified fascination—a human heart complete with ventricles and chambers. "*El corazón,*" I whispered.

A slow realization washed over me. I flipped through the flash cards once, twice—passed *la oreja* and *la nariz* without a second glance—but the line drawing of *el hombre* had vanished.

Grover still hung around my neck. I plunged my right arm into his furry blue body for comfort and worked his pink mouth up and down with my hand. The station wagon merged onto the freeway. Wind roared through the windows; still, I could hear the word as clearly as if my puppet had spoken it.

"*Salida.*"

TORTILLA FLATS

Shred cheddar or jack cheese, making sure not to grate your knuckles as you dream about *la libertad*. Open a bag of corn tortillas, and inhale deeply. Place six on a baking sheet. Know that to be truly authentic, you would grind the corn and mix the dough yourself. Resolve to buy a mortar and pestle and a tortilla press.

Sprinkle tortillas with shredded cheese. Top with sliced black olives and diced green chilies. Feel guilty that you didn't take the time to roast and peel the chilies yourself because you really wanted to finish that Steinbeck novel.

Place tortillas in oven, and broil until cheese is bubbly, but not burned. While you wait, listen to the laughter of your children as they sit in front of *Sesame Street*. Cut tortillas into wedges and place on a TV tray. Serve hot, garnished with a deep desire for someplace else.

2

IMPOSSIBLE DREAM

A WEEK AFTER SHE RELOCATED US FROM OUR STERILE, SWANKY LOS Angeles suburb to the beachside farming community of Oxnard, my mother traded her station wagon for a blue VW bus. Unlike the gated community where we'd lived with our father, the gritty streets of Oxnard allowed residents to assume whatever identity they wished. My mother longed to return to '60s bohemia. She did so via her new indigo ride with its red plaid curtains and eight-track tape player.

"Look, girls! Peter, Paul & Mary!" She held up a tape, thick as a sandwich, unearthed from a box marked BRIC-A-BRAC that sat among dishes, books, and old record albums for sale on our next-door neighbor's lawn.

The first week in our new town, we combed garage sales in search of home furnishings. In other people's yards, we, who had once been prissy devotees of the Sears home department, now reveled in cigarette-perfumed mattresses sans box springs, most of a twenty-piece dish set emblazoned with a green chicken, and the eight-track *The Best of Peter, Paul & Mary: Ten Years Together.*

"*¿Cuánto cuesta?*" my mother asked, holding the tape out to our new neighbor, who lounged in a lawn chair on his front porch.

Señor Lopez pondered the question and lifted a bottle of Budweiser to his lips before answering. My mother waited patiently. A gleaming red rooster crowed on the fence between our houses, his tail feathers glossy and green in the sun. From an unseen room in the house, I heard the sound of singing—a young male voice.

"We were very happy . . . that Harry married Mary," he sang. He repeated the phrase at a higher note and concluded with a final repetition, a pitch-perfect octave above the first.

His voice moved up a half step, but this time, the song changed: "We were very happy . . . that Harry married Larry. / We were very happy . . . that Harry married Larry. / We were very happy . . . that Harry was a fairy!"

"One dollar!" Señor Lopez hollered over the voice. The rooster crowed from his post on the fence between our houses.

"Fifty cents," my mother countered, undaunted.

Our neighbor swept off his straw hat and shook it in dismay. "*¡Ay, señora!* It's got 'Puff the Magic Dragon.'"

My mother turned the tape over and studied the playlist. "Ah. And 'Blowin' in the Wind.' I see your point. Seventy-five cents, then."

"*Bueno.*"

We listened to the tape as soon as we got home. That's what my mother told us to call the run-down ranch-style house we moved into with her new girlfriend, Patricia Sanchez. Invigorated by the music, Katie and I scampered, coltish, through their half-acre yard of overgrown grass. Monkeylike, we climbed the sprawling loquat and pomegranate trees and hung from our knees on thick branches.

The night after we left my father, we'd unpacked our boxes onto the orange shag carpet that smelled of cat pee. My mother had managed to fill up our suitcases with enough clothes and books that I suspected we weren't merely going on vacation. "How long are we staying here?" I asked her.

She smiled over my head at Patricia. "Forever," she said.

Forever. Already, I missed the community pool, my cat prowling through the rosebushes in my father's back yard. But a strange new excitement gripped me. We were moving, not just stagnant and waiting for something to happen.

I put on my favorite shirt with its alternating orange-carrot, brown-rabbit pattern and embraced my faded Toughskins jeans and beloved hardback copy of *The Velveteen Rabbit*.

"You girls will have this room." My mother and Patricia lugged mattresses to the refinished garage and set up milk crates on bricks to serve as our bookshelves and dressers. They decorated in the same scheme for my brother's tiny room down the hall. "We put Tim in there because it's next to the master bedroom," my mother told me.

"Actually, it's more of a *mistress* bedroom," Patricia chuckled in her growling alto.

My mother caught my eye and saw my confusion. My parents had never flirted in my presence. "I'd better unpack, too," she said quickly and pulled out a sculpture my father had given her for her thirtieth birthday.

Picasso's angular depiction of Don Quixote astride his steed, Rosenante, frightened and fascinated me. In one hand, the skeletal copper knight brandished a shield, in the other, an eight-inch metal spear. The weapon could be slipped out of his grip, but my mother forbade us to touch it. "Someone might poke an eye out," she said. Now she placed the sculpture carefully on a bookshelf beside the ripped orange couch she'd purchased from Señor Lopez for ten dollars.

"Such nice people," she mused as she ran a hand over our new couch. "His boy Kenny is seventeen. Old enough to baby-sit when I find a job."

Normally a statement like this would elicit a flood of questions about Kenny and why she was going back to work when she'd been a housewife for so long, but now my attention stayed focused on the sculpture. "I thought we left Daddy." I prodded the tip of Don Quixote's spear with my index finger. "So why'd you bring his present?"

My mother sighed. "It's not Don Quixote's fault that your father's a repressive misogynist."

A low chuckle rumbled from the bedroom. My mother hugged me to her for an instant. "Honey," she said, "why don't you take Katie and Tim into the back yard and scout out a good spot for a garden? We're not going to have much money until I start working, so we'll need to grow some vegetables."

She vanished into Patricia's room and closed the door. I wanted to place my ear against it, to understand further what had happened to my mother, but the thrill of growing corn and carrots won out over curiosity. "Come on!" I called to my siblings. "We're gonna be farmers!"

We lived in Oxnard for a month before my father found us. I went wild and barefoot, braided my hair like an Indian maiden, and planted a garden of sunflowers and corn next to a rickety chicken coop my mother stocked with baby Rhode Island reds.

She enrolled us in public school. I sat shy and rigid at my desk, surrounded by Latino kids with dirt under their fingernails, like mine. Some of them went to help their parents in the strawberry fields after school, according to the girl who sat beside me. I went home, where Katie and I begged quarters from our mother and walked down Hughes Drive to the 7-Eleven, past our neighbors, who sat on their porches smoking Camels or gathered around open-hooded Camaros while dogs on rope leashes lounged in the sun and Tejano music thumped from boom boxes.

"¡Hola! ¡Hola!" I cried as we walked by. "¡Buenos días!" I yelled out. When the sun beamed overhead I was careful to look at my Winnie the Pooh watch. If it was after twelve, I said, "Buenas tardes."

Some of the neighbors shook their heads and turned away toward tiny televisions propped on porch railings. Others buried themselves in copies of Hispanic News. But most smiled and called back, "¡Hola, niñas!"

"That means 'Hello, girls,'" I told Katie. Where before I'd felt envy, now I pitied my sister's blond ponytails. No one would ever believe her to be Mexican, while I—if I could just dye my hair black and roll my rs—had a chance.

I took as my tutor our baby sitter, Kenny. My mother hired him to watch us after school one day while she interviewed for a job with the local paper. "He's right next door," she said. "What could be more convenient?"

"Say 'rojo.' 'Rrrrrojo.' Rrrrrred!" Kenny coached me, leaning against my mother's worn living room couch, which used to be his father's. He wore tight blue jeans and a salmon-colored sweatshirt with the neckband shorn off Flashdance-style to reveal muscular brown shoulders.

"As soon as I graduate from high school, I'm kissing the Drama Club goodbye and heading for Hollywood," Kenny said, tossing his shoulder-length black hair to release a clovelike fragrance. "I'm gonna make it big, niñas. Just you esperen."

He rolled the r in "esperen" long and sensual around his pink tongue.

"Just you wait," I echoed. "Esperen." Trying to roll my own r, I choked and had to excuse myself to the kitchen for a glass of water.

Kenny pushed my mother's beloved copy of Man of La Mancha into Patricia's Beta player. I hugged my knees to my chest on the carpet and studied Peter O'Toole once again as he transformed himself and his sidekick from doomed Inquisition prisoners into knight and squire cantering across the arid plains of La Mancha.

"To dream the impossible dream . . ." Kenny leaped to his feet and sang the showstopper in a thrilling vibrato.

Katie and I jumped up beside him to join the song. "To fight the unbeatable foe. To bear with unbearable sorrow . . ."

My little brother Tim ran out of the kitchen with the spaghetti colander over his head like a helmet, a yardstick sword in his hand.

"To run where the brave dare not go . . ." Kenny sang.

He had a beautiful voice, or at least it seemed so to me. It was clear with just a hint of nasal. "You've gotta own the song, *niñas*," he told us, one sculptured eyebrow raised above a sardonic eye. "Style is everything."

My heart kept pounding long after the song had ended. After the movie was over, after Don Quixote expired in a stranger's bed and the narrator marched off to face his inquisitors, Kenny led us to the kitchen to make Frito Boats.

"Forget enchiladas and tamales," he told us. He dumped a can of chili into a saucepan and reached for a quartet of snack-size Frito bags. Carefully, he scissored them open along one long edge. "Actors don't have time to roast chilies and soak pinto beans."

He cupped his bag of corn chips in one hand and ladled warm chili straight into it. "A little *queso*, some olives and tomatoes, and a spoon, and you're good to go."

We ate standing in the kitchen, cradling our Frito Boats. "No dishes!" I crowed. "Nothing to wash but a pot and a spoon! It's *maravilloso!*" My *r* came out more of a croak than a trill, but Kenny knew what I meant. He smiled—his white teeth shining in stark contrast to his brown face—and for just a moment, I felt like a part of the Latino community in a city I'd fallen in love with. For a fleeting moment, I felt authentic.

The next Saturday night, Katie and I persuaded our mother and Patricia to take us out for a drive. "Please, Mommy, please can we cruise Saviers?"

Saviers Boulevard cut across Oxnard, linking pricey new beach homes to bullet-riddled shacks. Saturday nights the miles-long road became the asphalt version of a Madrid promenade. Young men and women in lowered sedans, hub caps and tail fins gleaming, cruised up one side of Saviers, made a U-turn at the cinema, and rumbled back down the other side. The *canciónes* of Santana and War blasted from rolled-down windows. Boys peered from under their hairnets or slicked-back dos. Girls vamped from passenger windows, their bangs moussed eight inches high, eyes lined in black, mascara so thick I wondered how they could blink without their lashes sticking shut.

"All right. We'll go cruising," my mother said at last. "We can stop at Sambo's for dessert."

"Yay!" Katie and I yelled in unison, running to the mirror in our shared bathroom. We yanked our bangs upward with a comb and lacquered them with Aqua Net. "Lemme use it. You're hogging it!" Katie reached for my mother's brown eyebrow pencil and spit on the tip, outlining her lids as meticulously as she attended to one of her many coloring books.

"If we're going, let's go!" Patricia called down the hall. "Sambo's closes at nine, and I've got a hankering for onion rings. *Vámonos*, ladies."

My mother helped Tim into the back of the VW bus. Katie and I climbed into the middle seat, Patricia in the front. My mother pushed *The Best of Peter, Paul & Mary* into the eight-track and started the bus.

"How many miles must one man walk . . . before they call him a man!" we sang out the window as the VW rumbled down Hughes Drive and my mother turned right on Saviers. The intoxicating smells of car exhaust and fast food mingled with the salt breeze off the ocean three miles away.

"Oh Stewball was a racehorse . . . and I wish he were mine," we wailed at red lights. Our voices pierced the thumping bass beat from lowered cars all around us, and dark eyes widened in shock as we trilled. "He never drank water. He always drank wine!"

In the back of the bus, Tim pushed aside the plaid curtains and flashed the *hombres* in the Chevy behind us the peace sign.

I loved living in Oxnard. At school, I traded PB&Js for cold tacos, happily snacking on buttered tortillas in exchange for my roll of Oreos. I was the new girl at school, but I made friends with the tough kids who met on the weekends to ransack half-built houses for shiny silver nails and sips of stale beer from discarded bottles.

At home, I sang and gardened and built forts. With pilfered nails in my mouth and a hammer plunged into the back pocket of my overalls, I walked into the living room one day to see if Patricia would let me borrow her cordless drill. My mother stood at the open door glaring at my father on our porch in his brown suit, his mustache lowered over his frowning top lip.

"Hello, Melissa," he said. "I want to take you kids out for dinner."

His eyes took in the peeling paint of the doorjamb, the dandelions growing a foot tall in the front yard, my bare feet and fingernails crusted with garden soil. "Right now."

The force of his tone caused my mother to step backward toward the bookshelf where Don Quixote stood guard with his spear. "Well . . . there's a Sambo's down the street," she faltered.

"Fine, Margaret," he snapped. "We'll be back in an hour."

I hadn't missed my father in the weeks we'd been apart. In my old life, he'd worked nine hours a day and commuted an hour and a half each way to his job. He took long business trips and spent free weekends washing his car and mowing the lawn. Reluctantly, I tugged on my sneakers, and Katie, Tim, and I walked out to the gold Buick.

"Daddy, Lupe's Taqueria is next door to Sambo's," I told him in the car. "Mommy won't mind if we go there."

"It smells like lard," he said, wrinkling his nose as he stepped out of the car and into the parking lot. He looked toward Sambo's bright sign depicting a little turbaned boy with pancakes and a tiger.

"Lupe's has free chips and salsa," my sister pointed out.

He sighed. "Fine, we'll go." My father helped Tim out of the car. "But girls, don't drink the water. I don't want you getting the runs."

From the corner booth at Lupe's, I could just glimpse the light shining yellow in Kenny's house at the end of our street. I could almost hear him running through his vocal exercises and practicing his English elocution.

Once, I'd heard him chastise himself out on his front porch. "It's *ask*, not *acks*, *tonto*."

"What's *tonto* mean?" I asked him later.

"It means stupid," he'd replied.

"Sit up straight, girls." My father's voice broke into my thoughts. "Katie, eat your . . . whatever that is."

I examined the rolled-up tortilla nestled beside scoops of rice and beans on my sister's plate. "It's a *flauta*," I said.

"Well, eat it," he told Katie. He turned his attention to me. "What's it like living with your mom and that woman—what's her name—Pat? Are you ready to come home?"

"*Oxnard es mi hogar*," I replied, just as Kenny had taught me.

"English," my father reminded me, his voice rising. Across the restaurant, our waitress began to walk toward us, caught sight of his expression, and drifted instead to the dessert case of revolving pie and cake slices.

"Oxnard is my home," I mumbled into my cup of *horchata*.

"You can't grow up parented by two women." He pushed his untouched plate of enchiladas away and raised a finger for the bill. "It's unnatural."

A month later, the custody judge echoed his verdict. "I must consider what's best for the children. A woman living with another woman, on a dangerous street with volatile neighbors?"

I pictured Señor Lopez with his Peter, Paul & Mary tapes and his rooster, thought of Kenny and his singing, of his salmon-colored sweatshirt and his bags of Fritos. I held on to my baby sitter's memory as a lifeline when I found myself back in my father's house with ironed skirts and blouses and a standing date at an exclusive after-school day care five days a week.

I promptly contracted head lice.

My mother fared no better. The judge mandated that she would be allowed to see us only every other weekend and one month during the summer. She could call three times a week. One night, she telephoned to report that she'd just returned from the hospital, where she'd had four stitches. "You know that statue I have of Don Quixote?" she asked me.

I nodded silently, gripping my father's phone in both hands. The cord just reached into the laundry room, where I could sit cross-legged on top of the washing machine and close the shuttered doors almost all the way, blocking out my father and his new blond girlfriend, who lingered over their glasses of merlot at the dinner table while my sister and brother watched reruns of *Little House on the Prairie*.

"I lost my balance last night and fell on the thing," my mother continued. "Don Quixote's sword embedded itself in my arm, and I had to have it surgically removed."

"What happened to the statue?" I knew the answer; I hardly dared to ask the question.

"That piece of trash? I threw it out," she replied. "Too dangerous."

I thought of the knight lying forlorn, separated from his weapon atop some landfill. With his fearsome sword, he'd seemed to me a symbol of hope and tenacity. But now he was gone. "Too dangerous," I echoed.

Each time I hung up the phone or watched my mother drive away on a Sunday night, I cried for hours into my pillow with my door locked against inquiry. My father avoided my bedroom those evenings, but one Saturday afternoon, a truck drove up and two men hopped out to deliver an ebony upright piano.

"Surprise . . ." my father said, his voice hopeful. "Guys, put it in the living room."

"I'll drive you to music lessons each week," his girlfriend promised me. "Your daddy says you love to sing."

But the house felt too quiet for music. Each evening after dinner, I perched on the polished ebony piano bench in the living room and gazed at the sheet music my teacher had given me. "Practice an hour each day," the elderly woman chirped every Wednesday at four, "and you'll play with symphonies right out of high school!"

She'd set me up with a book of classic songs for beginners. I plunked out notes to the melodies of "Für Elise" and "Moonlight Sonata," unimpressed with Beethoven and his angst. Different songs spun through my head—lyrics I longed to belt out until the windows of my father's house rattled. Instead, I clamped my foot down on the gold damper pedal to muffle the music and picked out a tune, singing the words to myself in a tiny voice: "We were very happy . . . that Harry married Larry. / We were very happy . . . that Harry married Larry . . ."

FRITO BOATS

Warm up with an irreverent song or two, then dump a can of chili con carne into a saucepan over medium-high heat. Grate the cheese of your choice—busy actors buy cheddar already shredded.

Open a small can of chopped black olives. If you've saved enough money for your relocation to Hollywood, consider springing for a sprig of cilantro or an avocado.

Cut open a snack-size packet of Fritos along one long edge. Cup the "boat" in one hand along with your dreams, impossible or otherwise.

Ladle the chili over corn chips, then sprinkle with cheese and olives, diced green onions, cilantro and/or avocado, and attitude. Grab a fork, and own your Frito Boat. Style is everything.

3 •

CHIMICHANGAS

THE FIRST YEAR AFTER MY PARENTS' DIVORCE, ALL FOUR ADULTS IN MY life turned themselves inside out trying to comfort my siblings and me with various attempts at creating a dinnertime ritual. Knowing that families are built or destroyed in that crucial half hour somewhere between 5:00 and 7:00 PM, they minced and chopped and boiled or scoured the yellow pages for decent takeout while I played them against each other with one goal in mind—to fill the growling emptiness in what I mistook to be my stomach.

For the first eight years of my life, I'd eaten beside my younger sister, Katie, at our white and yellow Formica table. Our chairs were vinyl and padded; they made farting noises when we bounced on them, which we did often. My father presided at the head of the table, my mother at the foot next to Tim, so she could help him cut up his chicken-fried steak or liver and onions.

When my mother left my father, Patricia replaced him in our dinner theater's cast of characters. We ate Patricia's chicken tamales and salsa *picante* while sitting cross-legged on the floor in the Oxnard rental my mother had managed to purchase with my grandmother's help. The Human League thumped from the record player. "Don't you want me, baby?" the lead singer crooned metallically.

"Isn't this fun?" my mother and Patricia prompted us. "Isn't this bohemian?"

"The carpet reeks," I observed.

"You'll have to hold your nose until we can afford a table." My mother ignited a stick of Nag Champa and waved it over me like the Pope bestowing a benediction.

She found a huge old farm-style table at Goodwill for ten dollars, but I only got to sit there two weekends a month, as the authorities had mandated my permanent residence at the ponderous oak slab in my father's dining room.

There, Dad sat at the head of the table, my sister beside me, with Tim just across the polished planks. But now a different woman, willowy and elegant, helped my brother to navigate the sudden appearance of incandescent pink poached salmon and asparagus gratin.

My father's blonde girlfriend had become his wife. Elsa turned out to be a gourmet chef who could stuff and roll a flank steak like nobody's business. She'd tie back her hair with a velvet scrunchie and throw her soul into cooking for us every night. But anxiety clamped my jaw muscles, and I often had difficulty chewing and swallowing anything tougher than a dinner roll. My stomach still rumbled after I'd mined the steak for stuffing and masticated a few stalks of broccoli. "Can you make Mexican food?" I demanded of my stepmother one evening. "My mom's girlfriend makes a killer mole sauce."

Elsa had been living with us six months, and I had yet to see her even attempt *taquitos* or tamales, or tacos and tostadas like those from Taco Bell, which had opened in L.A. that year. I adored the commanding gong that echoed on the television commercials and longed to heed the commentator's suggestion to "go south of the border."

But my new stepmother shook her head. "I don't know much about ethnic cooking."

I could see my father studying me from the couch in the living room where he'd retired to read the *Times* with his after-dinner brandy. I'd caught him listening in on my phone calls to my mother. He knew I yearned to return to her and Patricia, to the rough, raw excitement of their Mexican neighborhood, but the Bible lay on the toilet tank in his downstairs bathroom—a sure sign that I wouldn't remain in their den of damnation a moment longer than legally required.

The next week, he pushed through the back door, home early from work, and surprised Elsa in the midst of her dinner preparation. "Stop slicing and dicing," he commanded merrily. "I'm taking the family out for Mexican food!"

He and my stepmother kissed at length in the kitchen while my sister and I scurried to wash and primp and attire ourselves in the velour dresses Elsa had sewn for us on her Singer. My frock glowed like Santa Fe turquoise, Katie's like the smoky red of a good enchilada sauce. We stepped carefully to the garage in our polished Mary Janes—holding our sweatered little brother by his chubby scrubbed hands—and climbed into our father's Buick for the three-mile drive to Manhattan Beach.

"Take good care of it." He tossed his car keys to the dark-eyed valet who climbed into the leather driver's seat and winked at me. I returned the wink solemnly and followed my father up the marble steps to the restaurant.

Pancho's stood two stories high, a block from the ocean, with burbling fountains and white tablecloths and linen napkins. The waiters, like the diners around us, were Anglo. Aside from the valet in the parking garage below ground, I saw no Latinos. The cooks remained cloistered in the kitchen, and flamenco guitars—tastefully melodious over the sound system—obscured any disconcerting Spanish phrases that might have escaped from behind the swinging door.

I only pretended to read the menu laden with fancy fajitas and shrimp enchiladas. I craved the no-frills foods of Oxnard, the smells of which were magically replicated here, seventy miles away. "*Un taco, arroz, y frijoles, por favor,*" I ordered carefully when the waiter bent toward me in his black pants and cropped bullfighter's jacket with silver braided trim.

This was the meal my mother's neighbors brought her after their backyard fiestas: tacos, rice, and beans commingled on a paper plate, melted *cotija* cheese sticking to foil. Simple food, unadorned except for a stem of cilantro draped across the orange-hued rice like a Mexican four-leaf clover. Lucky food—it stayed with you all night (unlike Chinese chop suey) and left easily in the morning. But I kept my observations to myself at Pancho's and focused on the basket of warm flour tortillas the waiter had brought with a chilled dish of butter.

Candles in orange vases flickered on the round tables. My father ordered steak fajitas and nodded across the table at my glowing stepmother, who requested the catch of the day grilled with lime and tomatoes and chilies. Katie and Tim reclined like royalty in their plastic booster seats and ordered tacos from the child's menu. When the waiter brought our drinks, we clinked our highballed Shirley Temples together, mimicking the celebratory tinkle of my stepmother's margarita glass as it gently acknowledged the one in my father's red-knuckled hand.

"This is such a treat!" she trilled. "Kids, what do you say to your dad?"

"Thank you, Daddy," we chorused.

He smiled benevolently and passed the tortilla basket around once more.

While we were waiting for our meal, I excused myself to the restroom. I spent a long time looking at Pancho's impressive blue and red sombreros mounted above each toilet, then walked slowly back to our table, studying my family. They sat smiling, well-dressed, straight-backed, and possessive of the obligatory father and mother figures. To diners around us, we looked perfect.

Those nights I almost forgot about my mother. Instead, my mind strove to picture the Yucatán Peninsula off the southeast coast of Mexico. According to my stepmother, the ocean undulated bathtub-warm against white sand beaches, and tropical fish fluttered across elaborate coral backdrops.

"I'd love to vacation on the Mayan Riviera," Elsa sighed over her platter of cod. "People eat fresh fish tacos and drink margaritas in restaurants right on the sand."

"Who needs the Riviera?" My father leaned back in his chair and patted his stomach. "Any time you want a vacation, say the word and I'll take you to Pancho's."

But then he received the check. He raised his eyebrows at the waiter. "You've gotta be kidding."

The man bowed his head and murmured with firm deference. "I assure you, sir, I'm not."

My father sighed mightily and ripped his credit card from his wallet. He dropped it with a clatter onto the waiter's silver tray, then turned to my stepmother. "How do you feel about Taco Bell?"

Elsa grimaced behind her napkin. My ears rang with the imagined gong of a bell, and I smiled.

"Pancho's isn't Mexico," I declared to my sister on the way to our mother's house the following weekend. The restaurant bore no resemblance to the culture I knew from my mother's neighbors. Her house in Oxnard lay sandwiched between two abodes famous among local immigrants for their weekend fiestas. From inside the house we could hear mariachi trumpets blaring from competing stereos dragged outdoors for the occasion, and the Saturday morning breeze thickened with the smell of roasting poblano chilies and the men's high-pitched *gritos*.

"*Ay yi yi yi yi yi!*" they yipped, the frequency of their cries correlating to the lateness of the day and the number of Budweisers they'd consumed. I spied on them, peering into knotholes between my mother's fence and theirs. Glorious brown-skinned people surrounded picnic tables that buckled under the weight of casserole dishes and platters and bottles of tequila.

I could see kids through the knotholes; they scampered around in shorts and T-shirts, black hair gleaming as they played games of chase the family rooster. Sometimes my old baby sitter Kenny Lopez came home from Santa Monica College with a gorgeous man who wore gold earrings and Izod shirts. Once, the friend got stuck next to Kenny's fat old father as they gathered to hold hands and pray over the meal. Everyone else stood with heads bowed and eyes closed. From my post behind the fence, I was the sole witness to Kenny's father stuffing his hand into his jeans pocket so he wouldn't have to touch the younger man, whose handsome jaw hardened into stubbled stone.

"Why don't they ever invite us to their parties?" I asked my mother that Sunday morning. Already the *abuelas* on either side of us were clattering their giant cooking pots. They fried onions and garlic, the sacred smell of which blew into our open windows along with Spanish hymns sung in quavering old-lady sopranos. "If we were Catholic, we'd go to church like they do, and then have a picnic with our whole family."

My mother looked at me for a long moment. Her lips tightened. She reached for the yellow hexagonal package of Ibarra chocolate in the cupboard and broke off two triangles into a saucepan of milk. "We're

Unitarians," she said. "And your grandmother and great-grandmother live five hours away."

She gave the hot chocolate a vicious whisking and slopped it into two mugs, pushing one toward me. "Marshmallows?" I bargained.

She handed me the bag. Then suddenly, she brightened. "Let's have a picnic in our back yard!" she said. "Will you help me cook?"

Her culinary specialty was Midwestern food. She'd spent summers as a child with her great-aunts on their farm in Missouri and perfected the arts of fried chicken and garden-fresh green beans cooked—as Patricia said—"until they're good and dead."

That afternoon, we boiled russets and made cornbread. She sliced dill pickles and celery into her potato salad and pushed the bowl over to me. I arranged ovals of hardboiled egg across it in the shape of a daisy.

"Will you and Katie set the table?" My mother handed me the vase of wildflowers from the kitchen windowsill and dropped a Soft Cell album onto the record player. Marc Almond sang about this burning, yearning feeling inside him, and I wondered if he, too, longed for a huge casual family gathered around the red-checkered oilcloth of a picnic table.

What would the neighbors see if they grew tired of their own fiesta and peered through the knothole into my mother's back yard? I'd tied silverware up in cloth napkins with pieces of cornstalk from our garden and put out salt and pepper shakers shaped like cats. We sat—my mother at one end of the table, Patricia at the other—and shoveled in potato salad and fried chicken. Trees heavy with loquats and pomegranates shaded us from the sun, and chickens and cats wandered through the grass around our bare feet.

In an hour, my sister and brother and I would have to pack our overnight bags and load up in our mother's VW bus for the return to Los Angeles and our father's house for ten days. But for now, we chattered and laughed and sang fragments of songs that floated out through the back door. "Baby, baby—where did our love go? Oh, don't you leave me. Don't you leave me no more . . ."

That afternoon, Patricia told jokes. Katie did her impression of a dog chewing its fleas. My brother touched the tip of his nose with his freakishly long tongue, and I played the spoons. We even cajoled our mother into performing her rare King Tut dance—anything to distract ourselves from having to leave.

By the time we'd navigated beach traffic on Highway 1 and miles of red lights on Washington Boulevard, it was 6:00 PM. I stayed in the bus to say my goodbyes to my mother in my father's driveway. That way Ryan, the cute paperboy from my class, wouldn't see me crying if he happened to pedal by.

"I'll see you in ten days, kids." My mother steadied her voice and looked into our faces. "Remember, it's the quality, not the quantity, of our time together that counts."

Tim and Katie and I nodded and shuffled across the closely cropped lawn, past the drooping willow tree to our father's front porch. We stood and waved as our mother backed out of the driveway. Through the window, we saw her face crumple. She wiped her eyes on her shirt and wrenched the gearshift into first. We closed the curtains so we wouldn't have to watch the bus disappear around the corner.

Instantly, the warm, dizzying scents of cumin and oregano and cayenne embraced us. My stepmother stood in the kitchen doorway, wearing a floral apron and holding a wooden spoon red with sauce. Sweat beaded her upper lip.

She smiled kindly when she saw us. "Hello, kids! Dinner's ready, so go wash your hands, and come to the table."

Katie and I looked at each other. Three hours earlier, we'd stuffed ourselves with potato salad and green beans and the peach cobbler we'd helped to construct. I'd planned on locking myself into my bedroom and crying until I fell asleep, but the warm scent of flour tortillas beckoned. "It smells like Pancho's," I reasoned to my sister and brother as we washed our hands in our bathroom. "We've got to eat a little."

My father sat in his usual place at the head of the table. He smiled eagerly at us, but his eyes narrowed at my downcast mouth as I walked into the kitchen. "You're late," he snapped. "Your stepmom's had dinner ready for an hour. Tell your mother to get you here at five next time."

"All right," I mumbled, and sat down. Beside me, my sister kicked my foot in solidarity. But I couldn't stay miserable for long.

Our usually austere dinner table had been transformed. Candlelight danced across a white cloth, syncopated with Spanish guitars drifting over from the living room stereo. Margarita glasses brimmed with salt-rimmed slush. Shirley Temples in highballs held maraschino cherries floating in crushed ice. Bowls of beans and rice steamed on cloth trivets painted to look like fringed Mexican serapes. In the center of the table, my stepmother placed a platter stacked high with golden packages, the likes of which I'd never seen before.

"Chimichangas!" she cried. "They're fun to eat, and fun to say!"

She put one on my plate. Up close, I saw that it was a flour tortilla wrapped squarely around a filling of spiced beef and cheese, and then fried.

"Chimichangas!" I repeated. The word danced in my mouth.

Elsa passed a bowl of refried beans. Patricia called beans cooked in this style *"cordon blanc"*—that is, dumped from the Rosarita can into a saucepan and heated until the mixture melted into a brown slop. But I took a spoonful anyway and garnished it with shredded cheddar.

"Beans look like poop!" From his chair, my little brother cackled his delight. My sister snickered and bypassed the bowl. But what my stepmother lacked in terms of legumes, she made up for in twin alchemies of guacamole and salsa *fresca*.

My father glanced at Katie, who turned up her nose at the garlicky green glop mounded in a terra cotta bowl and ladled chunky tomato salsa on her chimichanga instead. "Kids, what do you say? Elsa's been cooking all day."

"Thank you," we murmured.

"Really, it's just a matter of chopping vegetables and frying tortillas." My stepmother ducked her head so that her shining blond hair nearly brushed her plate. "Girls, how was your weekend?"

"We had a picnic at Mommy's house, and it was real cool!" Katie piped up. "We had potato salad and chicken and . . ." She looked to me for help. "I forget."

"Me, too." I longed for solitude in which to savor the way my fork crunched through the golden-brown tortilla and allowed cumin-scented steam to escape. I wanted to ponder my stepmother's piquant salsa flecked with green onions and cilantro, how it tasted of backyard fiestas and trumpets and roosters. But across the table, my brother raised wistful blue eyes from his plate.

"I miss Mommy," he said.

Beside him, Elsa stared down at her chimichanga.

My father sat silent for a moment, his eyes studying each of us in turn. Then he scraped his chair back from the table and leaped up. "That damned asshole bitch cunt!" he yelled. "I hope she goes to damned fucking goddamned hell!" He flung the basket of tortillas across the table, and they fell to the floor, a scattering of soft golden discs.

I realized, mouth dropped open, that my father was attempting to cuss out my mother in alphabetical order. We sat frozen while guitars strummed gently from the living room. Elsa shrank into herself; she gripped her linen napkin and closed her eyes. I saw then that she was far away, lingering on white sands while the warm waters of the Caribbean drifted about her. I could almost see the cabana boy, handsome as my baby sitter's earringed Spanish friend, massaging her rigid shoulders.

My father stared at her a moment. In his face, I recognized rage and pain and unbearable sorrow. Then he turned on one heel and stalked out of the house. In a minute, we heard the Buick start in the driveway and screech down the street.

My siblings and I sat silent, unsure of what to do. "I'm going to go relax for a few minutes," Elsa murmured, breaking the spell. She picked up a thick Mexican cookbook from the counter and walked slowly to the couch. Then she sat, head bent so that her hair hid her face, and studied each lavish colored photograph.

Katie and I cleaned the kitchen. I bent and picked up tortillas from the floor, dusting them off gently. We microwaved them, then spread them with butter and honey, rolled them up, and ate them as we washed the dishes.

Much later that night, when my father had returned, after everyone else had gone to bed, I pilfered the last chimichanga from the refrigerator. In the dark, I slipped it into the microwave, grateful for the brief white light. I cradled the warm packet like a gift in my palm and marveled once more at how the luscious melted strings of cheddar cheese tempered the cayenne's hot bite.

CHIMICHANGAS

Close your eyes, and picture a breezy outdoor restaurant on the warm sands of the Mexican Riviera. In one pan, fry up a pound of ground beef with a teaspoon of salt and a quarter teaspoon each of pepper and garlic powder. In another, saute a chopped onion and a green pepper over medium-high heat until tender.

Add one and a half teaspoons of flour to the vegetable mixture. Whisk away lumps, and cook for two minutes. Add drained ground beef, along with two chopped tomatoes, a can of diced green chilies, and a quarter cup of water. Let mixture simmer for fifteen minutes while you imagine snorkeling among tropical fish.

Abandon your reverie to place half a cup of the meat-vegetable mixture in a line down the center of a flour tortilla. Fold the sides one and a half inches toward the center, then fold the bottom and top over until you've got a square package like a gift. Secure your offering with a toothpick.

Fry chimichangas in hot oil until they're the color of a tropical-vacation tan. Place in a baking pan, and spoon canned red chili sauce to cover. Sprinkle with grated cheese and diced green onion. Place chimichangas under broiler until cheese melts. Pass bowls of sour cream, guacamole, shredded lettuce, chopped tomato, and olives.

Serve with a green salad and refried beans cooked *cordon blanc*. Keep one hand on the tortilla basket.

4

THE ACORN

Before my parents divorced, the members of my family held no roles beyond those of Father, Mother, Oldest, Middle, and Youngest Child. But suddenly, our identities shaken, we struggled to define ourselves so that we might stand upon a more solid foundation should catastrophe strike again. My mother became the Maligned Lesbian. My father was the Exhausted Breadwinner, prone to fits of rage. My stepmother occupied dual positions of Housewife and Long-Suffering Optimist, while my sister turned Cheerleader and my brother retained his status as the Baby of the Family. As for me, I became the resident Genius.

School was my sanctuary. I set out on the mile-long walk half an hour early each day so that I might take shelter in the classroom as soon as my teachers unlocked the door. Mrs. Jansta and Mrs. Goethe team-taught fifth grade in a long stucco building dropped upon an arid, treeless playground.

Mrs. Jansta adored art; with her, we spent our days creating cars out of dried pasta, or reel-to-reel documentaries on California missions out of cardboard tubes and boxes and creamy rolls of accounting paper.

Predictably, Mrs. Goethe—whose name the eleven-year-olds struggled to pronounce phonetically, disbelieving such an array of vowels and consonants could translate into the unimaginative "Gerta"—adored books. On her days in the classroom, we listened to stories, our heads pillowed on folded arms. Some of my classmates fell asleep or grimaced at each other in shards of broken mirror hoarded from the playground, but I sat riveted on the biography of Sacagawea, the Shoshone girl who guided Lewis and Clark to the Pacific Coast.

"Weirdo!" my classmates taunted when I checked out biographies of Abigail Adams and Louisa May Alcott from the school library. I ignored them. Deep in other people's stories, I could forget about my yearning for my mother and Oxnard, about my father's wrath and my stepmother's cheerful resignation. I rushed home each afternoon with my books and lay prostrate on the carpet, following the shaft of sunlight as it meandered across the living room.

"She's a genius," declared Mrs. Goethe to my school principal, who arranged for IQ testing after I won a citywide essay contest. I sat—lank-haired and bug-eyed—across from a young woman who played word association games and pelted me with vocabulary and number problems. Soberly, she asked me what objects I saw in a series of ink blots and held up a poster, inquiring as to whether I could discern both the human profiles and the chalice.

"Not a genius, per se," she concluded, "but she does have a high IQ. A GATE kid, for sure."

GATE, Gifted and Talented Education, meant a reprieve from the tedious hours of math and spelling. Kids who fell under that acronym got to walk two blocks each Wednesday morning to a double-wide trailer lined with shelves of musical instruments and board games and a fully functioning kitchen. The GATE teacher, Ms. Schultz, wore her hair in dyed red ponytails. She taught us to make quiche and cream puffs, instructed us in chess, and showed us how to strum "Greensleeves" on the Autoharp. We conducted encyclopedia and file card research on Ronald Reagan and the birthing of the first test tube baby, crafting reports that we delivered to our classmates as confirmed members of Junior Toastmasters.

Grateful for the clearly defined parameters of my new role as Gifted and Talented, I upped my reading quotient to four books a week and began to keep a diary so that someone, someday, might write my biography. I entered another essay contest and won a set of encyclopedias. My father displayed the leather and gold-leaf volumes next to his series of uncracked Great Books on the oak bookshelf. At dinner, he tried to engage me in discussions on current events. "We've got ourselves a genius on one side of the table," he jerked his etched chin at me, "and on the other, a ree . . ."

I held my breath, but my father always stopped just in time, flashing a wine-infused grin at my younger brother. Still, I heard the chant in my head, voiced nearly every day by my classmates as we filed past the special education trailer for recess. "Retard. Dumbass. Idiot."

Retard was the worst of the insults. It occupied a place at the polar opposite of genius. But somehow, my brother and I managed to gaze at one another across the vast expanse of intellect and meet in the middle to make music.

My mother told me that Down syndrome manifested itself in varying levels, ranging from severe to mild. In my mind, my brother got off relatively easy. He seemed to me possessed of a simple wisdom akin to Lennie in *Of Mice and Men*. He could walk and talk, dress and feed himself. He couldn't read or do math, but he could compliment a pretty girl and dance a dead-ringer for Michael Jackson. I needed little else in a brother beyond these attributes and a willingness to sing backup vocals to my lead.

"Listen." I sat cross-legged on his baby-blue bedroom carpet those weekends we didn't visit our mother and strummed the worn-out nylon strings of an old guitar left in the closet by the house's previous owner. "Let's sing 'Puff the Magic Dragon.'"

My brother exhibited two facial expressions—a practiced pout and a sweet smile that caused even the crustiest of postal clerks to grin back. When I stepped into his room and picked up the guitar, wrenching my fingers into a G-chord, he bathed me in pure joy. "Okay, sister!" he cried. "I sing!"

Ms. Schultz had taught me three chords—C, E, and G. In duets, my brother and I ran through all the songs Peter, Paul & Mary wrote or appropriated from Dylan. Our voices shook with anger as we wondered aloud how many times must the cannonballs fly before they're forever banned. We teared up in synch at little Jackie Paper who came no more, causing Puff to cease his fearless roar. I practiced guitar until calluses hardened on my fingertips, and I dreamed of fronting my own folk band in a fringed miniskirt and leather boots.

"Shut up, you guys!" My sister pounded on her wall. "I'm trying to memorize the words to 'Maneater.'"

Katie, faced with one overachieving sibling and another barely able to tie his sneakers, compensated by becoming totally normal. She choreographed dance moves to Top 40 hits, pulled pink legwarmers over her blue jeans, and put on talent shows with a neighbor girl. One day, they appeared together in Tim's doorway in rubber bracelets and matching lime green lace tops. The neighbor girl wrinkled her nose at my brown braids tied with strips of leather. "Your sister's a weirdo," she told Katie.

My younger sister studied me, blond head cocked to one side, and stopped short of agreeing. "She's just a genius," she said and returned to her bedroom.

Separate rooms kept us apart at our father's house, but in Oxnard we shared a garage that our mother had converted into a makeshift bedroom. We slept on mattresses without box springs, carving out slim places for our bodies in nests of stuffed animals. We giggled long into the night, belting out the words to songs from *A Chorus Line*: "Tits and ass. / Bought myself a fancy pair. / Tightened up the derriere. / Did the nose with it, / All that goes with it . . . "

Our mother gave us free rein over the kitchen and her half-acre back yard. We constructed forts and rope swings in the fruit trees and grew pumpkins and sunflowers on a vast patch of soil. Tim was our gofer, fetching hammers and shovels with slavish devotion.

One night, my sister and I planned an elaborate meal of Mexican hot chocolate and cream puffs. While the puffs cooled and the chocolate thickened and skinned on the stove, we washed the custard off our hands and dove into the four-foot detergent barrel our mother had stocked with wigs and hats, gloves, and rhinestone necklaces discarded from my grandmother's costume shop.

"I get to wear the rabbit fur!" Katie cried, referring to a hip-length coat relegated to the dress-up barrel after our mother turned vegetarian.

"Be my guest." Eschewing elegance, I opted for a hoopskirt and a macramé vest, paired with purple feathered earrings.

"Those are roach clips," my mother's girlfriend observed, looking up from her book on the couch when we walked into the room to model our outfits.

"Patricia . . ." My mother shook her head and smiled at me. "Honey, your earrings look beautiful."

Our brother resembled a Munchkin, and we dressed him in a ruffled pinafore and a curly-haired wig to emphasize the similarity. "We're going to play charm school," I told him. My sister and I assigned ourselves the position of instructors and tapped our little brother as our protégé, Miss Sherri Tiptoes.

"Hold your pinky finger out like this, Sherri." Katie demonstrated with her mug of hot chocolate. "And cut your cream puff into tiny bites. Don't just stuff it into your mouth."

"I stuff my bra," Tim said, sending Katie and me into shrieks of laughter.

"He's so ree . . ." she began.

I held up my hand. "Ridiculous," I finished.

"Yeah." She nodded so her rhinestone tiara slipped over one ear. "Ridiculous."

At our mother's house, we were allies, bolstering each other against the inevitable arrival of Sunday afternoon at three and the trip down south to Los Angeles. But the moment we returned to our father's house—disembarked from the VW bus and walked up the front steps—we retreated into our separate bedrooms and closed our doors.

"You're wearing *that* to school?" Katie said as I appeared at the breakfast table one Wednesday in a leather headband and an ankle-length brown skirt.

"Ms. Schultz is teaching us about Indians today." I adjusted the pink feather stapled to my headband. "The GATE kids are going to the park."

If this privilege stung my sister, she didn't show it. "You're wearing Tim's slippers," she observed behind her box of Honeycomb. "They look weird."

"They're moccasins."

Surreptitiously, I studied my feet in my brother's leather and wool bedroom scuffs and addressed Katie behind my fortress of Frosted Mini-Wheats. "Conformity—now *that's* weird."

"You look beautiful, sister," Tim offered across the table. He sat shoveling in Raisin Bran, pretending to read the *Times*. Despite my attempts to teach him with flashcards and M&Ms, he could recognize only two words—"Tim" and "boobs." But he rushed onto his little orange

school bus with the same eagerness that propelled me down the sidewalk
to Ms. Schultz's GATE class that morning.

"The Indians who first lived on this land were Chumash," she told us
as we walked across the dewy grass to Holly Glen Park. She'd braided her
ponytails; they sprung from the top of her head like scarlet snakes. "They
lived off the land, taking only what they needed. They said a prayer for the
animals they killed and used every part of a deer or bear."

My classmates sat down in a circle under a vast oak beside the
playground, and she held up an acorn. "They mashed these into flour and
made fry bread."

I studied the burnished brown acorn in her palm. Within its hard
hull, I saw a woman in a leather dress hard at work with a mortar and
pestle, mixing acorn flour with water from a burbling spring now covered
by swing sets and slides.

My teacher produced a large Tupperware from her tote bag. "Today,
I've made fry bread with wheat flour and water. Indians would have eaten
theirs with venison, but I've brought butter and honey."

The GATE kids grinned at each other, collectively pitying our
poor normal classmates hard at work on spelling lessons back at school.
Gleefully, we passed around tubs of butter and honey. I bit into my
bread, still warm from Ms. Schultz's griddle, and thought I'd never tasted
anything so wonderful.

"What happened to the Indians?" I asked. Our fifth-grade history
book mentioned only briefly that Europeans had moved into what was now
Southern California. On page 242, Chumash lived in reed huts on the land.
On page 243, they were replaced by white settlers and log cabins.

"Genocide." Ms. Schultz frowned. "And forced relocation. The
government demanded that the Chumash move onto reservations. They
couldn't grow much on the hard-packed dirt around their new homes, but
some managed to survive."

I thought of my father's tiny back yard, how I struggled to grow crooked carrots in a patch of rocky soil. I bowed my head and imagined a procession of moccasin-clad Indians filing out of Holly Glen Park. Their pink-feathered headbands drooped low as they headed down 134th Street toward the desert.

"Up north, Chief Joseph fought the U.S. government to keep his tribe's land," Ms. Schultz told us. "He surrendered only after the white man slaughtered his people. Then he gave a famous speech in which he said, 'I will fight no more forever.'"

If my classmates' hearts also twisted at the chief's words, their blank expressions didn't show it.

"The Chumash wove mats out of pine needles," Ms. Schultz continued brightly. "Let's weave mats of our own now."

I knelt in the damp grass and scooped up green and brown needles, shivering with excitement. As I wove, I studied my classmates. Ian McNerny had curly hair and a gap-toothed, guileless smile. He sat beside Steven Sotherby, who struck me as impossibly handsome and kind. Maria Santos sat cross-legged, looking sophisticated and clever as her fingers deftly manipulated needles into a mat, while Thuy Lu concentrated so hard that the tip of her pink tongue stuck out.

This was my tribe. It didn't matter that the other kids referred to us as GATE Geeks, that they glowered with envy and disgust when we returned to school muddy and honey-scented while they finished taking a math quiz. We weirdos stuck together.

Come to a Birthday Party! I studied the invitation Thuy handed me that afternoon and shook my head. "I can't," I said. "That's my weekend to visit my mother."

"Visit?" Thuy blinked behind her thick, round glasses. "Why do you have to visit her? Is she on vacation?"

The other girls gathered in closer, waiting for my response. "My parents are divorced," I mumbled. "I live with my dad."

Maria's eyes glowed with pity. "Too bad for you," she said. "You must miss your mom."

None of my friends had divorced parents. Every girl in my classroom—evidenced by our end-of-year open house—had a mother and a father.

I lifted my chin. "I'm lucky," I told Maria. "I have *three* mothers." I held up a trio of fingers to represent my mother, her girlfriend, and my stepmother.

She recoiled, then tossed her black braid and addressed the girls. "That's weird."

And so I became the Weirdo who couldn't attend ice-skating parties or Girl Scout camp because I left town to visit some far-off, mysterious mother and her lesbian partner. Gradually, the invitations stopped coming. It never occurred to me to ask my parents if we might switch weekends on occasion, to accommodate my waning social engagements. My father said the custody judge had ruled that I could visit my mother the first and third weekends of each month. His word was law.

That summer, my father agreed to meet my mother halfway up the Pacific Coast Highway every other Sunday night, cutting her three-hour round trip in half. The first Sunday, he and my stepmother made a plan to dine on seafood at some oceanfront eatery and then meet us in Malibu.

"Be on time Sunday," he told me in front of my mother that Friday night. "There's a lot of traffic heading back to Los Angeles."

She eschewed a hot meal late Sunday afternoon and packed a basket with sandwiches and hard-boiled eggs. "We might hit traffic on PCH," she told me. "We'll have a picnic dinner."

"Isn't Patricia coming?" I asked as we piled into the bus.

My mother shook her head. "She and your father don't need to meet."

At once, I leaped into the front seat. "Shotgun!" I yelled.

"No fair." Katie sank into the middle seat beside our brother, deflated.

We picnicked on a wool Army blanket beside a sandy playground in Malibu that abutted a petting zoo featuring three red chickens and a black-and-white spotted goat. "Let's call her Frederica," my mother said. "She can be our Sunday night mascot."

We fed the goat bits of cheese and crackers from our spread and scratched the coarse hair between her silky ears. My sister and brother played on the swings and slide while I huddled next to my mother on the blanket. "Can't you go back to court?" I begged. "Can't you fight for custody?"

She sighed and pushed her hair out of her eyes. The late afternoon sun lit up the new silver hairs that sprung wiry from her scalp. "I can and I will," she promised, "but you know what the answer will be."

In my head, I saw the long line of Indians, heads bowed as they left their verdant acreage for unforgiving desert. "Ms. Schultz said it's important to fight the establishment," I told my mother.

At the park, my siblings laughed and spun on the merry-go-round with new friends they'd never see again. They devoured single-scoop cones at Swensen's while we waited for our father's Buick to appear in the parking lot next to the movie theater. I licked infinitesimally at my cone of Sticky Chewy Chocolate and prayed for it to be Friday night instead of Sunday.

When the Buick glided into the parking lot, my siblings kissed our mother and jumped into the back seat. I clung to her, hiding in the shadows of the VW bus. "See you in ten days," I mumbled.

She hugged me close. "Remember." She bent down and murmured into my ear. "It's the quality—not the quantity—of our time together that counts."

Head down, I climbed into the back seat of the Buick. "Hi," I mumbled to Elsa, who smiled kindly and handed me a package of oyster crackers saved from dinner. Tim sat beside me, waving at my mother as she pulled away in the bus. On the other side of him, Katie busied herself biting oyster crackers neatly in half and didn't look up.

"Cheer up." My father caught my eye in the rearview mirror. "Elsa made your favorite coconut cake. It's waiting for you at home."

But not even the promise of my stepmother's tender white cake, topped with fluffy coconut frosting and laced with piquant lemon curd, could cheer me. I leaned my forehead against the cool window and stared out at the oil rigs lit up in the ocean.

My father's smile darkened into a scowl. "Cool it, sister," he snarled.

Sympathy warm in her eyes, Elsa pulled out a cassette. "I brought your favorite tape," she said and pushed it into the player.

"Puff the Magic Dragon," "Blowin' in the Wind," and the rest sounded foreign and wrong in the leather and suede Buick. Folk music required a little shabbiness, a little bohemia. It required a Volkswagen bus.

When Peter, Paul & Mary ended their wistful harmonies, my own voice began to crackle and wobble over the car speakers, accompanied by discordant strumming on the old guitar: "If you miss the train I'm on, / you will know that I have gone. / You can hear the whistle blow five hundred miles."

On the tape, Tim moaned backup to my forced vibrato.

"Turn it off," I whispered.

Elsa clucked her tongue. "You'll never be a decent singer until you learn not to take a breath in the middle of a sentence," she chided.

"Turn it off!" I begged a little louder, as my voice launched into a cacophonic rendition of "If I Had a Hammer."

Tim broke into joyful song. My sister clapped her hands over her ears. "Turn it off!" she echoed. "Lissa's voice hurts."

"Please?" I begged.

My father met my eyes in the rearview mirror once more and held my gaze. He smiled. "Tim likes the music," he said and let my voice continue until the tape ran out.

The next morning, Elsa made waffles to celebrate the first day of summer, then settled down at the dining room table with the last of the batch and the *Times*. "I'm going next door to do a talent show!" Katie yelled and banged out the front door toting her Barbies.

My father, off work for the day, disappeared out the back door. A moment later, I heard the lawn mower growl to a start. I retreated into my bedroom with a biography of Pocahontas. I read until I finished the book, which ended with the Indian woman's death and a picture of her looking stiff and uncomfortable in an Elizabethan collar.

From the open window, I heard my sister and her best friend singing Sheena Easton's "Morning Train." Eyes aching, I wandered into Tim's room, where he sat lining up his Matchbox cars meticulously across the carpet. He looked up from his work. "Hi, sister," he said. "Wanna sing?"

I shook my head and slipped on his leather and wool bedroom slippers. "Let's go to the park. I'm going to teach you about the Indians."

"Okey dokey." He followed me into the kitchen, where I slapped together two peanut butter and grape jelly sandwiches. "I wish we could make fry bread," I muttered, but Elsa's kitchen was her castle. She allowed me to concoct PB&J—that was all.

I dropped two apples into my backpack. "The Chumash must've eaten fruit," I reasoned and led Tim out the back door. I helped him climb into our yellow metal wagon. "The park's a mile away," I told him. "I don't think you can walk that." I grabbed the handle and rumbled down the long driveway.

My father stood in the front yard, watering a newly planted weeping willow with the garden hose. He raised a hand in greeting as I approached.

"Want to come with me to the hardware store?" he asked. "I've got to pick up a few things, and we can stop at McDonald's."

Still angry about the cassette tape, I turned away.

"No thanks," I said. "The hardware store's boring."

At once, I felt a cold splash of water hit my head and shoulders. I gasped and stared at my father, but he'd already turned to water Elsa's jasmine bush.

Drenched, I hurtled myself and the wagon down the sidewalk. The hard rubber wheels bounced over cracks. "You okay, sister?" Tim asked.

I ignored him, and he launched into "Puff," his voice vibrating up and down with the wagon's flight.

I raced across the street against the light toward my school. I rushed past my GATE classroom with its curtains darkening the windows and a laminated sign hung on the door. SEE YOU NEXT FALL, it read. I pulled the wagon two more blocks, then bumped across the grass to Holly Glen Park. Several families had spread out blankets under the trees. Mothers presided over picnic baskets. Fathers pushed children on the swings and merry-go-round. I stopped the wagon under the big oak tree and pulled Tim out by his armpits. "We'll eat first, and then I'll teach you about the Indians," I said.

He sat cross-legged and ate his sandwich. I struggled to swallow mine. I'd forgotten to bring water, and the bread and peanut butter stuck in my throat. Near me, a girl my age played catch with an older boy; they had the same red hair and pale skin, so I knew they were brother and sister. Her balls went wild half the time, and he jogged over to demonstrate throwing techniques.

I wrapped up my half-eaten sandwich and frowned at Tim. "You should know that the Chumash Indians ground acorns into flour and mixed it with water for fry bread," I said.

I pounded an acorn into submission on a flat rock. Tim copied me, but caught his finger in between the stones and began to cry. A woman with hair the same nut-brown color as my mother's looked up from changing her toddler. For an instant, I met her eyes, then glanced away. "You're fine," I told Tim. "Now we're going to weave a mat out of pine needles."

I held his stubby fingers in mine, producing a crooked mat that fell apart as soon as he held it up to admire. "Ooops," he said.

I kicked the mat, scattering the needles across the grass. The sun shone down on my wet braids, drying them, but my moccasins remained soaked. "We could stay at the park until next Friday night," I told Tim. "Then we could send up a smoke signal so Mom knows where to find us."

"That's cool," he said and ran off to play on the swings.

I huddled in the grass, watching tree shadows lengthen across the field. Around me, families began to pack up their baskets and blankets. At last, only the woman and the toddler remained. She carried the baby to the swings and pushed him gently back and forth. From where I sat, I could hear her chatting with my brother.

I stalked over to Tim. When he saw me, he leaped out of his swing and scaled the slide. "It's time to go," I called up to him. "We've got to go back."

He shook his head. "I stay here."

"We can't." I climbed up the slide. "It's late. Dad and Elsa'll be worried. We have to go back now."

Again, he shook his head. "No way."

My throat tightened. "C'mon!" I gripped his shoulders. "We have to go."

"No!"

I shoved him down the slide. He landed at the bottom in cold, damp sand, immovable. "I not going," he said and folded his arms across his chest.

I bounded over to him. "What am I supposed to do?" I demanded. "I can't leave you. You're gonna be in such trouble when I tell Dad what you've done."

He shrugged and stuck out his bottom lip. "I not going," he repeated.

My head spun. I dug my fingernails into his arms and carried him to the wagon as he screamed. Across the playground, the woman cradled her baby to her chest and shook her head.

"Cool it, brother!" I snarled at Tim. Trembling, I yanked the wagon over to the water fountain. "Get a drink," I commanded. Out of the corner of my eye, I watched the woman pack up her baby and walk to her car. Only after her Honda had vanished down the road did I sink down, head in my hands on the sidewalk beside the restrooms. "I will fight no more forever," I whispered.

"Look, sister." My brother tugged on my sleeve. I pressed my palms into my eyes, blinking hard. Tim pointed to the fountain's handle. Below it, in a wet cemented crevice, sat an acorn. Its hull had split and given way to roots and a stem with two leaves pointing fiercely toward the setting sun.

Carefully, Tim plucked it from its hiding place. "Here." He handed me the acorn.

"No, you hold it," I murmured, trying not to see the fingernail marks—like tiny crescent moons—marring the reddened skin of his arms. "We'll take it home and plant it in the garden."

Wearily, I helped my brother into the wagon and picked up the handle. Then I plodded across the grass in my sodden moccasins, pulling my little brother behind me.

INDIAN FRY BREAD

Braid your hair, and put on your moccasins.
If you're out of acorn flour, pour three cups
of the white man's flour into a bowl. Add
one tablespoon of baking powder and half a
teaspoon of salt. Mix well.

Pour one and a half cups of stream water
warmed by the sun into the bowl, and mix
until you have a sticky dough. Knead the
dough on a lightly floured surface—not too
much, or it will turn tough and inflexible as a
homesteader on native lands. Place in a bowl,
and refrigerate for an hour.

Heat a griddle or frying pan over a wood
fire or, if you must, your kitchen stove. Add
a tablespoon of canola oil or butter. Retrieve
your dough, and scoop up a ball the size of an
orange. Pat the ball with your fingers until it's
a quarter inch all around.

Cook until it's golden brown on one side,

then flip it over and brown the other side, adding more butter or oil as needed. This should take about three minutes, long enough for you to belt out a passable rendition of the tits and ass song from *A Chorus Line*.

Repeat with the rest of the dough. Cool the fry bread slightly, then place the rounds on a pine needle mat. Eat them under an oak tree with plenty of butter, honey, and rage.

5 .

BLUEBIRD OF HAPPINESS

THREE TIMES A YEAR—AT CHRISTMAS AND EASTER AND ON THE
Fourth of July—my mother piled us into her Volkswagen bus with
organic licorice ropes and carob bars and dolls and eight-tracks of
Broadway musicals and drove five hours north to Monterey. My
grandmother lived on a forested half acre below Jacks Peak, along with
her mother—a former circus bareback rider and vaudevillian whom
everyone called "Grandmary."

"Hello, Melissa Marie," Grandmary quavered as we stumbled sleepily
through the door at 10:00 PM. "How's my little ray of sunshine?"

In Monterey, I glowed. I glowed because for these two women I was
the oldest grandchild, and adored. I glowed because their garage held
hoopskirts and hookahs and old gramophone records, because a trapeze
hung from their living room ceiling, left over from great-grandfather's

circus act. But mostly, I glowed because for two days, I got to live with my mother and her family.

A typical visit went like this: Our mother picked us up in Los Angeles after school on Friday, and our father and Elsa waved goodbye from the lawn. "Wear your jacket and a ski hat!" he'd yell to me, so my mother could hear as she backed the Volkswagen out of the driveway. "Your grandmother's house is cold as a witch's tit."

"Where's Patricia?" Katie asked.

My mother shrugged. Always, her answer was the same. "She wanted some time to herself."

I didn't mind. Without Patricia in the bus, I claimed the passenger's seat up front.

In Malibu, we rumbled through McDonald's for cheeseburgers, fries, and chocolate milkshakes. We pulled over at a rest stop every two hours so my mother could refill her cup of black coffee while we peed, and pulled up at last in my grandmother's driveway under a velvet-black, star-spotted sky. Grandma met us at the door, hair dyed newly red for the occasion of our visit. She hugged us stiffly, clucking henlike as she drew us into the chilly hallway. "You must be hungry," she chuckled. "Go into the pantry and see what you can find."

Katie and I looked to our mother for permission before scampering into the walk-in room off the front porch, where wonders awaited us. Here were dusty boxes of Mexican rice mix, instant flan, and packets of taco seasoning to sprinkle on bags of cubed potatoes from the freezer. Here were dented cans of tamales in red sauce, salty pinto beans, and diced green chilies. We filled our arms with processed bounty and added a frozen can of lime margarita mix, perfectly celebratory when blended with orange juice and poured into sugar-rimmed glasses.

It would be midnight by the time we shared our microwaved smorgasbord with Tim and my aunt and uncle, who'd come over to join the fun. "I love this place!" Tim said, putting into words what my mouth was too full to utter.

The next morning, we drank powdered hot chocolate from paper packets with our grandmother before she drove her Chrysler minivan to work. Grandmary nursed a glass of prune juice at the table and displayed a handful of photos. "This was your grandfather thirty years before his plane crashed." She handed me a scallop-edged picture of a man with a broad, mischievous smile and a long chin. He cradled an enormous accordion in his arms.

"He knew how to play one song," she told me. "'Red Sails in the Sunset.' It's all he ever needed for his vaudeville act."

I studied a later photo of my great-grandfather beside his doomed yellow Cessna and tried unsuccessfully to lift the accordion from its position of honor on the living room end table, my biceps aching from the weight of family history.

Midmorning, we ate Egg McMuffins on a picnic table outside Dennis the Menace Park and played until our breakfast threatened to reemerge as we clambered across the steam engine and slid down the long, bumpy slide. Then we drove to my grandmother's costume rental store. Grandma and her boyfriend of forty years owned the shop and adjoining dance studio on Lighthouse Road. My grandmother's costumes bore no resemblance to the sparse row of plastic capes and hats that appeared in neighborhood drug stores each October. Her clothing racks stretched deep into the back of her shop, each costume hand-sewn and meticulously researched from her many history books.

"I want to be Princess Leia!" Katie and I fought in the car over the floor-length white tunic and wig with twin side buns until I decided that Chewbacca's enormous brown shag costume was the better choice because it terrified my little brother.

"Wash your hands!" my grandmother cried as we skittered past her station at the glass counter with its tempting array of rhinestone jewelry, false eyelashes, and fake mustaches. We ducked under the beaded curtain that led to the back of the studio and ran past deer-hide loincloths and cotton togas, past Victorian gowns and checkered sunbonnets and metallic Martian dresses to the bathroom to scrub.

"When I grow up, I'm going to be a ballerina," Katie said, twirling across the cavernous dance studio in a tutu two sizes too large. Tim, in one sequined glove, executed a swift Michael Jackson spin and crotch-grab, cooing at his reflection in the tall mirrors. Having leaped from Cleopatra's jeweled headdress to Jane Austen's empire waists to Papa Smurf in a single morning, I announced to the stray orange cat lurking in the doorway of the dance studio, "I'm going to be an actress."

Beside my grandmother's shop stood my aunt's tiny blue and white sandwich joint, Hoagie's Heroes. At noon, we joined the lunch rush streaming out the door of her deli. We ordered the same thing, always—tuna for my mother and Tim, ham and cheese for Katie, turkey and Swiss for me. "Extra sprouts," I said and watched my grinning, double-chinned aunt pile them on high. She begrudgingly accepted the ten-dollar bill my mother handed her and wrapped a few black-bottom cupcakes in a paper bag for our dessert. We ate sitting on the warm wooden deck outside, listening to the screams of seagulls that wheeled overhead, breathing in the salt air from the ocean a few blocks away.

"Can't we move here?" I asked my mother.

She frowned over her tuna fish. "Your father won't allow it."

"We could stay with Grandma until Dad comes to get us . . . " I reasoned.

I pictured him stepping into the living room, ducking under the trapeze to be confronted by a fortress of women. Grandmary, my grandmother, my mother, and my aunt would stand in front of Tim and

Katie and me, linking their arms in solidarity. I could hear my great-grandmother's voice. "You're not taking the children," she'd croak.

He'd bend his head so I could see the submissive gray hairs at his temples. "You win," he'd say. Then I'd race out into the sunlit back yard and feed peanuts to Beaky, my grandmother's blue jay, who took them right out of my hand.

But mornings after the Christmas ham or Easter egg hunt or Fourth of July sparklers, we had to climb into the bus for the long drive back down south. My relatives stood in the front yard, smiling and waving, as my mother backed the Volkswagen down the driveway. Tears clouded Grandmary's eyes, and she tore off her spectacles and wiped them on her flannel shirt. "There goes my little ray of sunshine," she called after me.

Two hours into one of our trips back to Los Angeles—on a Monday following a Fourth of July weekend—the ancient VW bus gave one rheumatic cough, then sputtered and died on Highway 101 beside the oak-dotted fields of Paso Robles. From the back seat, Katie and I cheered. Tim clapped his chubby hands together in the passenger's seat. "The car is busted!" he chanted.

"Dammit, kids, play the quiet game!" My mother wrenched the key into the ignition, sweat beading her brow. Her Birkenstocks pumped the gas pedal and clutch, but the bus refused to respond.

"Hey Mommy," Katie giggled. "Don't bust a gasket!"

Per the rules of the quiet game, Tim and I pointed censorious index fingers at our sister. She merely shrugged and stuck her tongue out. Cars sped by us, their drivers so lulled by air-conditioning and interstate travel that they didn't bother to glance our way. My mother sighed and shouldered her fringed leather saddlebag. "Looks like I'd better go call a tow truck. My Visa's maxed out. I'll have to trade one of you kids for a ride to the gas station," she joked stiffly.

She slid past Tim and opened the passenger door. At once, an arid wind rushed in, rich with the scents of hot soil and car exhaust. "It's got to be a hundred and five in the shade," she muttered, fanning herself with the hem of the T-shirt my aunt had given her. A cartoon horse head dominated the front—underneath, bold blue letters read WATCH OUT FOR ROAD APPLES.

"Girls . . . " My mother looked at us for a long time, fear and necessity battling in her indigo eyes. "Don't open this door for anyone except the police."

She jumped down onto the steaming asphalt, pushed the lock button on the door, and stuck her head back in. "Make sure they show you a badge first."

I nodded soberly. "I will."

Katie and I scrambled to the back of the bus to watch her small, retreating figure as she trudged down the searing shoulder in search of one of the yellow call boxes that dotted the highway. A semi roared past her. The driver honked his horn, but didn't stop. My sister and I traded guilty smiles. A stalled bus cost money to fix, and that day, if my grandmother hadn't tucked twenty dollars into my hand, we would have been forced to eat her spongy red apples and pungent muenster cheese from my aunt's deli instead of our usual McDonald's fare. To my mother, a vehicle catastrophe of this magnitude meant taking on more housecleaning work. To me, it meant one more day, a blissful stolen twenty-four hours, to spend with her.

"Let's hide if the police come," I told Katie. "Otherwise, they might give us a ride back to Dad's house."

"What if it's Ponch and Jon?" my sister demanded. "Bet you'd open the door for CHiPs."

I shrugged and ducked my head with a dignified simper. Should Erik Estrada appear in his trademark tight pants and black leather boots, I'd be out the door and on his motorcycle in a second. "Not for Jon. He's a dork," I told Katie and tossed my mother's down jacket over my brother's head. "Tim, play the quiet game."

He began to snore, with elaborate snorting and flapping of lips. Katie ducked under the VW's foldout table. I crouched beneath our plaid picnic blanket and peeped through the bottom of the dusty window for squad cars. In the wake of thundering traffic, the bus trembled.

Ten minutes went by on my Tigger watch. Then twenty. Just when I'd given up on my mother making it back to the bus alive, she reappeared on the shoulder. "She's coming!" I hissed.

Under the table, Katie shrieked, "Is the fuzz with her?"

I studied my mother as she approached. Sweat dripped off her reddened face. Her mouth curved in a grim, downturned U. "Nope, it's safe." I unlocked the sliding door and met her with our emergency jug of water. "What happened?" I demanded.

She took a long drink and mopped her forehead with my panda bear beach towel. "I called Triple A," she panted, "but there's no mechanic available today. A tow truck's coming to pull us off the highway."

She took a deep breath and let it out so I could smell the onions she'd had on her Filet-O-Fish. "Looks like we'll have to stay in this hellhole overnight."

"Yay!" Katie and I crammed books and markers and dolls into our backpacks. "We love Paso Robles!"

In truth, we'd never considered the sleepy cow-town cohabitated by farmers and Mexican immigrants as anything but a place to stop for gas and a pee. A few motels and gas stations straggled down the main drag. Residents in shorts and flip-flops wandered along the sidewalk, taking refuge from the heat under wide-brimmed straw hats and the occasional sprawling oak.

The tow truck driver dropped us off in front of a dingy motel with a swimming pool, beside a windowless building that read TACO'S in faded green letters arched over the doorway. A heady smell of roasting corn seemed to emanate from the brick walls. "I'm hungry," I moaned.

"We'll have dinner later," my mother promised, eliciting another round of cheers. She checked us into a single room with two double beds done up in orange bedspreads and flat pillows. "You girls can change into your bathing suits." Her face reflected none of our jubilation. "We'll go swimming after I call your father and tell him what happened."

Katie and I rifled through our backpacks, searching optimistically for our nonexistent bathing suits. Our grandmother didn't have a pool, and Monterey remained at a constant sixty degrees and foggy, with an ocean too cold for anything but ankle-wading among the tidepools.

"Mom, can we swim in our Underoos?" I asked.

She waved me away. "It's a twenty-year-old Volkswagen," she snapped into the phone. "I'd buy a new car, but divorce fees cleaned me out."

She pressed a palm against the mouthpiece and nodded at the red and gold polyester clothing I waved above my head. "Help Tim get his on, too," she said.

I put a finger to my lips and pointed to the bathroom, signifying that if my father wished to speak with me, she should tell him I was otherwise occupied. She nodded and turned away.

"I'm aware that the kids have camp tomorrow," she said into the phone. "They'll just have to miss it."

I bit back my smile. Camp meant weaving plastic lanyards in the art shack and sing-a-longs to "Kumbaya" and nighttime dances where you weren't allowed to refuse a partner. Last year, I'd longed to get down to Olivia Newton-John's "Physical" with Flavio Flores—himself an Erik Estrada look-alike—and instead found myself shuffling to Air Supply's "All Out of Love" with a skinny drooling boy whom everyone called "Clown."

"I don't want to miss camp." Katie's bottom lip trembled. "Me and

Amber were gonna do the Go-Go's in the talent show and learn to shoot an arrow."

"Yeah, but now we get to have tacos for dinner!" I whispered.

She brightened a little. "And chips and salsa," she added.

"Tim, you get to be Batman!" I tossed my brother his blue and gold briefs. Underoos were all the rage that year. We all sat riveted when the commercial came on and the little mop-headed kid pulled up his multicolored underpants. Instantly, his skinny legs morphed into the giant metal gams of a Transformer from Saturday morning cartoons. "Underoos are fun to wear!" we sang with the jingle and begged until our mother stuffed them into our Christmas stockings with the requisite tangerines and chocolate Santas.

Due to a dearth of female superheroes, Katie and I both had Wonder Woman Underoos. In the motel room, we pulled on our red tank tops emblazoned with Lynda Carter's awe-inspiring gold eagle and shimmied into our royal blue briefs dotted with stars. Power surged through me. I wished the popular kids at camp could see me now, bold and strong and brilliant. Then they'd let me eat lunch with them behind the art shack, and Flavio would invite me to share his double kayak.

"We're ready for swimming, Mommy!" my sister trilled.

Flushed, my mother stood up. She gripped the phone so that her knuckles whitened. "Look," she snapped into the mouthpiece. "We're stuck in this godforsaken town until tomorrow. If you want the kids, you're gonna have to drive up and get them."

She slammed the phone down. Katie and I stared at her, horrified.

"Oh don't worry," she sighed. "Paso Robles is hours from L.A. Your father's not going to make an eight-hour round trip, not even to spite me."

"Good!" Tim shouted.

I didn't say anything. Out the open door, I could hear splashing and yelling from the pool. Guilty elation tightened my chest. "I'm sorry, Mom . . ." I began, but lured by the siren song of my peers, I ran after my sister in the simmering parking lot, threw off my towel, and dove. In the water, the bitter smell of chlorine embraced me.

Four other kids bobbed in the pool—three Latino boys who guarded the deep end and a red-haired girl in a sagging pink bathing suit who stood alone in the shallow water near the steps. "You're in your underwear," she observed as I came up for air.

"They're Underoos," I retorted. "So you can just go suck an egg."

Momentarily mollified, the girl turned her back to me and dog-paddled to the deep end. The boys surrounded her, sharklike. "You is Marco," the youngest child said in the accent particular to kids who'd learned Spanish first, and then English.

The girl clung to the side of the pool and allowed him to tie a wet T-shirt around her head like a blindfold. The oldest boy looked across the water at Katie and me. His eyes reminded me of the eyes of the blue jay in my grandmother's back yard—dark and sharp and soulful. "You playing?" he demanded.

"Of course," I said.

There was no way to resist Marco Polo, the game that could unify strangers in a swimming pool. Those who yelled "Polo!" forged an easy camaraderie in pitting themselves against the poor sucker who had to yell "Marco!" while swimming blindfolded and trying wildly to tag the others.

Immediately, I fell in love with the oldest boy. He didn't know me from my sixth-grade class, where I suffered nervous coughing fits that made my nose run and my eyes water until even the girls who called themselves my friends had to laugh and the teacher commanded me to go to the nurse. He didn't know that I'd been the most popular girl in third grade until my parents divorced and I had to go to three new schools in less than a year, where everyone had already formed cliques and I ate lunch alone and got chosen last for kickball even though my mother said I ran like a gazelle.

To this boy, I could be anyone.

When it was his turn to be Marco, I yelled "Polo!" extra loud, and he lunged toward me with his hands outstretched. His brown eyes peeked from under the T-shirt blindfold as he gripped one strap of my undershirt. "You've gotta see something," he told me. "Look below."

I ducked under and followed him to the bottom of the pool. For an instant, the boy's lips touched mine before he pushed off and surfaced, spraying water like a whale.

I swam to the shallow end, gasping and blinking.

"I saw you." The red-haired girl sat on the steps, ice-blue eyes flashing resentment. "He only kissed you 'cause you're wearing your underwear."

A deep confusion gripped me then. I glanced at my mother to see if she'd witnessed the scene, but she had her back to me, playing catch with my brother. What would she think if she knew a boy had kissed me?

Up until that moment, I'd assumed I'd grow up to be with a woman, just like my mother. But this kiss revealed a new truth. I liked boys.

I thought about how disappointed my mother would be when she found out. Then the boy splashed up to me. "Hey, we're playing volleyball now. We need you on our team . . . girl," he said. "What's your name, anyway?"

I studied him—how his smile stretched wide and mischievous above his long chin. In my head, I heard the lyrics that Grandmary had taught me: "Red sails in the sunset, way out on the sea. / Oh carry my loved one home safely to me."

At last, I relented. "My name is Mary," I said and caught the ball he threw.

Katie and I played with the boys until our fingertips puckered and shriveled and our eyes blazed with chemicals. The last beams of sunlight reached into the pool, and I swam through them, dizzy with romance and chlorine.

"Time for dinner, kids." My mother fished Tim out of the shallow end and wrapped a towel around him.

Katie swam toward her. "Can I get a soda, Mommy, please?"

I lingered in the deep end, clinging to the rough edge of the pool, my legs kicking languidly as I chattered with the boy.

"My parents own the motel restaurant." He pointed to the brick building. "It's the best one in town. My dad makes his own chili *verde* and chicken mole. He's cool."

"Maybe I'll see you there," I said so that the red-haired girl, still in the pool, could hear that I had a date.

"Where's your dad?" the boy asked me.

"At home," I mumbled, thinking fast. "He had to stay with our dog 'cause she's about to have puppies. My dad's Mexican, by the way," I added casually.

He snorted. "But you've got blue eyes."

I shrugged. "So?"

"And your sister and brother are blond."

My sixth-grade science class had not yet covered dominant and recessive genes, so I trotted out the line that always got a laugh on nighttime sitcoms. "Blame it on the milkman."

He allowed himself the barest glimmer of a smile. "You're cool, Mary. Well . . . see y'around." He leaped from the pool and hightailed it to his restaurant without a towel, leaving a feathery wet trail in his wake.

After our showers, my mother led us to a sticky red-cushioned booth in a dim corner of the restaurant. A waitress with a long black braid brought us chips and salsa and yellow plastic cups of ice water. My sister, brother, and I crammed our mouths full of the salty, still-warm tortilla chips.

"Eat up. They're free," my mother whispered. I hoped to sample the renowned chicken mole, but when the waitress appeared again, my mother ordered four-dollar taco plates for all of us. "*Los platos del día, por favor*," she said.

"*Y una Coca-Cola*," I added hopefully.

She frowned. "*¿Cuánto cuesta?*"

"*Un dólar,*" the waitress said.

My mother studied my siblings and me. For the first time that day, her face registered our excitement and she smiled. "*Tres Cokes,*" she said, "*y una Corona.*"

I shivered from joy and damp hair. I didn't see the boy anywhere, but the crisp crunch of taco shells and the play of cool lettuce against spicy beef distracted me. We would meet again, I told myself, the next time my mother drove us to Monterey.

The waitress appeared once more at my mother's side. "Dessert?"

"*No, gracias.* My car is in the shop," she explained, draining her beer. "*No tengo mucho dinero.*"

I blushed at our lack of funds, but the waitress nodded. "I no have money, either," she said. "I have four boys. *Mi esposo*—my husband—he leave to go back to Mexico. He take my oldest son with him."

They looked at each other with sympathy. For an instant, my mother's capable veneer cracked, and I shivered in the sudden blast from the air conditioner. I knew what it did to a girl to lose her mother. I was less sure of what it did to a mother to lose her daughter.

Over her shoulder, I saw a pair of fierce brown eyes flash from the kitchen doorway and vanish into the shadows.

Five minutes later, the waitress returned—not with the check, but bearing a dinner plate on which sat what appeared to be upside-down pudding. "*Es flan,*" she said, handing us four spoons. "It is . . . how you say? On the house."

We thanked her and dug in, smiling as the slippery pudding rich with caramel sauce tickled our tongues and throats. After dessert, my mother paid the bill and herded us back to the hotel room. Katie and I slid open the windows to invite in a tepid airflow before collapsing on one bed to watch television.

My mother paused in her channel surfing at a Shirley Temple movie. Shirley and her little brother, accompanied by bizarre human incarnations of their pet cat and dog, wandered through the lands of past and future in search of something called the Bluebird of Happiness.

Shirley Temple's bluebird was a squat German avian with a red breast, singing sweetly in its cage until it got out and headed for the hills. The pampered avian bore no resemblance to the scrub jays that patrolled my mother and Patricia's sprawling property. Our birds ate stale breadcrumbs and screamed threats from the fruit trees if the cats crept too close.

"This movie's boring," my sister yawned. Tim sat hunched over his pillow, asleep in his flannel pajamas.

My mother stood up to change the channel, but I leaned forward to peer at the screen. "Can we watch just five more minutes. Please?" The movie both frightened and fascinated me. Shirley and her brother navigated a raging forest fire, and a fairy led them through the "Land of the Unborn," where they met their future sister.

"Really, honey, this is gonna give you nightmares," my mother said when the kids met up with their grandparents, who had been temporarily liberated from their respective graves. She punched numbers into the TV. "Look, here's *Wild Kingdom*. The alligators are mating."

I watched the reptilian love-tryst with interest, but longed to know whether Shirley Temple ever discovered her bluebird. The next morning, I woke early. My mother slept frowning, one hand tucked beneath her chin. Determined to be her little ray of sunshine, I tried to make coffee in the Mr. Coffee plugged into the bathroom wall. But though the red light came on, no liquid would brew. "It's okay," my mother said, hugging me. "Coffee's free at the rest stops, and we'll eat your grandmother's apples and cheese for breakfast."

All that afternoon, as our Volkswagen headed down the 101 with its new starter, I couldn't stop thinking about *The Blue Bird*. "It was supposed to be another *Wizard of Oz*," my mother told me, "but it flopped. The film's one big cliché. Shirley Temple finds the bird in her own back yard."

"Are we picking up Patricia so she can drive down to Daddy's with us?" I asked as we passed Santa Claus Lane, dutifully saluting his mittened statue on top of the Date Shack. I stopped short of voicing what I really wanted to know: *so that after you drop us off, you don't have to drive back to your house all alone?*

My mother clenched her jaw. "Patricia moved out this weekend," she said shortly.

And now, a flicker of hope began to flame inside me. Without her girlfriend, my mother would no longer incur the wrath of the court system and my father. Without Patricia, couldn't we all move to Oxnard and live there full-time? I clenched my hands in my lap, giddy with excitement as we approached the strawberry fields that served as a gateway to the city.

But my mother flew past the exit for her now-empty house in Oxnard without a glance and continued down the freeway to Los Angeles. Katie and Tim dozed in the seat behind me. Suddenly, I tore off my seat belt and hurtled to the back of the bus. Through the window, I could almost see the yard full of trees and flowers and cats, could almost glimpse the flash of a blue feather in the sunset.

FLAN

Listen to the bluebirds outside your kitchen window as you preheat your oven to 350 degrees and grease a nine-inch round baking dish. Stir half a cup of sugar over medium heat in a heavy saucepan for about five minutes, until it turns golden brown. Do not get distracted by romantic longings for sweetness or the mixture will burn. Pour the hot syrup into your pan, and allow it to coat the bottom. You've made caramel, which will harden and melt again in the oven.

Daydream about the boy with the soulful brown eyes as you beat three whole eggs together with three yolks and two-thirds a cup of sugar until the mixture is smooth. Whisk in three cups of milk and two teaspoons of vanilla. Pour this custard into your caramel-lined pan. Set it inside a nine-by-thirteen-inch pan and fill the pan with hot water so that it comes halfway up the side of your round pan.

Bake the flan thirty-five to forty-five minutes. At that point, call out "Marco!" If the pudding answers "Polo!" it is ready. Alternatively, you may insert a knife into the center of the flan. It's done when the knife comes out clean. Cool the flan still inside the nine-by-thirteen-inch pan, then remove it and refrigerate in the round pan for at least an hour.

Locate and dust your best celebratory platter. Run a knife around the edge of the flan to release it. Put your platter over the top of your pan and then—gently as a first kiss—upend it so that your flan lands in the center of the platter. It should look magnificent, covered with caramel. Serve with dessert spoons, or spoon up flan to put into individual bowls. Enjoy while listening to "Red Sails in the Sunset" played on the accordion.

6

THE SQUEAKY
ANIMAL HAT CLUB

THE MEMORY OF MY GRANDMOTHER'S SPARE CLOSET LINGERED IN MY mind after we got back from Monterey. It had surrounded me, warm and dark and reeking of Avon jasmine perfume. The tiny utility flashlight I'd held in my hand highlighted the details of the costumes she'd brought home for mending. I huddled between threadbare Cleopatra tunics and torn French maids' uniforms, silent save for the whispering of pages being turned as I mined *One Hundred Years of Solitude* for erotica.

A baby sitter had introduced me to the novel—or, if not offering it outright, allowed me to skim through her copy at my father's house one night as she tucked my little brother into bed. On my father's orange couch, my eyes widened and my Kliban-cat nightshirt seemed suddenly too restrictive as I skimmed sex scenes involving men who approached women's bodies with caresses I couldn't fathom, but craved nevertheless.

My baby sitter took the novel home with her when she left that night, but I located another copy at the library in the adult fiction section. I tiptoed to the front of the library to find a trio of elderly female librarians manning the checkout counter; I knew they'd never let me leave with such a book.

Being forced to abandon the book when I'd just discovered it anew struck me as cruel injustice. But a few weeks later I spotted García Márquez on my grandmother's shelf, tucked among Agatha Christies.

I saw my chance. While my siblings napped and my mother and grandmother chatted on the back patio, I snatched up the novel and crept into the spare closet with my grandmother's flashlight. I skimmed over the various family dramas until I came to a scene between Aureliano and his feisty aunt, Amaranta Úrsula. My breath bottomed out as I read and reread, legs crossed tight, teeth imprinting my bottom lip as I imagined my pale, untouched body ravished by the hands of a Colombian man.

In the near-darkness, I struggled with lust and doubt. What did it mean that these scenes turned me on? Swooning over Aureliano, I'd unwillingly aligned myself with my father and stepmother, who locked their bedroom door late Saturday nights and didn't appear downstairs until midmorning on Sundays. I thought about how I'd snuck up to their room after school one day and discovered *The Joy of Sex* under the bed, its photographs relentlessly heterosexual and titillating. What would my mother say?

Shaken, I closed the novel and buried it under a crooked hoopskirt, resolving to keep my desire for men a secret from her and Patricia.

But Patricia had vanished. Always, she'd sat at the kitchen table, smoking an unfiltered Camel and drinking a bottle of Budweiser when we ran through the front door every other Friday evening. "Hello, kids," she'd rasp as we ran to hug her. "Who wants ice cream?"

Now the table stood empty. Patricia's pillow, encased in nicotine-stained green flannel, had been replaced by my embroidered blue cat-shaped cushion.

"Did she really move out?" I demanded. It was the first Friday in August. The queen-size bed had disappeared from her room. In its place was a single mattress on the floor, covered with a red-and-green-striped Army blanket.

My mother's eyes shone with a new, soft sorrow. "She's gone," she said and walked into the kitchen. I followed close behind and watched her take out a carton of ice cream and place a jar of fudge in hot water to soften. Her right bicep swelled as she ground a handful of walnuts with her tiny stone mortar and pestle.

Gone. I contemplated the word as I savored the fleeting combination of hot fudge and vanilla on my tongue. Did *gone* mean my mother would return to my father? Would my stepmother go as well, leaving us to live as a normal family once more?

"Are you moving back in with Daddy?" I asked her.

"Not a chance." She reached for a half pack of Camels, lit one, and stared out the window into the darkness. "Men are bad news."

All the way back to my father's house that Sunday afternoon, I thought of Aureliano's tender, skilled hands and hung my head in dismay. I thought of the boy in the pool in Paso Robles and resolved to never reveal my attraction to the opposite sex.

I found out about my mother's new girlfriend through the discovery of a pink furry hat. Sewn in the shape of a pig's head, complete with a snout and two floppy ears, it lay nestled on the top shelf of her closet. I pressed the snout. It squeaked.

"Mommy, why do you have this?" I carried it out to where she sat reading a Dr. Seuss book to Tim on the couch.

She looked up. "Oh, honey!" she cried, snatching up the hat. "You're not supposed to touch that."

I stared at her. "But it's a kid's hat."

She shook her head. "No, it's mine." Her cheeks reddened as she stuffed the hat into her jeans pocket. "I belong to a sort of club, and we wear these hats to meetings. They're not for kids."

Indignation flushed my face red. It hadn't occurred to me that my mother might enjoy a social life in my absence. I assumed she worked full-time and studied for her bachelor's degree on the evenings we weren't with her. But now I saw that she had friends, and a secret society—complete with an off-limits hat.

"Who's in this club?" I demanded. "Is it a Brownie troop?"

In our old life, she'd been a Girl Scout leader, organizing campouts and visits to retirement homes with homemade cookies and construction-paper cards. Panic gripped me. Had she adopted a new troop of girls in Oxnard? "It's not the Brownies," she sighed. "It's just four women who sit around and act silly. You'll meet one of them tomorrow," she added.

"So she has a pig hat, too?" I sputtered.

My mother turned back to her book. "She's the horse."

The next day, my mother's new friend raced down our street in a blue convertible Miata, speakers blaring Culture Club's "I'll Tumble 4 Ya." Tall, tanned, and athletic, she loped through my mother's front door in a red flannel shirt and cutoff blue jeans. "Lissa!" She grabbed my hand in hers. "I'm Annie. I've heard so much about you. You're the oldest, a bookworm, just like me."

I narrowed my eyes at Annie's firm grip, at her cropped hair and wide smile. Behind her, the adoration shining in my mother's eyes told me all I needed to know. "Ready to hit the tennis courts?" Annie bounced on the toes of her sneakers.

"She's going to give us all lessons," my mother announced.

My siblings rushed for the VW bus, already stocked with rackets and vacuum-packed cans of neon balls. I shuffled out the door, turning just in time to see Annie kiss my mother's cheek and squeeze her hand.

My palm burned as I remembered how Flavio Flores had touched my fingers for an instant the day before in PE class. Our teacher had made us square-dance to Kool & the Gang's "Celebration," and I was smitten. I looked at my mother and Annie and wondered what it would be like to dance with a girl.

On the tennis court, Annie sprinted back and forth, her serve graceful, her legs a blur. Our teams were uneven. With my sister and brother vying to see who could bounce tennis balls the highest in the court adjacent to ours, my mother stood alone on one side of the net while Annie taught me to serve on the other.

"Toss the ball up with your left hand as you swing the racket in your right hand. Up, over, and serve!" she chanted. But my ball flew wild, again and again.

Whenever my mother had to chase my wayward serves and volleys to the far corners of the court, I studied Annie. "I'd love to join your squeaky hat club," I said. "I love animals."

"Sorry, kiddo." She ruffled my hair. "Women only. I'd better go help your mother."

She jogged to meet my mother on the other side of the net. I threw down my racket. Wasn't I a woman? Even now, a too-large maxi-pad chafed the sides of my thighs.

My mother looked up at me as the racket crashed onto the concrete. "Annie's made chili. We're going to her house for dinner."

"Chili!" my brother echoed, clapping his hands.

"I thought Katie and I were making Frito Boats," I grumbled.

She crossed the court and put an arm around me. "Honey, you can stay home if you want."

I shrugged off her embrace. "I'll go," I muttered.

Annie's tract home was remarkable only for the fact that three women shared it on a suburban street otherwise teeming with mom-and-dad families, whose tricycles and kickballs littered the lawns. We walked into the kitchen, where a Crock-Pot of chili simmered on the tiled countertop. "Serve yourself!" Annie handed me a ladle and a mustard-colored bowl.

I peered into the pot. Kernels of corn hid among pinto beans and diced green chilies. "What's that meat stuff?" I demanded.

"Texturized vegetable protein," Annie said. "Your mom's a vegetarian, so I created this recipe for her."

"It's the best chili in the world," my mother assured me from the table where she sat with Annie's two housemates. I didn't have to ask who they were. The way they whooped and joked in their flannel shirts and baggy blue jeans convinced me that I was breaking cornbread with the other two members of the Squeaky Animal Hat Club.

In spite of my jealousy, I had to admit that Annie made a great chili, not too spicy, yet warming to the stomach. The TVP mimicked meat without any of the guilt I often felt when confronted with cow, pig, or bird in my bowl.

"So what do you think?" My mother cocked her head to one side.

"It's delicious," I mumbled, spreading honey-butter over another square of homemade cornbread.

She beamed at me as if she'd made the meal herself. "Annie puts a secret ingredient in her chili."

My sister peered into her bowl. "What is it?"

Annie shook her head. "I'll never tell."

Katie pursed up her lips. "But Mommy knows."

One of the other women elbowed my mother in the side. "That's because she's special. Let's go watch *Poltergeist*."

My mind settled on that word, *special*. Not even the horror movie, shown on Annie's new Beta player, could distract me from my angst.

Obviously, Annie was special to my mother, too. I slumped on the orange shag carpet and studied the quartet of women as they laughed when the maggot-infested pork chop crawled across the counter. They mimicked the tiny exorcist woman's voice and hollered at their own imitations. I suspected their club wasn't so much about being a woman as it was about liking women. How hard could it be to shift my desire from boys to girls?

I stared at JoBeth Williams freaking out on the television in her T-shirt and underwear. "She's so hot," I said experimentally.

My observation elicited silence. And then all four women burst out laughing.

At the end of September, the third Friday night of the month, my mother picked us up in Los Angeles and sped back up north, flying past our usual stop at McDonald's in Malibu. The Miata stood in the driveway. "Annie's here!" my sister cried and ran up the newly mowed lawn to the front door.

I straightened the tail of the blue flannel shirt I'd bought for a dollar at a garage sale. The day before, I'd hacked the legs off an old pair of Levi's and fringed the ends meticulously with a needle. In this outfit, which I'd completed with a careless ponytail, I greeted Annie and prayed she'd recognize me as one of her own.

She didn't appear to notice my transformation. "I've made chili," she said. "Wash your hands, and grab a bowl."

I savored the meal even as I puzzled over its secret ingredient. Savory, yet sweet. I ate another serving in wonder. "We're going to have movie night," my mother announced as I cleared the table. "*Seven Brides for Seven Brothers*."

"Again?" I dropped the bowls into the sink. "Can't we watch *La Cage*

Aux Folles instead?" *Seven Brides*, formerly my favorite musical, now struck me as shamelessly boy-meets-girl. But already, Howard Keel was belting out "Bless Yore Beautiful Hide" from the living room, where my sister and Annie had spread out blankets and sleeping bags and pillows.

I sat beside my little brother, who sang incomprehensibly to every song, and ate from the communal bowl of popcorn. Perhaps the film could serve as a litmus test of my sexuality, I reasoned. Fourteen couples sang and danced for an hour and a half; surely I could find one of the gingham-clad girls more attractive than the broad-shouldered Benjamin Pontipee, after whom I'd historically lusted.

I settled on his girlfriend, a tall dark-haired woman who bore the unfortunate name of Dorcas. "She's so beautiful," I exclaimed.

On the couch, my mother and Annie said nothing.

When "June Bride" came on, and six women danced around in their corsets and bloomers, I cast a surreptitious look at my mother. "Oh man, that Dorcas is so sexy!" I breathed.

My mother's brows drew together. Beside her, the corners of Annie's mouth twitched. "She ends up marrying the most handsome man in the movie," she said. "That Benjamin Pontipee's pretty hot stuff."

Katie executed an enthusiastic wolf whistle. I shrugged, blinding myself to the actor's chiseled chin. After the movie, my sister and I pirouetted around the living room. I clasped my hands under my chin and sang Dorcas's lines, casting out the image of Benjamin square-dancing with me in the Oregon wilderness. "By the light of the silvery moon, / Home you ride, side by side . . ."

My mother applauded from the couch. "Someday you'll make a beautiful bride," Annie told me, "with your curly brown hair flowing, and a long white dress."

I snorted. "Unless I fall in love with a woman."

My mother's smile faded. "A woman?"

"Sure." I lifted my chin and tossed my ponytail. "Like you."

Now I could almost feel the pressure of the too-small, furry hatband around my head. My mother stood up. "Bedtime," she said and carried my brother off to his room.

Annie wiped her hands on her jeans. "I guess I'd better get going."

I began folding up blankets and sleeping bags. "Can I ask you something?" I said.

Annie sat back down on the couch. "Shoot."

"When did you know you were . . . well . . . gay?"

She picked up a pillow and thumped it thoughtfully. "When I was seven," she said at last. "I had a crush on a girl in second grade. I tried like hell to like boys, but you can't alter nature. How about you?"

"What d'you mean?" I rolled up a sleeping bag, hiding my face.

"When did you know you were straight?"

"I didn't. I mean, I don't. I mean . . . I don't know," I stammered. "I like women."

Annie regarded me soberly over the pillow. "It's a difficult life," she said. "I'm not sure your mother would wish it on you."

I shrugged, feigning carelessness. "Well," I said, "you can't alter nature."

Still, the next weekend, I thought I had succeeded. My father invited his boss to dinner, along with the man's wife and two children.

"The girl is a freshman in high school," Elsa said as I helped her scour the house with lemon-scented rags. "The mother is Spanish, and very elegant. I hope she likes seafood."

For days, my stepmother had debated the merits of fish over beef, rice over potatoes. She shopped the afternoon before the dinner for the freshest produce possible. My sister and I surveyed the menu, written out in her beautiful hand and stuck to the refrigerator with a magnet.

"Poached salmon with dill sauce." Katie wrinkled her nose.

"New potatoes with butter and dill," I read, already planning how I'd scrape the herb off my spuds with a fork.

"Salad with blue cheese dressing." My sister and I winced in unison. Not even homemade rice pilaf with hazelnuts could convince us that the supper would be appetizing. "Can we have hot dogs?" Katie asked.

Elsa nodded. "I've already boiled them for you."

"Salmon tastes like dog," my brother observed from the table, cramming half an Oscar Mayer into his mouth.

I ladled sweet pickle relish over my wiener on its whole wheat bun and regarded my bowl of baked beans, sans dill weed, with gratitude. The doorbell rang as I took a bite.

Elsa looked up from her salad spinner. "They're here!" she cried. "Half an hour early, and your father's still in the shower!"

She unclasped her ponytail and shook out her hair on her way to answer the door. "This is Mr. and Mrs. Lowe," she said as the family filed into the dining room. "And their children, Natalia and Georgie."

Mr. Lowe looked like every other businessman I'd ever seen, stiff and smirking in a three-piece suit. His wife wore her raven hair pulled back into a bun, revealing diamond earrings the size of pencil erasers. She wore a suit as well—a tailored skirt with heels. The boy, Georgie, had her black hair and wide smile. Under the table, my sister stepped on my foot. I ignored her and greeted his older sister.

"Hi!" I lifted my arm and waved. The bun I was holding, laden with pickle relish, gave way in my hand, and my hotdog slipped to the linoleum.

"Ooops!" Natalia bent to pick up my dinner. "There you go." She placed the dog on my plate.

I bent my head so that my hair swung forward to hide the new pimples dotting my cheeks. "Thank you."

My heart began to pound. Natalia was fourteen. She had unblemished skin, smooth as melted chocolate ice cream, and a silky black pageboy.

"You're welcome," she said, and the syllables evoked the sweet strumming of Spanish guitars in a cobblestone courtyard. Her breasts swelled delicately under her blue Izod shirt, its collar turned up around her slender neck, and her ankles glowed—an inch of tantalizing skin between the hem of her pegged blue jeans and snowy socks.

She was so lovely that my chest tightened in agony and euphoria. At last, I was a lesbian.

Natalia looked at her mother. I looked at my stepmother. Would the adults include her in their feasting on salmon and rice pilaf and the dreaded blue cheese, or would she be relegated to my sister's bedroom with the rest of us?

"Would you like to have dinner with us, Natalia?" Elsa held out a hand for her jacket.

"Thank you," she replied. "I've already eaten."

That was my cue. "Come on!" I leaped up from the table and grabbed her hand. "We have a new video game in my sister's room."

That year, Centipede, Pac-Man, and the rest had moved out of Chuck E. Cheese and into private homes—affordable for the middle class, but my father never bought anything he could get for free. A coworker had presented him with a box of inch-long microchips, each representing a different video game, and he showed us how to lock their tiny metal teeth into a disc fitted into the console in lieu of a cartridge. "We have Frogger!" I said.

"I've never played it." Natalia smiled kindly and tucked her legs under her on the carpet.

To cover my excitement, I handed her the joystick and showed her how to navigate the one-dimensional frog across a busy highway so as not to become roadkill. Her French manicure made her seem so sophisticated. "What's your perfume?" I whispered.

"Jean Naté's After Bath Splash," she replied.

I resolved to buy a bottle the next day.

My sister, meanwhile, appeared to be equally captivated by Natalia's brother. They shoelaced her stuffed rabbits together back-to-back and held them down on railroad tracks composed of the Little House on the Prairie series as my brother rolled his toy train across the carpet.

"No! No! No!" Georgie cried, emulating a damsel in distress.

Katie took on the deep voice of a sadistic train conductor. "It's curtains for you, ma'am."

I turned my back on them, indicating my elevated age and rank to Natalia. "Where do you go to school?" I asked.

She frowned delicately as a truck smashed her frog into an X and then disappeared from the screen. "Saint Bonaventure," she said. "It's Catholic. My parents won't let me go to the public school. Saint Bonnie's is all girls."

I took a deep breath and considered what that meant—that Natalia must be a lesbian, too. I pictured myself inviting her to my mother's house, sitting around the living room with her and Annie. Each of us would wear a furry animal hat as we gossiped about Billie Jean King's short skirts.

"I bet you like tennis," I said.

Natalia shook her head so that her hair swayed against her neck, releasing the scent of her citrus perfume. "Swimming."

"Do you listen to Culture Club?"

She raised trim black eyebrows. "Madonna."

"Oh. She's my favorite, too," I lied. "I just love that song, 'Holiday.'"

At the mention of one of her beloved forty-fives, my sister leaped to her feet. "Hol-i-day-ay!" she sang, expertly gyrating her hips and shoulders. "Cel-e-bray-ate!"

Natalia clasped her hands in admiration. "Wow, Katie. You've got the moves."

Dismay dampened my effervescence. I couldn't join Katie in her dance; Flavio Flores had lately remarked during PE class that I moved like Herman Munster. I shrugged. "Yeah," I told Natalia, "but I've got the brains."

"I can see that." She put down the joystick and stretched out her legs. "So do your parents have a liquor cabinet?"

I nodded. "Sure. It's next to where we keep the board games."

I glimpsed the bottles of gin, rum, and whiskey whenever my stepmother concocted drinks for herself and my father. Alcohol held no interest for me. My attentions were focused on the top shelf, where my father kept wide containers of superfine sugar for rimming glasses, plus jars of candied citrus peel and maraschino cherries. "Would you like a cherry?" I asked Natalia.

She snorted delicately and lowered her voice, glancing at Georgie and Katie. "What I could go for is a couple shots of crème de menthe. Can you score us some?"

Crème de menthe. Wasn't that what Elsa poured into the drink she called a Grasshopper? It reminded me of Drano. "Is it alcohol?" I whispered.

She smiled. "Of course it is, silly. All the girls at school drink it. Go see if you can find the bottle."

I closed my eyes and pictured the path to the liquor cabinet. It stood just beyond the dining room table. I knew Elsa would invite Mr. and Mrs. Lowe into the parlor after dinner. The French doors were usually locked to preserve the Asian-print couches and glass elephants, but she'd opened it for the occasion.

"I guess I could jump over the counter so nobody sees me," I said.

"So do it," Natalia urged.

I looked deep into her brown eyes. They were placid, like those of a cow. My gaze drifted down from her partially unbuttoned polo shirt to her ankles. Confusion clouded my mind. Did I love her . . . or did I just want to be her?

I slipped off my shoes and stepped out into the hallway. I could hear the adults in the parlor. I smelled French roast and knew they'd moved into the coffee-and-brandy part of the evening. I tiptoed down the hall, through my bedroom, and into the kitchen.

Remnants of the salmon feast littered the counter. If I rounded the corner of the kitchen, I'd be in full view of the parlor. I couldn't remove the platter and plates from the counter without the telltale clink of china. But how could I leap over the fish?

For an instant, I wavered. No girl, no matter how cool, was worth getting caught by my father with a bottle of alcohol. But now I heard Annie's voice in my head. "It's a difficult life," she said.

"I can take it," I muttered and vaulted over the counter. I combat crawled to the liquor cabinet, grabbed a green bottle, and retraced my leap, heart thudding as I tucked it under my T-shirt.

In my sister's room, the three younger kids had strung the luckless rabbits from the overhead light and were pelting them with tennis balls. Natalia lounged on my sister's bed, picking at her cuticles. When she saw me, she brightened. "Did you get it?"

I bent toward her, hiding the bottle in my cupped forearms. "Here it is."

She examined the label and shook her head. "Silly girl," she chided, "this is vermouth. Still . . . " She uncapped it and we leaned in to sniff the sickly sweet liquid. "Gross," she said.

My heart sank. "I'll go get the right one," I whispered. I turned around to find my stepmother standing in the doorway. My hand flew to my mouth.

"I thought you kids might like to join us for dessert," Elsa said.

In my peripheral vision, I saw Natalia's foot nudge the vermouth bottle under the bed. "We'd love to," she said and led us all out of the room.

Our families gathered on opposite sides of the dining room table. I studied my father's tailored boss, his sophisticated wife flanked by their urbane offspring. They struck me as intact, happy, magnetic enough to rate one of the full-page Nordstrom ads in the Saturday *Times*. Across from them, indelicately scooping up pie à la mode with our forks, my family sat fractured and fractious, worthy only of modeling for the Sears catalog.

Over her pie, Natalia caught my eye and tilted her head a cool half inch toward the liquor cabinet. The door stood slightly open, and I could see the crème de menthe glowing green in its clear bottle.

She winked one long-lashed eye at me and smiled. I bit my lip to keep from grinning. I thought of Aureliano from *One Hundred Years of Solitude*. Would the touch of Natalia's hands seduce me as the image of his had? I tried unsuccessfully to break into goose bumps.

"So, Natalia," Elsa said. "How is school going for you this year?"

My new girlfriend turned to my stepmother. "It's going well, thank you. I really enjoy my history class."

History. We would sit over twin glasses of crème de menthe and discuss the plight of the Native Americans, the sad record of lesbian mothers. But Natalia continued.

"I've been dating a junior from the all-boys' school down the road."

Elsa's pie, so delectable with its crumb topping and golden-spiced apples, abruptly nauseated me. I scowled down at the ice cream melting in a puddle on my plate. *Natalia's straight,* I thought. Then followed another thought that I found even more troubling. I was relieved.

"We've got to be going," my father's boss said. "Elsa, thank you for a marvelous dinner." He shook my father's hand.

"*Muchas gracias.*" His wife kissed my stepmother on both cheeks. "*¿Niños?*"

Natalia and Georgie shook my father and stepmother's hands. "Thank you," they echoed.

I followed them to the door. "Well, goodbye," Natalia said and reached to hug me.

I pressed up against her and felt neither titillated nor repelled. Suddenly, I just wanted her gone.

In October, my mother pulled into my father's driveway with Annie in the passenger's seat of the VW. "Where am I supposed to sit?" I grumbled.

She hugged me. "Honey, there's plenty of room in back." She handed me her fringed leather purse. "Will you count out change for four McDonald's sundaes?"

"Katie can do it." I shoved the purse toward my sister and strapped myself into the middle seat, sweating in my blue flannel shirt.

Even hot fudge didn't sweeten my mood. At my mother's house, I stalked to the converted garage bedroom I shared with Katie and threw myself down on my mattress with a copy of *Gone with the Wind*.

My mother walked in. "Honey, don't you want to watch *Oklahoma!* with us?"

I didn't look up from my book. "I'm reading," I muttered, steeling myself against the heart-wrenching romance between Scarlett O'Hara and Rhett Butler.

At breakfast the next morning, I pulled on my cutoffs and stalked out to eat Annie's blueberry pancakes in silence. "Pass the syrup," Katie told me.

I shrugged. "Get it yourself."

Annie sat beside my mother and handed me a plate of sausage. "Oscar Mayer's Little Smokies," she said. "Your mom tells me they're your favorite."

I eschewed the plate. "I'm going vegetarian," I snapped.

She nodded. "Well, it's a good thing I'm making my chili tonight. Why don't you come with me after breakfast? I need to pick up the secret ingredient."

Instantly, Katie petitioned Annie with her wide blue gaze. "I want to know what it is!"

"Lissa's the oldest." Annie wrapped a Little Smoky up in a pancake and took a big bite. "She deserves a few privileges."

Glumly, I finished my breakfast and set out with Annie down Hughes Drive. At the end of the four-block street stood Saviers Boulevard with its trio of fast-food restaurants beside a Safeway. We walked past Taco Bell and Kentucky Fried Chicken. "Turn here." Annie guided me into a Wendy's. "It's not too early for French fries and Frosties, is it?"

I surveyed her, suspicious. "I guess not."

Annie ordered large fries and medium Frosties for both of us and grabbed a handful of condiment packets. We sat at a yellow laminate table with our food and faced off. Annie took a long pull from her straw. "I really like your mother," she said at last.

I sprinkled salt on my fries. "I really like her, too."

She reached for the salt shaker. "I'd like to move in with her," she said, "but only if it's all right with you."

I searched her face for signs of sarcasm. Finding none, I sat and stared at my Frosty. If Annie moved in, my mother wouldn't have to make the long drive up and down Pacific Coast Highway by herself four times a month. She wouldn't have to spend ten days alone in her house between our visits. Still, I glared down at my soggy fries.

"I don't care if the whole darned Animal Hat Club moves in," I muttered.

Annie lifted her Frosty cup to toast mine. "I'm so glad, Lissa. You've got a wonderful family."

I shrugged and sucked at the thick chocolate milkshake so violently that the insides of my cheeks ached. I had a wonderful family two weekends a month. Tomorrow, I'd have to return to my father's house, and Annie would get to live with my mother full-time.

We finished our snack in silence and threw away our cartons and cups. Outside, I headed for Safeway.

"Where're you going?" Annie waved me back to her.

I stopped. "I thought we were going to get that special ingredient for your chili. What is it, anyway?"

She reached into her jacket pocket. "I've got it."

She opened her hand and revealed six packets of Wendy's hot chili sauce. I stared at them splayed out on her palm.

"That's it?" I yelped.

She grinned. "That's it."

I plodded home beside her, resigned. There was no storage in my makeshift garage bedroom, so I slipped into my mother's closet and closed the door. Her flannel shirts and worn blue jeans surrounded me, warm and soft. If I closed my eyes, I could almost hear her heartbeat.

My stomach ached. In the darkness, I shrugged off my own flannel shirt and balled it up in my fist. I shoved it far back on the top shelf of the closet, hiding it and the pink furry pig hat from view.

ANNIE'S SPECIAL CHILI

Fringe the ends of your cutoff blue jeans, and put on a flannel shirt. Soak one cup of texturized vegetable protein in boiling water to cover. If cow in your bowl doesn't trouble you, substitute a half pound of browned ground beef for the TVP.

Sauté a chopped onion in a soup pot. Crank up Kool & the Gang's "Celebration" and sprinkle the onion with salt. Add two cloves of crushed garlic. Dump in an eight-ounce can of tomato sauce, and add one tablespoon each of cumin and coriander, plus half a teaspoon of chili flakes, a teaspoon of salt, half a teaspoon each of paprika and chili powder, and a can of diced green chilies.

Add the soaked TVP, and prepare the secret ingredient. First, clear the kitchen area of onlookers. Then, using a pair of sharp scissors or your teeth, open six packets of Wendy's chili sauce and carefully squeeze them into the soup pot. Discard the evidence immediately.

Add two fifteen-ounce cans of chili beans. Taste, and adjust flavoring. Note that the longer this chili simmers, the better it will taste. It's especially good paired with MGM musicals. Pass shredded cilantro and cheddar cheese for each individual bowl. Top with a squeaky animal hat, and enjoy.

7

THE MATCH

ON AN ARID SUMMER MORNING IN MID-AUGUST, A MONTH BEFORE I began eighth grade, my father loaded my siblings and me into the back of his Buick and cranked up the air conditioner. My stepmother settled herself in the passenger's seat with a James Michener novel and her binoculars, as Dad wedged five suitcases into the trunk.

I regarded my younger brother, crammed between my sister and me, with dismay. Tim and Katie were to be my constant companions on the four-day drive from Los Angeles to Ohio to visit my stepmother's parents. My sister and I had diaries and latch-hook rug kits—mine Peter Rabbit, hers Holly Hobbie—to break up the monotony of the trip. We also had a game—a set of sixteen plastic cubes, each with a common roadside object printed on it. The goal was to spot each item and then turn the cube upside down. When all sixteen were upended, they formed an American flag. I found the cat and the tree before my father backed out of the driveway.

"Why can't we just fly to Ohio?" I asked as he merged onto the freeway. "We'd be there by tonight."

"And a thousand dollars poorer." He glanced at me in the rearview mirror and winked. "On a road trip," he observed with the barest hint of sarcasm, "we all get a chance to enjoy each other's company."

I rolled my eyes. My stepmother smiled over her shoulder. "When you get home," she said, "you can tell all your friends you've been in nine different states!"

Her enthusiasm shamed me. "That's cool," I lied and affected an eager and expectant observation of Interstate 110 through the window. We passed LAX, and later the giant Felix the Cat who presided, grinning and waving, over Felix Chevrolet. "Daddy, sing your song," Katie begged.

"Yeah, Pop." Tim leaned forward and tapped him on the shoulder. "Sing!"

My father smiled, pleased at the request. He cleared his throat and boldly proceeded to bastardize the lyrics prefacing the old Felix cartoon. "Felix the Cat . . . / the wonderful, wonderful cat. / He laughs and dances, jumps and sings. / He plays around with his little things!"

On the other side of the car, Katie bent double with laughter. Elsa sighed and opened her book. Beside me, Tim sat up straight and grinned sweetly. "Cat balls," he announced.

I hunkered down in my seat, worrying. My cat, Julius, orange with white stripes, slept at the foot of my bed every night. Elsa had hired our baby sitter to walk him around the block twice a day and give him his Friskies and a dollop of tuna, but what would he do without my daily brushing and petting?

"What if Orange Julius runs away?" I demanded of the front seat as we left Los Angeles.

My father snorted. "Don't be such a worrywart." He swerved into the carpool lane and set the cruise control to eighty. "You're just like your mother."

This was not high praise, coming from him. But much as I wanted to disagree with his assessment of her, I had to admit he was right. In my head, I ticked off a list of those items that caused her the most angst: balloons, the propane tank on the Coleman stove, champagne corks, the plastic fin on surfboards, and my walking across the top of the monkey bars barefoot.

In my head, my mother's round, cheerful face morphed into that of a warthog's. She snuffled about, hooves pawing the dirt with anxiety. I saw myself a miniature warthog beside her and winced.

"I'm not worried," I declared to my father, "but you know how Tim loves that cat."

"If Julius is there when we get home," Elsa said, "I'll take you to the mall and buy you an Orange Julius to celebrate."

"I want to go!" Katie whined.

Tim looked at us blankly. Having lost the thread of the conversation, he resorted to his old standard. "Cat balls," he repeated.

Elsa ignored him and slipped her Supertramp tape into the cassette player. My father retreated into silence. I reached for my Peter Rabbit diary and extracted the tiny gold key from the ribbon around my neck. Furtively, I slipped it into the lock and clicked it open.

My English teacher had assigned us Oscar Wilde's *The Importance of Being Earnest* the previous spring. Carefully, I'd copied Gwendolyn's lines on the first page of my journal: "I never travel without my diary. One should always have something sensational to read in the train."

But reading through my own diary, I found only a scribbled account of boys I had loved, boys who had not noticed me in math or English class except to make fun of my lime-green A-line skirt dotted with pink hippos. "Hippo Girl!" they called me when I walked up to the chalkboard to do long division or parse sentences, until mournfully, I folded up the beloved skirt and tucked it into Elsa's Goodwill bag.

"We'll stop twice a day, for lunch and dinner," my father told us that first leg of the trip. "Use the bathroom then. Otherwise," he jerked his head at the empty Folgers can on the upholstered ledge behind the back seat, "there's your potty."

My stepmother smiled patiently. "Don't listen to him," she told us. "That can's in case one of you gets sick."

Gingerly, I slid the can from its position above my head and over toward Katie, who stuck out her tongue at me and put it behind Tim's head. Elsa returned to her book.

I studied her serene profile. Was she excited to be traveling to see her parents? We'd met them once when they flew out to meet us shortly after she'd married my father, and she hadn't seen them since. In the past few weeks, she'd sewed Katie and me organdy sundresses to wear in Ohio's sultry summer heat. Mine was pale green, off the shoulder with a flounce at the bottom. Katie's was a strappy pink number dotted with purple butterflies. Elsa had sewed herself an outfit, as well—a button-down linen blouse with cuffed short sleeves and a matching fitted skirt. The ensemble, light blue with tiny white flowers, showed off her hips and her talent for buttonholes.

For the road trip, however, we all wore T-shirts and shorts. My thighs stuck to the seat, sweaty in spite of the air conditioning. I climbed out of the Buick that first afternoon at a McDonald's in Arizona, and a wall of heat hit me in the face. I gasped from the force of it.

"You can each order a cheeseburger, small fries, and a small drink," my father declared inside the restaurant. From his billfold, he produced a crisp twenty-dollar bill. "We'll spend twenty dollars a day on lunch and thirty on dinner."

He ordered a Quarter Pounder and large French fries, while Elsa requested a Filet-O-Fish sans fries and a large Diet Coke. We ate together in a plastic booth, then filed back into the car for another five hours of driving.

My father parked that night at a hotel somewhere near the Arizona border. "You'll share a room with Katie and Tim," he said and unlocked the door to a room that smelled of cigarettes and cleaning supplies. He handed me a key affixed to a plastic cactus. "Elsa and I will have the room next to yours."

I'd assumed Katie and I would room together and Tim would be with him and Elsa. Now I could see my role as baby sitter. "But where will we all sleep?" I demanded. "There are only two beds."

"You'll sleep with your sister," my father said and unlocked his door.

I shook my head. Katie rocked herself to sleep each night, and Tim thrashed around until his twisted bedsheets threatened to strangle him. "I'll sleep on the floor," I muttered.

"Fine," my father said. "Let's go eat."

A diner stood beside the hotel. We ate burgers and fries and drank red plastic cups of milk while my father and Elsa drank red wine. Outside, after dinner, the air was still hot, even in the dark. My siblings and I piled onto one double bed to watch *Wild Kingdom* and *The Wonderful World of Disney* on the hotel TV.

"Lights out at nine," my father told me. "My alarm will go off at six. I'll wake you at six thirty, and we'll leave at seven sharp." He closed the door between our room and his.

Katie nudged me with one bare foot. "I'll bet they're doing it," she whispered.

I shrugged and concentrated on the image of Jim Fowler wrestling a boa constrictor on the screen. I missed my mother. I didn't want to spend three more days trapped in a car, with only the prospect of a boring week in Ohio before embarking on another road trip back to Los Angeles.

Restless, I slid off the bed and walked to the window. I pulled back the stiff gold curtain and stared into the darkness. I longed to leave my siblings and wander outside to walk in the hot, dry wind alongside Interstate 40 until Burt Reynolds from *Smokey and the Bandit* pulled over and offered me a ride back to Oxnard. Instead, I walked back and sat on the bed beside Katie.

When Tinker Bell had cast her final spell over the Disney castle's animated turrets, I turned off the television and tucked Tim into bed. Katie crawled into the other bed and scooted over to one side. I pulled off her bedspread. "I'm sleeping on the floor," I reminded her.

She shrugged and tossed me a pillow. "More room for me," she said and turned out the light.

"Goodnight, sisters," Tim called from his bed.

"Sleep tight," I whispered, echoing our stepmother's bedtime ritual. "Don't let the bedbugs bite."

Yellow light from the outside hallway streamed in through a gap in the curtains. Stale cigarette smoke emanated from the bedspread. I imagined tiny insects crawling over it, but I couldn't bring myself to climb in beside Katie. I stared at the light a long time and finally fell asleep.

The next morning, my father shook me awake in the dim gray dawn. "You kids can come into our room for breakfast," he said.

I stood up, shoulders and hips aching from the hard floor, and stumbled into the room with Tim. Elsa opened a red and white cooler to reveal tiny cans of orange juice and a carton of milk. She produced single-serving cereal boxes and a package of chocolate-covered mini donuts. I took three and sat on the king-size bed to watch TV. From what I could gather over Tim crunching Frosted Flakes in my ear, people in Lebanon were at war. Blood had been shed.

That morning, my family's own personal war began. Katie wandered into the room at quarter till seven with her blond hair in her eyes. "I need to take a shower," she announced and opened a package of Froot Loops.

From the vanity mirror, my father shook his head. "Tonight." He brandished his comb at the digital clock on the nightstand. "It's six forty-five. We need to be on the road at seven."

"But I need to wash my hair. I'm filthy." My sister glared at him, her eyes sleepy but aggressive chinks of blue.

In the mirror, he stared her down. "You're ten," he said. "You don't even sweat. Now get dressed, and get in the car."

She snatched up her box of Froot Loops and stomped into the other room.

At seven exactly, we climbed into the Buick. Katie glowered under Tim's L.A. Dodgers cap. My brother clutched a melting chocolate donut in one hand, which he proceeded to smear on the seat behind me. I scrubbed at it with a paper napkin, gave up, and strapped on my seat belt, trying not to sit back. "Thanks a lot, Tim," I muttered. Elsa raised her eyebrows.

"Everyone okay back there?" my father asked in a voice that suggested we'd better be. I attempted a bright and sunshiny attitude. "Let's play the travel game," I told my siblings and took out the plastic cubes.

"That's stupid," Katie challenged. She closed her eyes and leaned her head against the window as my father pulled out of the hotel parking lot. Tim and I attempted to play the game, but we found only cars and the occasional telephone pole. A vast desert stretched out on either side of us, broken up by saguaro cacti, their spiny arms imploring me to stop and explore the flat, rocky terrain. But my father sat rigid in the driver's seat, staring straight ahead, his fingers curled around the steering wheel with no indication that he might apply the brake pedal.

How could he stand the boredom, I wondered. He had no books, no games to distract him. What was he thinking about, as we hurtled toward his in-laws in Ohio?

He'd gotten along with Elsa's parents when they'd visited. He'd complimented my new grandmother's hand-sewn blazer at the airport.

At home, he'd shared single-malt scotch with my grandfather. But I'd overheard him, the night before we left L.A., asking Elsa to reconsider the trip.

"The kids can stay with their mother," he told her upstairs in their bedroom, "and you and I can fly to Mexico for a week."

There'd been a silence, and then my stepmother said, "But I miss my family."

So here we were. At noon, we disembarked at another McDonald's and ate once more at a plastic table. We watched other travel-weary families stagger into the restaurant. I sipped my Coke and yearned for a chocolate milkshake. I peered at the menu above the cashiers and calculated the difference in cost. "Excuse me, please," I told my father and slipped out of the booth. "I need to use the restroom."

Instead, I excavated the coin return slots in a trio of pay phones, searching for spare change.

"Any luck?" Elsa paused on her way to the ladies' room and smiled at my index finger stuck in one of the slots.

"Fifteen cents." I fished out a dime and nickel. In the car, I bent down to lift the edges of the floor mat, in case an errant nickel had slipped down.

"What'cha looking for?" Katie bent down and peered under her floor mat.

"None of your business," I told her.

She shrugged. "Whatever. Oh, look. I found a quarter!"

I sat up, sudden nausea souring my throat. I felt the effects of eating my cheeseburger and fries too quickly, without really chewing, and I stared straight ahead, willing myself not to need the coffee can above Tim's head. I couldn't read, couldn't work on my Peter Rabbit rug. If I tried, my stomach did flip-flops.

Finally, out of desperation, I fell asleep shivering in the air-conditioning. I woke up in New Mexico when my father drove up over a curb and pulled into a hotel with a restaurant beside it, all done in split rails and pictures of cowboys.

"I should've brought my lasso," my father observed as he returned from the lobby with two keys. This time, they were affixed to tiny bronze boots. He tossed me one, and we lugged our suitcases up a flight of stone stairs.

As soon as I unlocked our door, Katie stalked into the bathroom and closed the door. I heard the shower start. "Okay to take Tim to the pool?" I asked Elsa.

She nodded. "I'll meet you down there," she said. "It's still light out. We can catch a few rays of sun."

My father unlocked his door and put one arm around her shoulders, already bronzed in her baby-blue tank top. "Give us half an hour," he told me. "Don't take your eyes off your brother in that pool."

"I won't," I muttered. I helped Tim change into his bathing suit and walked him down to the pool. In the shallow end, we practiced floating.

My stepmother appeared an hour later. She pulled off her sheer beach dress to reveal a new red bikini. I bit my lip and looked down at my pale thighs, which looked even whiter in the pool. No one around us—not even the elderly couple in the Jacuzzi—would mistake me for Elsa's daughter. She looked like a supermodel.

"Your father wants us to meet up for dinner in half an hour," she said and swam down toward the deep end of the pool with an elegant butterfly stroke. She returned and took Tim's hands. "Let's go under, Timmy," she suggested.

I waited until her head was under the water, then climbed quickly out of the pool in my sagging blue one-piece and wrapped a towel around my waist. "I'm going to go shower," I told her.

We reconvened, refreshed and showered, in a semicircular booth at Gaucho's Restaurant. Black velvet pictures of cowboys astride bucking broncos lined the red walls. An older woman in a fringed red skirt and vest, with a black cowboy hat perched atop her gray braids, handed us leather-bound menus. Her nametag read CAROL in letters formed from braided rope.

"What'll it be, partners?" she asked us.

I searched the child's menu for anything that wasn't a cheeseburger and fries. "A toasted cheese sandwich," I said at last. "And a Shirley Temple."

"Ribs," my siblings said in sync.

My father shook his head. "Not at eight dollars a plate. They'll each have the child's Gaucho burger."

Katie shot him a disgusted look and stalked off to the bathroom, her hair bouncing in a perfect, silky bob.

My father and Elsa ordered chicken. It arrived with my sandwich and Katie's and Tim's burgers. Elsa cut into hers and wrinkled her nose delicately. "It's pink," she said.

My father leaned over to inspect her plate. Then he cut into his own chicken thigh. "Pink."

The waitress appeared. "How's everything?" she asked.

My father held out his plate, followed by Elsa's. "The chicken's pink," he said. "Have the cook stick these in the oven some more."

Under her cowboy hat, the woman's eyes grew round. "Yes, sir. I'm sorry, sir. I'll be back shortly." She disappeared with the plates.

I studied my sandwich, studded with plastic frilled toothpicks, and refrained from eating while Elsa and my father drank white wine. In a few minutes, Carol returned. My stepmother cut into her chicken, paused an instant, and forked a piece into her mouth. My father regarded her with lowered eyebrows. He hacked into his own poultry with his fork and knife. "Pink!" he growled and waved Carol over.

"This chicken isn't done!" He thrust his plate toward her, and a slice of julienned carrot slipped down onto the toe of her boot. In the booth beside us, a young couple with an infant in a red plaid carrier stared at him, then stood up and moved to a far table.

Carol flushed under her hat. "My apologies, sir. I asked Cook to put it back in the oven. Maybe it just needs a few more minutes?"

The yellow circles around my father's pupils seemed to flash fire, and I shrank in my seat. Kids at school laughed about how their parents got mad and smacked them with a wooden spoon or a hairbrush, but I saw no humor in my father's fury. His temper was unpredictable, fickle. Although he'd never hit me, anger wrenched his arms and face and fists into something terrifying, and I cowed before it.

"Yes," he told the waitress, his voice sinister and soft. "It needs a few more minutes . . . ma'am." He drew out the last word so that it mocked this woman almost my grandmother's age.

I wanted to switch places with her, to give her my comfortable padded seat and the rest of my Shirley Temple, even the cherry. But I stayed where I was and tried to think of a joke to defuse my father's fury. All I could come up with was a punch line to the worn "Why did the chicken cross the road?"

To get away from my father.

Katie and Tim kept eating, oblivious to the diners around us now staring at our table and discussing us. But Elsa looked down at her pink-painted nails, her lips pressed together and her cheeks flushed.

Carol stared at my father with her mouth open. Finally, she snatched up both plates and rushed to the kitchen. She was gone longer this time. By the time she returned, my American cheese had congealed on my plate, and my pickle had warmed.

My father cut into his chicken. I imagined Carol holding her breath, along with the people sitting around us. I held my breath, too, and watched my father with my hands clenched under the table.

He took a bite and shrugged. "It's fine," he said and waved the waitress away.

Elsa picked at her dinner, and I attempted to eat my cold cheese sandwich, but I hid most of it in my napkin. Carol brought the bill and set it at arm's length next to my father's elbow. "Again, I'm awful sorry about the problem, sir," she said.

He didn't reply. He just finished his carrots and drained his wineglass. She walked off, and he extracted a few bills from his wallet. "No tip?" my stepmother said.

"Are you kidding?" My father laughed. "That chicken was tough as a hunk of rawhide."

That night, as my siblings slept, I huddled in my cowboy-riddled bedspread on the hard hotel room floor and cried into a pillow that reeked of bleach. My mother felt so far away. I couldn't talk to her; the hotel phone made only local calls. What was she doing tonight? Was she missing me terribly, too? At last, tear-stained and exhausted, I fell asleep.

The next morning, I woke up at six and shook my sister's shoulder. "If you get up now," I whispered, "you can take a shower."

Her eyes, initially affronted, registered my meaning. In an instant, she flew up and out of bed and into the bathroom. "Thanks!" she whispered back before shutting the door.

Tim woke up, and I helped him into his clothes and shoes, then turned on the TV. While my sister showered, I sat at the desk and opened the drawer. I studied the comment card beside the Bible. "How'd we do?" it read in ropy font. Below, there were lines to rate the comfort of the beds, the cleanliness of the room, and the quality of Gaucho's restaurant.

I thought of Carol, and of the negligent cook who had caused her distress. I wanted to write her a note, to praise her in some way, but the drawer held no pen. A matchbook lay in the glass ashtray on the desk; after a moment's thought, I extracted one match and struck it, then blew it out to reveal a burned black end with which I began to scratch out my comments. "Sorry," I began before the thing crumbled.

I reached to light another, but my father appeared at the door and sniffed. "What's on fire?" he demanded as Katie walked out of the bathroom in her shorts and T-shirt, her hair wrapped in a towel turban.

His hair stood on end, and his eyes looked red and strained. I wondered if he'd slept the night before, or if he, too, felt wrecked by insomnia. Behind my back, I folded the comment card and slipped it into the back pocket of my denim shorts. "Nothing's on fire," I said, moving to the bed.

Tim looked up from the TV. "Hi, Pop," he said. "Let's eat."

But my father sniffed mightily and stalked around the room. He examined the heater and reached up to take out and reinsert the batteries in the smoke detector. He paused at the desk and looked down at the glass ashtray where I'd laid the burned match. Scowling, he held it up between his thumb and forefinger. "Who lit this match?" he asked me.

I cowered under his gaze and began to tremble. "I don't know," I replied.

My father's eyes glittered with fury. "Who lit this match?" he repeated, glaring at Katie. "Was it you?"

She turned from the mirror to stare at him. "Daddy, why would I light a match?" she asked. "That's so totally lame."

I longed for my little sister's courage, for her ferocity. She wasn't afraid of our father.

The sharp edge of the comment card bit into the small of my back under my T-shirt. I took Tim's hand to hide my terror. "I'll help him get breakfast," I said and moved toward the door.

My father held up a hand. "No one's eating until one of you confesses to lighting this match," he said.

Katie shrugged and combed out her hair. "I'm not hungry anyway," she said.

Tim stuck out his lower lip and pouted. "Want donuts," he muttered.

My stomach rumbled, but I stayed silent. "It wasn't me," I whispered.

My father flexed his fists, and I closed my eyes, waiting for the blow. But he turned on his heel and headed for his room. "Goddamn kids," he muttered. "Meet me at the car in ten," he said and closed the door.

In the front seat of the Buick, he and Elsa drank coffee out of Styrofoam cups and ate red apples and string cheese. Katie read her Sweet Valley High book. I gazed hungrily at the mozzarella. Finally, my stepmother passed back a package of donuts and three cans of orange juice. "We can't let them starve," she told my father.

I held my breath, wondering what he would do, but he merely gripped the steering wheel and kept driving.

"Girls," Elsa said as she passed us each an apple, "I'm deeply disappointed in whomever of you isn't telling the truth."

Katie sighed and bit into an apple. I nibbled my donut and prayed to be anywhere but where I was. *Two more days*, I thought and opened my book.

Elsa's parents' house towered grand and white above a sloping lawn—a lush chartreuse expanse so vast that her father cut it from his riding mower every weekend. My new grandfather was a big man, white-haired and gentle. He shook hands with me as we piled out of the Buick and said he was pleased to see me again. Then he shook my father's hand. "I've got steaks waiting to be grilled, and beer in the cooler."

My father nodded, relief relaxing the tension in his face, and walked off.

Elsa's mother also had white hair—tight curls above cheerful blue eyes. "Let's get you some tea and cookies," she said to my siblings and me. I followed her into the big blue and white kitchen, glad to be absolved of cheeseburgers and fries. "How was the trip?" she asked Elsa, pouring tall glasses of peppermint tea.

My stepmother smiled at me like a co-conspirator and gracefully inclined her head toward my father's, just visible in the kitchen window. "Long," she said.

"Well, you're here now." Her mother opened the oven door to reveal a tray of chocolate chip cookies that made my stomach ache with hunger. Maybe this visit wouldn't be so bad after all.

My mother's mother revered packaged convenience foods; upon opening a can or box, she was wont to break out in a spontaneous soft-shoe on her sticky kitchen floor, belting out "A Bushel and a Peck" from *Guys and Dolls*. Elsa's mother was Betty Crocker incarnate. Her white tile floor gleamed. Instead of tearing open some Doritos or Oreos, she slid the cookies off the pan and onto a duck-embossed plate for us.

"Lissa, would you like to help me make a salad?" she asked.

I cut up avocados and cucumbers at the counter beside her and looked out the window at my father standing beside the grill. He had a beer in one hand, and he smiled and laughed as my step-grandfather flipped the steaks. I caught his eye through the glass, and he winked at me. For an instant, I wondered why I hadn't just confessed to lighting the match. Then I thought of the terrible yellow circles surrounding his pupils, and I shuddered.

That evening, we ate steak and fresh corn on the cob and my salad on the long covered porch. Katie and I balanced our plates sitting side by side on the green-and-white-striped porch swing. As the sun began to set, a flash of scarlet flew across the yard.

"A cardinal," Elsa told me. "I've missed them."

We didn't have cardinals in California, nor did we have the tiny light-filled insects that appeared at dusk to flit about the shadows. "Fireflies!" Katie and Tim cried and launched themselves off the porch to chase them. I followed, suddenly buoyant and hopeful in the waning heat.

"Who wants chocolate–peanut butter milkshakes?" my new grand-mother asked from the porch, and we raced inside to watch her alchemize milk and vanilla ice cream, chocolate syrup and peanut butter in the blender. "A girl needs a treat now and then," she said to Elsa and toasted her daughter's glass of milkshake with her own.

Our first three days in Ohio passed in a slow, lazy haze of late-morning waffles and croquet games on the wide lawn, in afternoons spent reading and drinking iced tea with sugar and fresh mint from my grandmother's window box. After lunch, while Katie and Tim rolled down the long hill, I crept into the cool, white-carpeted living room and examined the bookshelves. There I discovered James Herriot and lounged in an easy chair, fixated on the stories of a country vet with his hand eternally stuck up some poor cow's bum as I sucked butterscotch candy from the crystal dish on the end table beside my chair.

By the fourth day, I couldn't read any more. My head ached with words. The air-conditioning in the big white house caused goose bumps to rise up on my arms and legs, but outside the air hung thick and heavy. I retreated to the shade of the front porch and sat waiting for something to happen.

Elsa and her mother sat on the swing, discussing my grandmother's new overlock sewing machine. "It finishes seams like a miracle," I heard before I stopped listening.

"I miss home." Katie wandered out to the porch, nursing a glass of iced tea. "There's no one to play with."

I caught the affront. "So go get Monopoly," I sighed. "We can play it out here."

My sister wrinkled her sunburned nose. "That's boring."

Elsa's mother stood up and brushed her hands off on her green polyester shorts. "I think I'll go call Mrs. DiMarco from next door," she told us. "She has eight kids. Some of them are your age, and they have a backyard swimming pool!"

"Yay!" Katie ran inside and appeared a minute later in her pink flowered bathing suit with one of Elsa's mother's fluffy pink towels.

I moved more slowly. At twelve, I knew you couldn't just invite yourself to a stranger's pool. But that's what we did, as soon as I'd changed into my navy-blue one-piece. "We'll take care of Tim," Elsa said. "You girls go have fun."

Her mother walked us down the sloping lawn to the shabby reddish house next door and knocked. At once, the door flew open.

Three kids stood on the doorstep—a big black-haired girl my age and identical twin boys Katie's age. Their hair hung in their eyes like crow wings. Each boy took one of my sister's hands. "Mommy says you want to swim in our pool!" they said. "Let's go!"

I blushed at our presumption, but the big girl shrugged. "I'm Rita," she said. "Are you really from Southern California?"

I nodded and cast a last longing look at Elsa and her mother as they turned and walked back to the house. "I'm from near Los Angeles," I explained.

The girl clutched her hands to her chest. "Oooh—have you seen any movie stars?"

"I stood beside Goldie Hawn and Kurt Russell at the LAX baggage claim once," I said.

"That's cool," Rita said. "Want to go swim?"

"Okay." I followed her through a house littered with clothes and shoes and books and toys to an equally cluttered back yard taken up by an enormous pool. Two kids played on a slide near the deep end. Two boys busied themselves diving for plastic rings, and two older girls stretched out in bikinis on lawn chairs. All of them had dark hair and beautiful olive skin.

"Are all these kids your brothers and sisters?" Katie demanded. She dog-paddled in the deep end with the twins, who nodded.

"Yup," one boy said, "but we're done now. My mommy says eight is enough."

Rita groaned at the pop culture reference and elbowed me in the side. "Let's dive." She padded toward the diving board. "Can you do a backflip?"

I couldn't, but I could do a somersault, which earned me her respect. We began an Olympic-style competition with her older brother until Mrs. DiMarco appeared at the side of the pool. She was a broad-hipped woman with a big voice to match. "Melissa! Katie!" she cried. "I called your grandmother. You're staying for lasagna."

My sister and the twins cheered, and Rita high-fived me. I couldn't help smiling. I longed to be part of a big Italian family like the DiMarcos. They hollered at and fought with each other, but everyone seemed to regard their collective overwrought emotion as a big joke.

Mr. DiMarco walked into the back yard in a brown three-piece suit and tie. "Hi, Daddy!" the twins exclaimed and splashed him from the pool.

"Jesus, Mary, and Joseph!" the man yelled. "You want to ruin the only decent suit I've got?"

The twins giggled, and Rita ran up to kiss his cheek. "Oh, Daddy, go take a load off," she said.

I stared at her from my perch on a torn plastic lawn chair. Why did Mr. DiMarco's anger seem good-natured and comic, while my father's made me cringe in fearful silence?

Beside me, Rita's two older sisters looked up as Katie and the twins shook their hair like wet dogs. "You're getting burned," one girl told her.

I looked at Katie's arms and then at my own reddened shoulders, and I pulled a towel over my pink thighs. I knew without looking that my nose had burned scarlet.

Another sister cocked her head at me so that her hair cascaded across one shoulder, an obsidian waterfall. "It must be hard to be a WASP in Los Angeles," she said.

"A wasp?" Katie drew her blond eyebrows together. "My sister's not an insect."

I played it cool, waiting.

"White Anglo-Saxon Protestant," the sister said. "You have no heritage. Not like us Italians."

"We have heritage." Katie looked to me for confirmation.

Rita sat cross-legged beside her. "Oh yeah? What church do you go to?"

Now my sister looked worried. We didn't go to church. One time only, my mother had taken us to Sunday school in a basement decorated with B-52s posters. We'd made animals out of pinecones. I closed my eyes and struggled to remember the name of the church. "We're Unitarians!" I said at last.

Rita and her older sisters exchanged a bewildered look. "Okay," she said, "but where are your parents from?"

Katie looked to me again for assistance. This time the question proved to be too much for me. We possessed two sets of parents, and numerous grandparents. I suspected that between them we came from all parts of the globe. "I don't know," I admitted.

Rita stared at me. "Then how do you know who you are?"

"Dinner!" Mrs. DiMarco appeared at the back door in an enormous red-and-white-checked apron and clapped her hands. At once, eight kids swept Katie and me into the house on a chaotic, ravenous tide.

At the long dinner table, savoring spinach lasagna and garlic bread, I contemplated Rita's question. At twelve, I'd begun to learn who I was by who I wasn't. I wasn't Italian or black or Mexican. I wasn't Catholic or Jewish or Protestant. I wasn't tan or pretty or cool. Nothing distinguished me except perhaps for the red nose that I studied in my grandmother's guest bathroom later that night.

Dismayed, I dabbed Noxzema on the burned skin and prayed it would fade by tomorrow when Rita came over to show me the local park. Her mother hadn't offered us dessert. I longed for one of my grandmother's chocolate–peanut butter milkshakes. They could be my defining food, I reasoned, much more charismatic than spinach lasagna and garlic bread.

In the living room, my father and stepmother relaxed with her parents and their after-dinner drinks. I listened to them laughing from the bathroom and went out to tell them goodnight. For a moment, I stood in the doorway and watched them. They talked much more loudly than usual, and my new grandmother giggled like Katie. Suddenly, I remembered how my father used to sit with my mother in her mother's Asian-print living room, the three of them sipping her famous sangria while my great-grandmother drank her evening concoction of whiskey and honey and apple cider vinegar.

"What's wrong, Lissa?" Elsa stood up and peered at my nose. "Does your sunburn hurt?"

I shook my head and turned away. "I'm fine," I muttered and crept into the spare room, where Katie was already stretched out on one bed fast asleep. I looked at the white telephone on the nightstand. Did I dare call my mother?

I dialed her number.

"Hi, Mom," I said. "It's me."

"Honey," she cried into my ear. "Annie and I are having a party right now. I can barely hear you. Can I call you tomorrow?"

I hung up without answering. In bed, I read James Herriot until I fell asleep. I woke up later to the sound of my father's voice, furious on the other side of the wall.

"If they liked him so much, then maybe you should've married him!" he cried.

My stepmother murmured something unintelligible. In my head, I saw the yellow circles, and I trembled.

"What?" my father snapped. "What did you say?"

Again, my stepmother spoke, but I couldn't make out her words until she said, "No. Please don't."

I burrowed under the pillow and tried to drown out their voices. Had he hit her? Had her parents heard them, and if so, what did they think of us? After a while, the voices stopped, and I fell back into a fitful sleep.

I stayed in bed late the next morning, reading and listening to determine the mood of the house. We were supposed to head back to Los Angeles in two days. Would Elsa's parents ask us to leave this morning, instead, and would Elsa stay with her mother? I hoped not. I knew I couldn't survive the car ride home with only my father and siblings for company.

Tim's laughter floated through my open bedroom door. I heard Katie ask Elsa a question. My new grandfather's deep voice answered, calm and reassuring. At last, I slid from the bed and tiptoed into the hall.

Elsa and my father had the room next to me. The door stood open, and I peered in, looking for clues. At first, I saw nothing out of the ordinary—just open suitcases and an empty wineglass on the dresser. But then I spotted Elsa's skirt and blouse—the blue ensemble with the white flowers—lying crumpled on the floor. The skirt had been ripped down the middle; it splayed open ungraciously on the carpet, its edges ragged and the hem hanging loose. The blouse was missing buttons, and one cuff had been torn loose. I thought of how Elsa had spent an hour picking out the pattern at the fabric store, labored weeks to cut and pin and sew the outfit.

Looking at the ruined clothing, I felt a sudden rage begin to gather into my face and arms and fists. It propelled me across the room, and I snatched up the skirt and blouse. All at once, I didn't care if he yelled at me, didn't care if I got smacked.

I stood up and caught sight of my eyes in the mirror above the dresser. The yellow circles around my pupils seemed to flash fire. I turned and stalked out to the kitchen.

My family sat at the table eating pancakes. My grandmother stood frying bacon at the stove. I held up the torn clothing.

"Who did this?" I demanded. "Tim? Katie?"

My siblings looked up at me, bewildered. Elsa blushed and glanced at her father. My own father glared at me, a half smile frozen on his lips. I stepped toward him, brandishing the skirt, and he shrank back in his seat. "Did you do this, Daddy?" I said.

He shook his head. "It wasn't me," he said.

WASP MILKSHAKE

When the last cardinal has gone to bed and fireflies light up the night, drop three scoops of vanilla ice cream into your blender and fill it halfway with milk. Being careful not to stain your hand-sewn sundress, drizzle in a good-quality chocolate syrup—as much as you like because a girl needs a treat now and then. Follow this with two tablespoons of peanut butter, and blend it all together while you belt out the theme song from *Felix the Cat*. Savor your milkshake and your WASP heritage while reading James Herriot's memoirs.

8 •

ETHIOPIA

ETHIOPIAN JOKES REPLACED POLISH WISECRACKS MY SECOND YEAR
of junior high, and Marc Cleary memorized them all. Thirteen-year-olds
with Eastern European last names must have felt relief when he—the
merriest and most shameless among our troupe of eighth-grade jesters—
turned his focus away from Polacks and their apparent inability to screw
in a lightbulb and onto the starving country in Africa. At lunch, Marc
strode up to a gaggle of girls at a picnic table under a eucalyptus tree.
"What do you call an Ethiopian who swallows an acorn?" he asked. He
regarded us over our cafeteria trays and brown paper bags, his full lips set
earnestly. His voice resonated across the schoolyard, deep and nasal. He'd
mastered the art of the pause; he allowed a full five seconds of silence to
heighten the tension of a joke while his copper eyes gleamed wickedly
behind large horn-rimmed glasses.

In vain, I tried to guess his punch line. My great-grandfather had worked as a vaudeville acrobat and comedian throughout the 1920s and '30s. My great-grandmother, Grandmary, distracted the audience from her husband's tendency to drop his juggling pins with her quick, sharp-witted patter and her saucy scarlet smile. Each time I visited, she recounted her show business days and the act, which she still knew by heart. With a calculated casualness, she'd feed him lines leading into each joke.

> **Grandmary:** I sure do miss my chickens back on the farm, Hap. But you know, one of my hens has been fighting with the others. She's just bad, through and through.
> **Hap:** Why, Mary, your hen's so evil she lays deviled eggs!

Maybe heredity compelled me to bat my stubby eyelashes at Marc and dutifully repeat the question that led to his punch line.

"I dunno," I'd say. "What *do* you call an Ethiopian who swallows an acorn?"

"Pregnant," Marc intoned solemnly.

I despised comics who laughed at their own jokes. "It's unprofessional," my great-grandmother scoffed when we watched Jerry Seinfeld smirking during his set on *An Evening at the Improv*. I admired Marc's deadpan delivery as that of a consummate comic.

But Marc was a greedy joke teller, not content until the members of his audience guffawed so hard that they spit up their cafeteria peas onto their mashed potatoes. We knew the joke wasn't truly funny. We'd been raised on images of starving children gazing out from classroom copies of *National Geographic*. Terrified to do otherwise, we snorted with laughter.

"Why do Ethiopians bathe with their arms out?" Marc demanded.

The five or six girls at my table giggled and shook their ponytails in bewilderment. Marc raised his heavy eyebrows at me and indicated, with Groucho Marxist genuflection, my cue.

"I dunno." I gazed up at him wearily, hungrily, and folded my arms on the sticky picnic table. "Why *do* Ethiopians bathe with their arms out?"

"So they won't go down the drain."

Even the most politically correct among us capitulated under the force of Marc Cleary's charm. We tittered with laughter. We wiggled with mirth. He allowed himself the barest flicker of a smile, then smoothed down his tight brown curls and moved to the next table of girls, leaving me exhilarated and ashamed.

I recognized Ethiopia as destitute—felt the injustice as I dumped half my ham sandwich and a mealy red apple on the mound of food heaping the fly-festooned trash can beside our lunch table. Still, I played straight man to Marc's incessant comedian. To not do so—to defend this African culture—would be to invite ridicule.

At my suburban Los Angeles school, the coolest thing you could be was Latino. Kids just up from Mexico—tough, self-assured boys and girls called Jorge, Alejandro, and Marisol—were the most popular kids. We Anglos looked on with envy, lamely practicing our Cheech and Chong accents: "Holy sheep shit. You wanna get high, man?"

Only one black student attended our junior high. David Jenkins towered over the rest of us, six feet tall. Murky circles of sweat stained the underarms of his Lakers T-shirt. His biceps swelled large as my father's. Once, he hurled a desk across the room. He cursed, too—sharp-edged, sex-tinged words I'd never heard before. "You've got some fucking nerve taking up all our time with this shit," he told our math teacher when she assigned us one hundred long division problems for homework.

Mrs. Carr, with her elegantly coiffed white hair and rigid aristocratic jaw, who permitted us to say "damn" and "hell" because they appeared in the Bible, sat down at her desk and wept.

"She's so Ethiopian," Marc Cleary said at recess. At once, a black hand clamped down on his shoulder like a talon.

"What'd you say about Africa, shithead?"

From then on, Marc looked around to determine David Jenkins's whereabouts before he launched into his repertoire.

The Latinos, goaded by their Catholic upbringing, tended to favor slurs against homosexuals. "Faggot!" the boys yelled when someone squirted ketchup across a favorite Izod shirt during a cafeteria food fight. "What a dyke," the girls hissed when one of our classmates appeared with a Princess Diana bob hacked too short and a dearth of Bonnie Bell strawberry lip gloss. I thought of my mother and her new girlfriend, Annie, and I trembled.

"Annie and I would like to come to your graduation, honey," she told me over the phone.

"It's just eighth grade," I stammered. "You'd have to drive an hour and a half for a twenty-minute ceremony. That's so silly."

"But . . ."

"Really, Mom." I thought of her Birkenstocks and flannel shirts, of her girlfriend's baggy Levi's and makeupless good-natured face. In junior high, being the daughter of a lesbian hippie who drove an ancient VW bus was akin to having herpes or orthodontic headgear. If my classmates learned of my mother, they'd tear into me like vultures.

"You don't need to come to graduation." The words wrenched themselves from my lips, followed by a second lie. "I probably won't even go."

But I did go, and I watched with envy as Marc danced with all the Latina girls in their purple and turquoise chiffon while I sat in a high-necked white dress cradling a plastic cup of punch and sorrowfully hummed along with Elton John's "I Guess That's Why They Call It the Blues."

• ●

The hierarchy of race followed us to ninth grade. Suddenly, students from three different junior highs found themselves sharing classes and hallways and locker rooms in an immense, sprawling high school. Marc and I joined the track team—the only Caucasian runners in a group of African American kids and others from Mexico, Spain, Ecuador, and Venezuela. In high school, Marc had abandoned his Ethiopian jokes and now sported silkscreened T-shirts with images of Che Guevara and César Chávez. "Chicano power!" he'd yell during our mile-long warm-ups around the track.

"I thought you were Irish," I said, catching up to Marc the second week of practice, matching the pace set by his muscular, newly hairy legs.

Around us, our teammates chuckled as they ran. The October sun beat down on the spongy, pinkish track, and spots danced in front of my eyes. Marc took hold of my arm and pulled me onto the football field, away from the others. "Hey, White Girl."

He laid his arm against mine. For an instant, I admired the chiaroscuro of my pale freckled skin blending into his arm, which was the color of coffee with cream. But he gave my wrist a cautionary twist. "You wish your dad was Mexican like *mi padre*."

"Your last name is Cleary," I reasoned, gripping my burning skin. "That's Irish."

Marc snorted. "*Ay, caramba*. It's my mom's name, Casper. Face it—you're white."

"*¡Beso mis nalgas!*" I slapped my butt and made a kissing sound with my lips.

Marc rolled his eyes. "You kiss your butt? Oh, Casper . . . please don't try to speak Spanish. It just embarrasses us all."

I began to wear long sleeves and spandex running tights. I smeared on foundation two shades darker than my skin color. My whiteness had become a mark of humiliation, a stigma that doomed me to a lifetime of despair—much as Ian Jones from Freshman English was condemned after he sneezed and green snot shot across the room and onto our teacher's copy of *Lord of the Flies*.

"You'll run the three thousand, Melissa," Coach Bravo told me before our first track meet.

"But Coach," I said, "That's two miles. I want to sprint. My dad competed in the four hundred in high school and won almost every race."

His mouth twisted in amusement below his dark mustache. "Darling, you're better suited to distance running. The black kids have sprints and hurdles covered, got it?"

I got it. The darker your skin, the higher your position in track's social echelon. Now David Jenkins ruled the school with his record-breaking time in the four hundred. He occupied the coveted position at the back of the bus and chose what music we'd listen to on the way to our first Saturday all-comers meet. If the fourth replay of George Michael whining "Careless Whisper" over the bus speakers made me want to hurl his boom box out the window, one look at his regal bearing in his scarlet tracksuit silenced me.

Marc Cleary, meanwhile, showed an uncharacteristic slavish devotion to David, who referred to him as "homeboy" and allowed him to haul his gym bag to the field. Marc plied him with sodas from the snack stand and shared his jumbo bag of M&Ms. After the meet, he offered me up for David's consideration as we waited for our bus in the parking lot.

"Hey, White Girl."

Marc swept the Hawthorne High Cougars' cap from my head and tossed it to David. "Hey, White Girl. Why're you so white?"

Again, that practiced pause, those teasing eyes behind thick-lensed glasses. I stood among the other girls in my red shorts and sweat-stained white jersey and closed my eyes, willing myself to come up with a witty punch line.

"I dunno," I mumbled at last. It had something to do with my French and German ancestors on my mother's side, with the British folks on my father's side, all of whom had conspired to come to this country with the sole purpose of making my adolescence a living hell. But I said none of this to Marc.

He remained silent as well, raising hopeful eyebrows toward David, who condescended to his own amusement, slapping his huge hands on his knees as he grinned at me. I saw then that I was a capper—in vaudeville slang, the joke that got the biggest laugh.

In high school, Marc's punch line was me.

Our school tracked freshmen into honors courses or vocational classes in a top-secret process known only to administrators and teachers. Was it Mrs. Carr who deemed Marc and me fit for Honors Math with a class full of Asian students, while David Jenkins, Jorge, Marisol, and the rest found themselves relegated to Woodshop and Auto Repair? At fourteen, I didn't attempt to solve such complex riddles.

"Hey, White Girl." Marc snatched my great-grandfather's tweed cap off my head after Algebra class and threw it to another boy. "We're studying for the math test at Tuan's house tonight at seven o'clock. Wanna come?"

"Absolutely!"

I reached for my Trapper Keeper and wrote MARC, 7 PM on the inside flap. While he busied himself playing keep-away with my hat, I turned the *a* in his name into a heart.

"You should invite your friend." He tossed my hat back to me and studied a jet screaming overhead on its way to LAX. "What's her name . . . Angelina? You know, the Mexican chick you hang with."

He was referring to my friend Angie. She ran track, too, relegated to the three thousand because of chronic shin splints and asthma.

"Okay, I'll invite her," I said, "but she's not in Honors Math."

"Yeah, but she's hot."

I chose to ignore this observation and allowed my heart to skip a beat that night as Marc and I crowded into Tuan's tiny bedroom with our notebooks of quadratic equations.

Half an hour later Angie appeared at the door. "Any room for me?" Her silky black hair swung across her eyes. She spoke with a slight accent and the expert enunciation of someone who navigated two languages with grace.

"Come in!" Marc scooted so close to me that our legs touched. At once, my shin burned as if ignited. Under my eyelashes, I studied the play of our light and dark ankles against Tuan's navy-blue carpet. We looked like a clothing ad for Benetton.

"Hey, White Girl."

Fearing he'd read my mind, I leaped away from Marc and overturned my Coke. He sighed and waited patiently as Tuan got a towel. When I'd mopped up the spill, Marc began again. "Hey, White Girl. Why can't you do math?"

Soda soaked my denim skirt. I ducked my head, cheeks flaming. Marc gazed blankly at Angie, worked the pause, and waited for my straight man's response. When it didn't come, he proceeded without a glitch.

"'Cause white people ain't got no algo-rhythm."

"Sweet!" Tuan slapped Marc five and they went back to chanting the algebraic order of operations. I stared out the door at Tuan's sparsely decorated living room. Beneath one window stood a stone statue of a Buddha. A bouquet of incense sticks and a plate of orange slices sat on a shelf beside it. It reminded me of the altar Angie's family constructed for Día de los Muertos, with photos of departed family members and candles and pastries set on tiny plates.

If I had a discernible culture like Tuan's or Angie's, Marc might stop teasing me. But I had a vaudevillian great-grandmother who wore silk robes over hoary overalls, a grandmother who made Smurf costumes for a living, and a lesbian mom who subscribed to *Ms.* and *Mother Jones.* I was screwed.

A rich, spicy smell drifted down the hall. Tuan's father appeared, holding a tray with four bowls and spoons. "For you." He ducked his head shyly and stepped into the room.

My friends and I cradled the deep bowls of broth adorned with thinly sliced carrots, cabbage, and broccoli. Tuan passed a plate of slivered basil leaves, bean sprouts, and crescents of lime. We watched him add these to his soup and followed suit, dipping our spoons into the bowl to mix the condiments with long strands of noodle.

"What's this stuff?" Marc demanded with his mouth full.

"*P-h-o.*" Tuan spelled out the name of the soup. "Pronounced *fuh.*"

"What the *pho?*" Marc responded automatically, but the joke ended there. Apparently nothing was funnier than being white.

The next Friday, my mother picked my siblings and me up in her bus. "What d'you want to do this weekend, kids?" Barefoot, she pressed the clutch and accelerator, goading the VW into fourth gear as we headed up Pacific Coast Highway.

"I want to make cookies," I said, "to take to school on Monday."

"Me, too," my sister said.

"Chocolate chip? Oatmeal?" my mother tried.

I shook my head. "No . . . something more ethnic."

At home in her kitchen, we flipped through the pages of her battered *Joy of Cooking.* "Mexican Wedding Cakes?"

I clasped my hands to my chest. "Perfect!"

Katie and I baked four dozen cookies and packed them into tins. I brought the tiny baked balls of dough, flecked with walnuts and rolled in powdered sugar, to school that Monday. "Want one?" I held the tin out to my friends in the hall during passing period. Angie and Tuan took a cookie, and Marc popped a whole one into his mouth. For a moment, I thought my baking had silenced him at last. But then he swallowed, making room.

"It's pale doughy stuff and powdered sugar, just like you." He gazed soberly at Angie. "Melissa's made White Girl Cookies."

My friend suppressed a smile and whacked Marc on the arm with her Hello Kitty purse. "You're an asshole," she said. But she walked with him to her next class, leaving me to overturn my tin of cookies into the nearest trash can.

Miserable, I attempted to talk with my mother about Marc. "He makes fun of you constantly and puts you down in front of your friends?" She sat in her cutoff jeans and flannel T-shirt, studying my prone figure on her couch as if she weren't quite sure how this blow-dried and lip-glossed ingenue had sprung from her loins. "Honey, you've gotta have some self-respect."

"Self-respect won't keep you warm at night," my great-grandmother said from the kitchen table. Grandmary had taken up residence in Oxnard with my mother and her girlfriend that summer, toting Vicks Cough Drops in her overall pockets and folded manila envelopes full of vaudeville memorabilia in the deep pockets of her silk robe.

Intrigued, I pulled up a chair beside her. "What do you mean, Grandmary?"

She pulled out publicity photos and newspaper clippings of my great-grandfather's death in an airplane crash when I was four. "Marriage of convenience." Her blue eyes glowed, stoic. "Hap needed me to set up his jokes, but he was a loner . . . self-involved. You know, Melissa Marie, most laughter's dependent on someone else's pain."

She produced a square, scallop-edged photograph of a smiling, dark-skinned man leaning elegantly against the side of an elephant. "Pedro Morales," she said. "I guess you could say I had a thing for the Latins."

"I do, too!" I studied Pedro's handsome face, the fine cut of his linen suit. Could it be that I was part Latino, after all?

I pictured Marc's reaction to this news. He'd scoff at me, and then I'd pull out the photo of Pedro. "This is my great-grandfather," I'd say proudly.

My great-grandmother's old wrinkled lips curved into a shadow of their once-sensual smile. "I remember the play of white skin against brown, the murmur of Spanish phrases as he . . ."

"That's enough, Grandmary." My mother thrust a book into my hands. "*The Feminine Mystique*." She recited the title. "Read it."

I tossed the tome on the table. "Excuse me, but didn't you stay married to my father for eleven years?" I snapped.

My mother pursed her lips. "Don't be fresh," she retorted.

In the end, I read her book. But women's liberation offered me nothing close to the thrill I felt upon returning to my father's house in Los Angeles and finding a note on my pillow. MARC CLEARY CALLED. ASKED IF YOU WANT TO GO FOR A RUN.

"I do!" I said over the phone to Marc.

On a sultry July evening, he jogged the mile from his house to mine and appeared on my front porch with diamonds of sweat sparkling below his tight curls. He'd left his glasses at home, and his brown eyes squinted, unsure, as he bent toward me. Then he laughed and pinched my cheek.

"White Girl, let's run to the beach. You need a tan."

His skin glowed a rich, dark brown. We jogged the two-mile stretch of road to Manhattan Beach, and I looked sidelong at his muscled arms and chest, visible under his jersey. We splashed through the surf still wearing our Nikes and collapsed on sand that held the memory of midday heat, along with cigarette butts and candy wrappers. The molten disc of sun melted into the indigo ocean as dark figures leaped and glided through the waves.

"Dolphins!" I cried.

"Would ya look at that." Marc squinted again. "Freakin' magnificent. Where were you this weekend, anyhow?"

"With my mom," I mumbled.

"Hunh. Why don't you live with her?"

I chewed my lip. Suddenly, I was tempted to tell him everything— how my father and the cops had shown up at my mother's house five years before and taken me from her because of her relationship with a woman, how I was only allowed to see her two weekends a month because the judge thought homosexuality was contagious, how I missed her with an ache I shoved so far beneath my consciousness that it surfaced only as bitter words hurled in her direction.

Instead, I lied. "My mom's a travel writer. She's away a lot."

"So's my dad," Marc said gruffly.

I nodded, emboldened by his disclosure. "D'you . . . d'you want to go running again tomorrow?"

"Absolutely."

The next night, we ran to the beach again. No dolphins dotted the waves, and fog obscured the setting sun. But Marc touched my arm for an instant, his fingers warm. "Wanna go back to my house?"

"Absolutely."

At his back door, he untied his shoes. I kicked mine off and surreptitiously swept on a coating of cherry Chap Stick.

"Hurry up, Casper!" He pulled me into the kitchen.

His mother stood at the stove, pouring macaroni into a pot of boiling water. She turned as we walked in and pulled her red hair into a ponytail off her pale neck. Her green eyes assessed me, and I saw from whom Marc had inherited his piercing gaze. "Nice to meet you, sweetheart," Mrs. Cleary said. "Marc talks about you a lot."

Glowing, I accepted a glass of water and followed Marc into the living room. An Irish flag covered one wall. Across from it hung another— vertical green, yellow, and red stripes with a yellow star in a blue circle. Marc steered me toward the hall. "So . . ." he said casually, "is your friend Angelina seeing anyone?"

I laughed to hide my dismay. "She's a lesbian," I said quickly. "I don't hang out with her anymore. She's a . . ." I hissed out the accusation. "She's a dyke."

"Hey, Marc?" His mother appeared in the kitchen doorway. "Your daddy called this afternoon. Come here a sec."

"*Ay, caramba.*" Marc yanked open a door and jerked his chin. "That's my room. Wait in there."

But I lingered in the hallway. Family photos lined the walls. There was Marc as a child, already wearing thick glasses with a mischievous smile. There was his red-haired mother, slender and laughing in a touristy Polaroid as she bent to kiss the Blarney stone.

I recognized her again in another photo and thought she held the toddler version of Marc in her arms. But who was the man beside them? He stood handsome and dark, with full lips and curly hair. Not Latino. Black. On his soldier's jacket was a patch depicting the unfamiliar flag hanging in the living room.

From the kitchen, I heard Mrs. Cleary's voice. "Your dad's gotta stay in Ethiopia another week. His mom's selling their house, and he's trying to persuade her to move to the States."

I scurried into Marc's bedroom, cheeks flaming. He walked in and stared at me. "*Ay caramba*, White Girl. Your face's red as an Injun."

"You're Ethiopian?" I demanded.

For an instant, he froze. Sweat trickled down the sides of his face and collected at his collarbone. Then he broke into a broad grin and sat down beside me. "So?"

"But you made fun of them . . ." I stammered. "In junior high, you . . ."

"White Girl, you think too much. I make fun of you, too."

He pulled me toward him, and the sour smell of his sweat filled my nostrils. I recoiled with a mixture of horror and hatred and agonizing compassion. But when he pressed his full lips against mine, I let him.

WHITE GIRL COOKIES

Ponder your sentence of a lifetime of despair, then preheat your oven to 325 Fahrenheit. Chop one cup of macadamia nuts in a blender or food processor, duly noting their whiteness. Cut two sticks of cold butter into one-inch cubes. Add them to the nuts, and mix until smooth.

Hold one-fourth cup of powdered sugar against your skin to check for any faint difference in hue, then add to blender with a tablespoon of vanilla. Mix, and add two cups of white flour. Process until just blended. The dough will be very pale.

Flour your hands, and roll the dough into one-inch balls. Place these about an inch apart on an ungreased cookie sheet. Bake fifteen to twenty minutes, or until the bottoms of the cookies are as brown as the eyes of the boy you love.

Cool cookies on racks for ten minutes. Heap insult upon injury by rolling warm cookies in sifted powdered sugar. Let them cool, and roll them once more in powdered sugar for additional humiliation.

9 •

Trapped White Space

I lived for high school. Hawthorne High required freshmen to take only six classes, but I signed up for first-period creative writing and seventh-period cross-country, ensuring that I'd leave my father's house at 7:00 AM and not return until dinner. His anger, unpredictable and random, infuriated me—in part because I worried that I might be to blame.

I mourned for my mother every other Sunday evening when she dropped us off on his doorstep, and my sullen silence lasted long into the week. But at school I could forget my problematic home life. I reveled in my honors math and English classes, in lunchtime gossip with my friends, and in the exhilaration that came from putting pen to paper and winning an essay contest sponsored by the public access TV station and then publishing a poem on the poetry page of *Cat Fancy*.

I knew I'd achieved the pinnacle of success—a coveted spot on the high school yearbook staff—when my stepmother appeared in my bedroom one evening with the unprecedented gift of new pajamas. "Your old ones are so ragged," she explained, the aristocratic planes of her face a careful blank. "And these were on sale at Mervyns."

Everyone knew that senior staff on the yearbook kidnapped new members for a 4:00 AM initiation in late spring. The editor called parents beforehand to work out details like which door would be left unlocked, and which teens slept in the nude and required a nudge in the direction of sweatpants for this one critical morning. Rumor had it initiation would be this week, and so my heart leaped as I examined my stepmother's purchase.

"She bought me shorties! Light blue with lace trim," I told my mother over the phone, "with white Keds to match!"

If this news broke my mother's heart, separated as she was from me by seventy miles and a court order that forbade me to live with her and her girlfriend, she kept it to herself. "That's wonderful, honey," she said. "Promise you'll take pictures of your El Molino initiation."

El Molino was the name of the yearbook, and the collective term for the dozen or so kids on staff. The noun translated as "the windmill." I wasn't sure how a machine used to pump water and grind grain related to the stories and photos that would commemorate the best years of our lives, but I longed to wear the staff's red sweatshirt silkscreened with a yellow windmill. Under the application question "Why do you want to be on El Molino?" I wrote in fervent dark letters: BECAUSE THE EXPERIENCE WOULD BE SO PROFOUND.

Senior students selected freshman writers and photographers to replace them so that the staff maintained a zero-growth policy. In a ritual handed down over years, the upperclassmen ushered in new members by embarrassing the crap out of them.

By prearrangement, the morning after the presentation of my new pajamas, two senior girls crept through my father's unlocked back door and appeared at my bedside. "Do you solemnly pledge your eternal faith to El Molino?" they asked in unison.

In the dim light, I blinked at their red sweatshirts silkscreened with yellow windmills. "Whuh? Whosat?" I yawned, feigning surprise. I'd been awake since three o'clock, in order to shower and blow-dry my hair, brush on gold eye shadow, and iron my pajamas before arranging myself beneath my floral bedspread as if in sweet slumber. My alternate extracurricular choice, had my talents not rated El Molino, was Drama Club. Even now, in the midst of my euphoria, I rehearsed the part of the sleepy, startled ingenue just in case. "I'm on Yearbook? Really?"

The seniors hauled me out of bed by my perfumed armpits. "C'mon, Sleeping Beauty. We're taking you to the park for a makeover."

This was Los Angeles. Twenty kids congregating predawn at Holly Glen Park without any weapons save a can of shaving cream was a relatively dangerous endeavor on our parts. But the transients and gang members who patrolled the park's perimeters merely cursed and staggered over to Tiny Naylors coffee shop when we screeched up in the seniors' vans and Camaros with Silly String, perfume, glitter, and all manner of humiliating costumes for us rookies.

The hazing traditionally ended at Denny's, where we hunkered down at a long table, reeking of Gillette and Love's Baby Soft. The seniors treated each of us to Grand Slams, provided we sang our school song alone, and a cappella, to the delight of the early-morning diners around us. When it came to my turn, I leaped onto my chair in my full-length pink rabbit costume and trilled exuberantly. "Oh scarlet and gold. Our colors unfold. / Forever flying high . . ."

Suddenly, the girl beside me jumped onto her chair as well and added her alto to my soprano. "Our praises to sing. Forever to ring / throughout dear Hawthorne High."

We finished the song in harmony. Amid the applause, a senior girl named Betina presented us with two platters of eggs, sausage, and pancakes. "Pay attention to my little sister." She nodded at my singing partner, who sported a giant black beehive topped with shaving cream and glitter. "Rose'll teach you everything you need to know."

Rose wore a giant rainbow-striped muumuu and matching rainbow stickers on her pale, heart-shaped face. I wrapped my purple feather boa more securely around my neck and watched her stuff an enormous bite of blueberry pancake into her mouth. "So what do I need to know?" I asked.

Instantly, the girl was all business. "The copy's in twelve-point Helvetica except for headlines and photo captions," she recited with her mouth full. "If we're on Friday night deadline and you don't know the name of someone in a photo, use one of your grandparents' names." She leaned in close to me, her brown eyes solemn. "And always avoid trapped white space."

My stomach soured at the smell of cheap perfume mixed with the bitter odor of unbrushed teeth, but I forced myself not to recoil. Feeling suddenly young and callow, I hesitated. "What's . . . what's trapped white space?"

All around us, kids laughed and shrieked, but Rose's dark eyebrows furrowed over foreboding eyes. "That's when photos or textboxes are poorly placed," she confided, "so you have a white blob that goes nowhere on the page."

I nodded with equal gravity. "I'll remember that."

By what alchemy are best friends created? Rose and I had little in common aside from El Molino and a love of John Hughes movies. I lived with my father and stepmother in a coolly elegant tract house complete with a hot tub and a parlor gleaming behind glass French doors. Rose lived a mile away in a tiny ranch-style home with her parents and three high-pitched sisters.

That summer, we hung out at her house every day and ate stacks of

Saltines mortared with cream cheese while we watched *The Breakfast Club* and *Sixteen Candles*. We searched for our identities in Molly Ringwald's pout, in Ally Sheedy's sly smile. "I'm gonna marry Judd Nelson," Rose proclaimed, stretched out on the threadbare couch in her Jordache shorts and Culture Club concert T-shirt.

Not to be outdone, I tossed my head so that my oversize fluorescent pink hoop earrings swayed. "Well, I'm going to marry Emilio Estevez."

When we ran out of movies to inform our sense of self, we pedaled our Schwinn Cruisers to the Manhattan Village. Ninety-five cents in small change jingled in our shorts pockets as we leaned the bikes against the stucco walls of the new Häagen-Dazs shop and sashayed inside to order mint chocolate chip cones and ogle Daniel Jimenez, our freshman class president turned summer ice cream scooper.

"Let's go to your house," Rose begged when, lobster red from an afternoon on the beach, we were forced to cover up and retreat from the sun. But the stuffiness of my father's parlor hung like an opulent albatross around my neck. I thought about my stepmother's flashy china cabinet and my own spacious bedroom and bath compared to the converted garage that Rose shared with three sisters. Her entire family navigated a single sink and toilet.

"My stepmom's having the place fumigated," I groaned. "It smells like crap. Let's go to your house."

We rode home and ran up her lopsided porch steps, banging through the screen door. At once, a delicate savory scent surrounded us. "Oh my god!" I squealed, heading for the kitchen. "What's that awesome smell?"

"*Chaulafan.*" Rose kicked off her lime-green Converse beside a TV blaring a Spanish soap opera. "Let's score a bowl from my mom. But Mel . . ." She held up one hand and her glossy red fingernails stopped me in my tracks. "Let me do the talking."

Rose and her mother conversed in rapid-fire Spanish, lisping their *z*s and punctuating their syntax with hysterical shrieks and occasional peals of laughter. "Are you Mexican?" I asked the first time I heard them speak. I'd listened to Spanish for years at my mother's house—I still recalled the melodious dialogue I'd caught as I spied on backyard fiestas through the knothole in our fence. But their accent seemed different, and yet I wasn't well-versed enough to place it.

Rose lifted her chin, eyes flashing. "We're *Ecuadorean*. My parents came to the States just before I was born."

Her mother clung to the old country. She cooked Ecuadorean food every night and refused to speak English.

This afternoon she stood at the stove, red apron tied over a drab housedress, alternately stirring something in a pot and frying an omelet. "*Hola*, Mommy," Rose said when we walked into the kitchen, bending to kiss her mother's wrinkled, powdered cheek.

"*Hola*." Her mother turned from the stove to appraise me through sharp black eyes. "*Ay, dios*." She shook her graying hair mournfully. "*Tu amiga tiene zapatos muy feos*."

In my second year of Honors Spanish, I immediately recognized the words "Oh god," "friend," and "shoes." I looked down at my Keds. Were they too small? Too old? Too white? At last I remembered what *feo* meant. Ugly.

"*Ay*, Mommy, shut up!" Rose unraveled a string of impassioned Spanish, so fast I couldn't follow it. She grabbed two bowls from the dish rack and handed me one. "I told my mom you'd never tasted *chaulafan*, and that your stepmom made killer chicken and dumplings last week and gave me a bowl."

"But that's not true," I whispered as she plunged a wooden spoon into the pot. Rose had never been in my house, and while chicken and dumplings was my stepmother's specialty, she had only tasted the dish lukewarm at lunch when I'd brought it in my red plaid Thermos with two spoons.

My friend shrugged. "Hey, it got us a snack, didn't it?"

And what a snack. I'd never tasted anything like her mother's rice, seasoned with soy sauce and flecked with bits of ham, steak, and chicken. "*Aquí, niñas.*" Her mother scraped thin strips of omelet into our bowls and sprinkled diced green onions on top.

"*¡Es muy delicioso!*" I cried through a mouthful. "*¡Gracias, señora!*"

Rose's mother stared at me a moment, then turned back to the stove, one hand pressed against her mouth. Only her raised eyebrows betrayed her amusement at my attempt to talk my way into a culture with which I'd fallen obviously and madly in love.

"C'mon, dork." Rose pulled me into the den, and we collapsed on the carpet with our bowls. She aimed the remote control at the VCR, one finger poised above the Play button. "But remember," she said, her brows lowered over suddenly sober eyes, "you owe me chicken and dumplings."

Aside from chicken and dumplings, what did I have to offer Rose in terms of a charismatic culture? My grandmother's house, with her costumes and vaudeville memorabilia, more than made up for the lack of style at my father's. Even now, as a sophomore in high school, I'd don hoopskirts and Egyptian headpieces and swing on the trapeze suspended from her living room ceiling. But Grandma lived six hours north of Hawthorne—too far for a slumber party with Rose, and anyhow, show business wasn't culture. Neither was my mother's vast garden and chickens, or her girlfriend's Maxfield Parrish posters and art deco lamps. Still, I tried to persuade Rose that I understood her world.

"In Oxnard last weekend, my mother and I went to this big fiesta downtown," I told her the first week back at school. "We had tamales and listened to mariachis." I pronounced the *r* in mariachi as a soft *d*, hoping to convince her of my potential as an honorary Latina.

"Can I go with you to your mom's house?" Rose asked.

For a moment, I was tempted to invite her. But my friend wore a gold cross on a chain around her neck, and I'd seen the photo of her in a confirmation dress and veil on her parents' bedroom wall. As far as I knew, the Catholics had no place in their doctrine for my mother and her girlfriend.

"Sorry—my mom said no friends over," I told Rose. "She's writing a novel, and anyone new might scare away her muse. Let's go see what your mother's making for dinner."

At school, Rose and I collaborated on our first story for the yearbook—a piece on the popularity of car washes as fundraisers for the yearbook's Student Life section. Another sophomore named Delia Enriquez shot the photos.

Delia owned her own thirty-five-millimeter Nikon, eschewing our yearbook's prehistoric cameras. "I know my way around a darkroom, too," she bragged.

"I'll bet she does." The boys on staff elbowed each other and eyed Delia's snug Sergio Valentes. It was no secret that the yearbook photographers regarded the school's darkroom as their personal den of iniquity, complete with fifths of bourbon, condoms, and joints hidden inside developing tanks. Delia integrated immediately, producing flawless photos that she handed to Rose and me with suspiciously reddened eyes.

Rose looked up from her electric typewriter and praised Delia's work. "*Tus fotos son bonitas. ¿Quieres comer con Melissa y yo?*"

Delia flashed a wide, lipsticked smile. "*Sí, gracias.*"

Stunned into silence, I studied the way her diamond earrings sparkled under glossy black curls. But the moment she sashayed away, I recovered my voice. "Did you just invite her to eat *lunch* with us?"

"Why not?" Rose shrugged.

Every afternoon since the first week of our sophomore year, Rose and I had eaten lunch together under the David W. O. Niles tree. Niles had been our age when he died in 1982, just two years before our arrival at Hawthorne High School. We spend our lunch across his memorial plaque under the tree, which read: "Tomorrow glows with the promise of joys yet to be."

For half an hour five days a week, we shared food and discussed Marc Cleary from Honors English, whom I'd kissed, and Stuart Li, who had felt Rose up before the Christmas dance while he pretended to pin on her orchid. We talked endlessly about our plans to attend UC Santa Barbara together, where we'd read classic literature on the beach in matching bikinis.

But suddenly, here was Delia.

"My mom made *taquitos*. Want some?" Delia asked.

She lowered herself delicately to the grass in her lace miniskirt and leggings and proffered a Tupperware lined with crisp rolls of pork-filled tortilla. Rose took one. At once, another, tinier Tupperware appeared with guacamole.

"*Ay dios*, your mom can cook!" Rose said through a mouthful.

I thought of my mother's cobbler made from home-grown apricots, of her oatmeal chocolate chip cookies and her potato salad—the recipe handed down from my great-aunts on their Missouri farm. "My mom and I made cream puffs last weekend," I began, but Delia's words cut through mine.

"*¿Ven a mi casa el sábado, sí?*" she said to Rose. "*Todas mis amigas vienen.*"

The heat rose in my cheeks as I translated slowly. "Come to my house on Saturday—all my friends will be there."

I looked at Rose. What did she know that I didn't know?

She shifted her body slightly away from me. "*Claro que sí,*" she replied to Delia's invitation in a low voice, ducking her head. *Of course.*

Tears welled up in my eyes. To hide my confusion, I stuffed an entire *taquito* into my mouth. It was delicious.

"What's happening Saturday?" I demanded on the phone that night.

"Delia's having a rehearsal and a slumber party," Rose sighed. "It's the night before her *quinceañera*. She didn't think you'd be into it."

"Of course I'm into it!" I fumed. "What's a *quinceañera*?"

"It's a fifteenth birthday party for Mexican girls," she explained. "Delia wears a white dress, and fifteen couples waltz around her after her godparents present her with a Bible and a tiara and scepter."

"A *tiara*?" I yelped. "A *scepter*? What is she, some kind of princess?"

"Pretty much." I heard the tap of Rose's fingernails against the phone.

"I'll score you an invitation," she said at last, "but let me do the talking."

Saturday evening, Rose picked me up in her father's ancient Pontiac. Her learner's permit sat on the dashboard. I regarded the white slip of paper and the fact of her birthday six months before mine with envy and wished that my father shared her parents' disregard for the rule that mandated an adult in the car at all times.

"Let's go!" She tossed my overnight bag into the back seat and burned rubber down Sepulveda Boulevard. "We're late. Traffic sucks on the way to Delia's house Saturday nights 'cause the airport's so close."

"Oh, so you've been there before?" I folded my hands together primly and stared straight ahead, my heart breaking in my chest.

"A couple times." Rose screeched in front of a slow car. The driver honked and she shot him the finger. "*Ay, que* asshole!"

Delia's family lived in a neighborhood I'd never been to before. Houses crowded the narrow streets under an LAX flight pattern with a few ragged arborvitae to soften the concrete. Spanish music spilled from open doors, and rusting cars sat decaying on dandelion-infested lawns.

"This looks like my mother's neighborhood in Oxnard!" I said.

Rose pulled up alongside a crumbling curb. "I wouldn't know." She navigated a broken beer bottle in front of us, and a ragged orange cat sleeping in the street behind her car. "You've never invited me there."

She shouldered her bag and led me to a white house incongruous for its fresh paint and rose garden. "No one hears if you knock at the front door. They all hang out on the back porch." She swung open a gate. "We can go through the side yard."

She led me past a hot tub to a wide patio. Girls and boys waltzed expertly under strings of multicolored lights shaped like chili peppers. The guys wore suit coats with long tails, and white spats over black shoes. The girls danced in fuchsia satin dresses and black velvet headbands. "Our shoes haven't come yet!" Delia bustled up to us in a full-length slip and a crinoline skirt. "They're being FedExed right now so they'll get here first thing in the morning. Your dress is in my bedroom, Rosita. ¡Ándele, chica!"

I watched Rose disappear into the house. Twenty-nine pairs of brown eyes stared at me. I smiled brightly. "Hi! I'm Melissa!" I chirped.

The boys nodded mutely. The girls continued to look at me, suspicion pursing their lips. In a moment, Delia returned with Rose, now resplendent in her own satin dress. "Emilio's going to be your partner," Delia told her.

A short, handsome boy in a white fedora shook Rose's hand. "*Mucho gusto*," he murmured. Rose's pale cheeks flushed. She glanced at me, and then looked away.

"We're practicing the waltz right now, so jump in," Delia commanded.

I looked at her, waiting. She ignored me.

"Can I help with anything?" I said at last. A 747 screamed overhead, drowning out my words. Delia shook her head and walked off. I shrank into a corner and watched the girls twirl in a graceful waltz. Rose had told me they were called *damas*—maids of honor—Delia's cousins and friends. Why wasn't I among them?

"It's 'cause I did the Funky Chicken at the Sadie Hawkins dance, right?" I whispered to Rose when the song had ended and the dancers flocked to a cooler for cans of soda.

"It's not that . . ." she said vaguely, saved from further explanation by the appearance of an older, curly-haired woman in the doorway.

"*Ay*, Mommy, you made Rose's favorite!" Delia led the onslaught of kids to the platter her mother held out. "I swear," she told the girls, "Rose ate twenty *taquitos* last weekend when we were watching *Pretty in Pink*."

I stood apart from the group, a bewildered smile frozen on my face. Rose busied herself retying a bow on her dress. Delia's mother gazed at me, her double chin spreading under her smile. "*¿Quien es la gringa?*" she asked her daughter.

My Honors Spanish teacher liked to speak reverently of the magical moment that occurs when someone has truly learned another language. The words enter her ear, foreign no longer.

That night, the magic walloped me. I knew instantly what Delia's mother had said.

Who's the white girl?

"So I wasn't invited to dance because I'm Anglo?" I asked Rose later, pulling her into Delia's bathroom and shutting the door behind us. "And you're best friends with her now because she speaks Spanish."

"It's not that . . ." Rose lifted the lid off a small fabric basket on a shelf and extracted a pair of tweezers. She squinted at her eyebrows in the mirror. "It's . . ." She plucked a stray hair and stood staring at the tweezers in her hand. "It's that I know where Delia keeps her tweezers, and I don't even know if you have a pair!"

I stared at her, dismayed. "What are you talking about?"

She tossed the tweezers into the basket and opened the bathroom door. "*¿Quien es la gringa?*" she repeated. "I don't even know who you are."

The next morning, I reached for the phone to call my stepmother and beg her to pick me up. Before I could dial, Delia tottered over to me in her fuchsia high heels and dropped her Nikon into my hands. "We need an extra photographer," she said. "Doesn't have to be anything fancy. I just want some candids. Give it your best shot, okay?"

"Okay," I echoed, helplessly flattered. I sat at the back of St. Mary's Church and snapped photos of the *quinceañera*. Delia reclined in state near the priest's podium, ensconced in white tulle that fluffed around her like cumulus. I listened, mystified by the priest's Spanish as he urged her to accept the Bible and tiara and scepter along with a diamond bracelet and a gold ring. Fifteen boys in tuxedos and fedoras stood soberly to Delia's right. To her left were the girls in their satin dresses and fuchsia pumps. My best friend stood next to Delia, holding her bouquet.

I shot endless rolls on the lawn outside the church. Delia alone. Delia with her parents. Delia with her *damas* and the boys. At last, Rose took the camera from my hands and gave it to Delia's mother. "You get in this shot, too." She pulled me in beside her for a group picture with all the couples and squeezed my hand before dropping it to link arms with her dancing partner.

I didn't see the photos until our yearbook came out at the end of the year. To raise money for its printing costs, we'd sold ads for the back pages to businesses and individuals. Delia's family had purchased a full-page spread.

LA QUINCEAÑERA DE DELIA ENRIQUEZ, the header said above a close-up of her dress and tiara. A group shot filled the bottom of the page. In it, Delia brandished her rhinestone scepter surrounded by three rows of beautifully dressed young adults who radiated confidence. But a flaw marred the photo. If you looked closely, you could see it poorly placed in the second row to the left . . . a white blob going nowhere.

CHAULAFAN

Begin by learning to pronounce the word—
it's *chow-la-fawn*. Practice until those around
you can keep a straight face. Cook four cups
of white rice in eight cups of boiling, lightly
salted water. Allow to cool.

In your high-heeled fuchsia pumps,
whisk four eggs in a bowl. Sprinkle with salt
and pepper and fry into a thin pancake in a
large frying pan while your daughter's Anglo
friend looks on reverently. Slide omelet onto
a dinner plate, and cut it into thin strips, two
inches long.

Fry the rice with four tablespoons of soy
sauce. When your daughter's friend asks in
Spanish why you're using an Asian ingredient
for Ecuadorean food, simply chuckle to
yourself, and add one and a half cups of diced
cooked pork or chicken, or a combination of
the two. Add strips of egg, one cup of peas,
and sliced green onions as you listen to the
soundtrack from *The Breakfast Club*.

Cook mixture until it is heated through.
Serve in a tense room, along with a pot of
chicken and dumplings.

10.

YOUNG AMERICANS

DURING MUCH OF MY SOPHOMORE AND JUNIOR YEARS OF HIGH school, writer and director John Hughes provided what I believed to be a definitive answer to the adolescent conundrum "Who am I?" His film *The Breakfast Club* not only offered comedy, romance, and a hit single but also presented me with a multitude of complex characters from which to craft my identity.

"A brain, an athlete, a basket case, a princess, and a criminal," he labeled the members of his hip young quintet, forced to serve Saturday detention together in the high school library.

"You're lucky," my mother said after I made her watch the movie on VHS the following spring. "When I was a teen, we could be good kids with Troy Donahue and Sandra Dee, or rebels with James Dean and Rita Moreno. Nothing in between."

"Were there lesbians in the movies?" I asked.

From the couch, Annie snorted and rolled her eyes. "Ha! They either died or converted to heterosexuality."

"So how did you figure out who you were?" I asked her, mystified.

My grandmother, down from Monterey for a visit, can-canned out of the kitchen in her magenta robe and fuzzy slippers. "We are what we are!" She belted out the lyrics from *La Cage aux Folles*. "Honey." She paused in her high kicks to chuck me under the chin. "Forget the movies. Look for your identity in the theater."

She pronounced it "thea-tah," and I groaned. "Grandma," I said, "with all due respect, *La Cage* is about drag queens. I'll stick to John Hughes."

Ally Sheedy gave me hope. Little girls who grew up with Cinderella, who prayed for redemption from braces and knock-knees via the handsome prince, were granted a final chance in Sheedy, who—after eight hours of Saturday detention—emerged from under her feral hooded parka an indisputable hottie.

Somewhere within me, a similar butterfly longed to materialize, if only I could persuade an Emilio Estevez look-alike to coax it from its shy and pimpled cocoon. When it became apparent that no one from my high school was willing to take the chance, I settled for a boyfriend in Phoenix.

Five juniors and seniors from our yearbook staff traveled to Arizona for a Journalism Education Association conference. There, we marveled at saguaro cacti and the possibility of Gila monsters and attempted to seduce or be seduced by students from other high schools. The focal point of the weekend was supposed to be a writing and photography competition; teachers gave us a topic and an hour to craft it into something approximating journalism. An awards ceremony followed three hours later, preceding the obligatory hotel ballroom dance.

I won first place for yearbook feature writing. A lanky brown-haired boy named Mike DeFazo took first place for newspaper features. Fate and our Journalism teachers propelled us together for a commemorative photo with our unwieldy gold-plated trophies. "Congratulations," Mike told me in a breathy falsetto, under which I thought I could detect an emerging baritone. "We should go out sometime."

Mike wore a black angora beret. I recognized him from the hotel room next to mine; with both our doors open, I'd heard him playing classical guitar with a gentle confidence that eluded the boys at my school. Deep within his soulful brown eyes, so like those of Emilio Estevez, I could discover my worth. "We *should* go out," I agreed.

Later that evening, we danced together to Beatles oldies in the ballroom and hugged goodbye outside the hotel. "I'll trade you my hat for your scarf," he said. "Then we can each have something that the other has worn."

I unwound the gossamer pink fabric from my head. "That's so romantic," I whispered with tears in my eyes. I clutched his black beret to my cheek. "Well . . . good-bye."

From our separate states, Mike and I began to write to one another. Three times a week, he sent me thick letters filled with philosophical ramblings and professions of his love. He called nightly until my father threatened to cut off the phone service.

"I have enough to worry about without some *fairy* tying up the line," he growled. "Twice a week. He can call you twice a week."

Thwarted, Mike and I resorted to communicating through telepathy, which we'd discuss on our next call to see if the other person had sensed specific phrases or emotions.

"I was thinking of you as I scrubbed dishes at the greasy Mexican food restaurant for the unwashed masses," he told me.

"I was thinking of you while I was baby-sitting on Friday night," I replied, "and wondering how soon I might be able to afford a plane ticket to Phoenix."

Southwest Airlines offered round-trip fares between LAX and Sky Harbor for forty-nine dollars. After a month of baby-sitting, I'd earned enough for a ticket. I called an agent and booked a flight.

"You're going to Arizona?" Rose stared at me in shock when I told her of my travel plans. We sat on the floor of her den, watching *Pretty in Pink* for the tenth time and eating cookies.

"Well, of course," I said. "My boyfriend lives there."

"But . . ." She knit her dark brows over disapproving eyes. "A date is dinner and a movie, not a weekend in some guy's trailer a million miles a way." She reached for another Chips Ahoy! and shook her head. "Honestly, Mel, what are your parents thinking? My mom won't even let me go on a bike ride with a boy unless he comes over for dinner first."

It hadn't occurred to me to ask my parents' permission to travel to Phoenix. They were busy with their own lives. I left the house at six most mornings and stayed at school working on the yearbook until dark. Some days, I didn't even see my father or stepmother. Why would they care if I left for a weekend?

The Thursday evening before my flight, I approached my father in the driveway where he stood washing his Buick. "I'm going to Arizona tomorrow to visit my boyfriend."

He paused a moment and regarded me. A flicker of worry passed over his face. Then he shrugged and plunged his sponge into a bucket of soapy water. "Don't do anything I wouldn't do," he joked.

Buoyed, I approached my stepmother. "Like I told Dad, I'm taking off for Phoenix tomorrow," I said casually. "I'll be back Sunday night."

Elsa turned from the stove and appraised me. "You've just turned sixteen," she said. "Don't tell me you're flying across the country to shack up with some boy for the weekend."

I reached to stir her white sauce before it boiled over. "It's not across the country. It's only a one-hour flight. And I already have the ticket."

She snatched the wooden spoon from my hand. "Well, I'm not taking you to the airport. And your father won't, either."

The airport was five miles away. I could walk it, but I phoned my mother instead. "When you come to pick up Katie and Tim tomorrow evening, can you drop me off at LAX? I'm going to Phoenix for the weekend."

"What for?" she asked.

I sat on my bed and twined the phone cord around my toes. "To visit my boyfriend," I said.

"Mike?" she replied. "Oh, that's wonderful. Tell him he can stay with Annie and me when he comes to California.

The next day, I pulled my hair into a headband and put on a sleeveless lace camisole, mimicking Ally Sheedy's outfit in the last scenes of *The Breakfast Club*. I stepped off the plane at Sky Harbor, tentative as she'd been when she stepped out of the girls' bathroom at her high school.

"Hello, my love," Mike said as he approached me at the gate. He wore flared jeans and a pink fuzzy sweater. He'd wound my pink scarf around his neck, hiding his Adam's apple. He bent and kissed me awkwardly on the lips.

"It's funny," I giggled, speaking too quickly. "Up until now, we've only hugged once at the hotel. Um . . . are you wearing lipstick?"

Mike shrugged. "My grandma got a sample. Ziggy Stardust wears it. So does Boy George. What's the problem?"

"No problem." I bit my bottom lip, wishing I'd put on lipstick myself instead of relying on cherry Chap Stick for color.

Mike loaded my backpack into his ancient red Toyota, and we headed for the arid trailer park where he lived with his grandmother. "My mom has a horse ranch three miles away," he told me. "She lives with her second husband and my two half sisters."

"Why don't you live there?" I asked.

His pale face tightened. "She doesn't like boys," he said. "She was seventeen when she had me, and she gave me to my grandma to raise."

Sympathy overwhelmed me. If Mike were a John Hughes character, he'd be the handsome, go-getting editor of the school paper, able to hold down a part-time job and a long-distance girlfriend, emoting about his tragic past only once near the end of the movie.

I reached across the stick shift and squeezed Mike's hand. "I love you," I said.

He stroked my cheek with his long fingers. His nails gleamed with a glossy pink polish. "I love you, too."

In his double-wide trailer, he introduced me to his grandmother, who only looked up from her tiny television, set on a bookshelf in the living room, and croaked, "Good to meet you. I bought Pop-Tarts."

"Oh," I replied. "Thank you."

I followed Mike into his bedroom at the end of a long, dim hall and appraised the decor. Posters of Morrissey and David Bowie covered the walls. A guitar and amplifier dominated one side of the tiny room. A desk and chair pressed up against a narrow cot, opposite which stood a closet open to reveal a tangle of clothes and textbooks.

"Come here, you." Mike pulled me down beside him on the bed and began to kiss me. I'd made out before, most recently with a senior who took me to see *Platoon* and then French-kissed me sloppily until—plagued by images of napalm and grenades—I begged him to take me home. Mike's kisses unnerved me, as well. I didn't enjoy them as much as I'd expected to. They were too delicate, like tiny lost butterflies.

"Let's just cuddle," I suggested.

He sighed and reached for his guitar. While he played an expert rendition of "Yesterday," I lay back on his cot and reveled in my good fortune. I had a handsome, talented boyfriend. When I lifted my head from his pillow, I pretended not to notice the streaks of pink lipstick on the linens.

A month later, Mike stepped off the plane at LAX, and we climbed into the back of my mother's VW bus. "Thanks for picking me up," he told her.

In the driver's seat, she nodded. "I like your jacket."

He smoothed down the fringes of the new white faux leather. "It's like the one Mia Sara wears in *Ferris Bueller's Day Off*."

Mike shared my obsession with John Hughes's latest movie. In Oxnard, we borrowed the bus and drove to the mall to see it again. "Mia's so hot," Mike said of Ferris's sultry girlfriend.

I lay my head against his cashmere sweater and contemplated how to change my image. I had a closet full of thrift store clothes, à la Ally Sheedy. Now, I'd have to embrace Mia Sara's haute couture.

Back in the VW after the movie, I attempted to mimic her sloe-eyed vamp. "Let's drive over to the Navy base," I suggested languidly. "There's a good spot to park near the beach."

"Excellent," Mike said. "We can put the bed down in the back."

We did, and he climbed on top of me. I tried to thrill to his touch. "Have you ever noticed that the characters in John Hughes's films don't have sex?" I said, gazing carefully over his shoulder. "They just kiss."

Mike rolled off me. "So what are you saying?"

I sat up and adjusted my blouse. "Maybe it's just that this is my mother's bus," I reasoned. "It doesn't put me in the mood. We should try making love someplace else."

Up until now, I'd guarded my virginity. None of my four parents had talked with me about intercourse, and I wasn't entirely sure how it worked. I knew what went where—but I wasn't sure why I'd want to have sex beyond retaining my boyfriend.

Mike wasn't so much tender as he was determined, and his insistence made me nervous. "I just don't see why it's such a big deal," I told him that night as I tucked him into bed on my mother's couch, ignoring his pleas to "Do me."

In the living room, lit up by a street light, he turned a shade paler. "I promise you," he whispered, "it's a big deal."

"All right," I sighed. "We'll keep trying."

Over the next six months, over the course of four visits back and forth, we tried in my grandmother's damp garage, surrounded by hoopskirts and Chewbacca masks from her costume shop. We tried in Mike's trailer after his grandmother had gone to bed. We tried in his mother's king-size bed while she was on vacation in Hawaii.

The last spot was the worst. I lay prostrate, legs spread, and stared past Mike's pale buttocks at the portrait of his chic mother and tawny golden-haired half sisters. "Just do it," I said. I longed to sit beside him on the easy chair in the den, watching *The Adventures of Buckaroo Banzai Across the 8th Dimension* and eating Pringles, but he could barely contain his euphoria.

"Really? We can actually have intercourse?" He glowed, but his smile abruptly faded. "I don't have a condom."

I blinked at him, relieved. "Too bad," I said, but he brightened.

"Wait!" he cried. "I'll be right back."

He disappeared down the hall. In a moment, he'd returned with a Ziploc Baggie. "Perfect!" he crowed.

I watched in disbelief as he slipped it over his penis. "You've got to be kidding."

He frowned. "I filled it with water to test it. It doesn't leak."

Exhausted, I surrendered. Mike entered me via the bag, and I bit my lip to keep from crying. I'd imagined my deflowering would occur in a daisy-filled pasture at dusk, with the man I intended to marry. Instead, I lay rigid on a stranger's bed, my eyes squeezed shut against the pain.

Finally, Mike rolled off me and slunk to the bathroom.

I lay on the bed and wondered what was wrong with me. Other girls had sex with their boyfriends—they talked about it constantly. Slowly, I stood up and walked to the bathroom. I tapped softly. No answer, and then a breathless falsetto said, "Come in."

I pushed the door open to find my boyfriend clothed in his white-fringed jacket and his sister's plaid school skirt. He leaned toward the bathroom sink, applying red lipstick. Rhinestone earrings dangled from his lobes. I saw the truth then. Unlike me, Mike knew exactly who he was. And I knew, as I waved goodbye to him for the last time from the dim window of the Southwest 737, that the distance between us had grown impossible to navigate.

Artie Ramirez nailed Judd Nelson's role in the senior-class production of *The Breakfast Club*. He smoldered and taunted, a tough-talking juvenile delinquent nursing a heart both wounded and optimistic. Artie understood the complexity of John Hughes's darkest character. After the performance, everyone whispered that he'd kick ass in Hollywood if he could only lose his double chin and that weird Darth Vader breathing.

Artie suffered from chronic asthma and insomnia. Locked in a constant battle with the principal, he teetered on the edge of expulsion due to poor attendance. "Who cares if I can write a five-paragraph essay or find the square root of pi!" he fumed to the other members of the Drama Club. "I'm an actor!"

I'd joined my school's thespians after Mike and I broke up. What a trick to be able to transform oneself from a lunchtime misfit loitering, black-clad, on the steps outside the theater to a presence worthy of standing ovation on Friday and Saturday nights. Aspiring to such a transition, I dyed my hair red, auditioned for *Bye Bye Birdie*, and found myself with a brief cameo as a tap-dancing secretary. Artie played the main character's father. "I wanted the role of Conrad Birdie," he grumbled to me, "but the drama teacher said I wasn't the rock star type."

I wrapped my arms around him. "You rock my world," I whispered in his ear.

To my astonishment, Artie had chosen me to star as his girlfriend in his final three months of school. I envisioned him a fierce yet tender Judd Nelson to my naively captivating Molly Ringwald. But Artie entertained a different perception of our roles. One night, he showed me the film *9 1/2 Weeks* in his mother's dark, musty living room. "Study these characters," he lectured me. "They're the real thing. Enough of this John Hughes bullshit. Ever notice that his only Latin character is a car thief?"

Artie reclined behind me as I sat on the threadbare Asian rug and tried to immerse myself in the story of a sad, sadomasochistic relationship. He rubbed my back in slow, hypnotic circles as I dutifully observed Mickey Rourke's power over Kim Basinger.

Later, he took me to Denny's for chili-cheese fries. In the booth, he handed me a flat box tied with a ribbon. "I got you some clothes," he said.

"*Got?*"

I eyed the box. Artie worked part-time in a gentlemen's clothing store at the Manhattan Village—an outlet so elegant and restrained that his boss never suspected a gentleman might help himself to the inventory. But what could he find for me there?

"We have a sister store," he said. "Honestly, you can't go around in polka dot skirts and kitty cat earrings forever," he continued. "If you want to be an actress, you've got to make the most of your sex appeal. You've gotta work it."

I blinked at him across the platter of French fries. I had sex appeal?

Elated, I accepted the box and slipped into the restroom. In the stall, I lifted the lid to find black stretch pants, an off-the-shoulder pink shirt, and obsidian heart earrings adorned with pink bows. Even as a cross-country runner, I'd never worn pants so snug, but I shed my beloved thrift store circle skirt and pulled on the outfit. The smudged mirror above the sink reflected sudden curves and cleavage. I pocketed the maligned gold felines and thrust Artie's new earrings into my lobes.

Two elderly women walked through the restroom door as I stepped out. They looked me up and down and clucked their tongues. But Artie beamed when he saw me. "Much better." He reached across the platter of now-cold fries and fluffed out my hair. "Now you're perfect."

My heart thrilled to his benediction.

He showed me how to remove the screen from my bedroom window without bending the frame so our nighttime trysts might go undetected by my father and stepmother. Artie's mother owned a white BMW, which he borrowed after she went to bed. I listened for the engine's purr outside my window at midnight and leaped out to join him on the warm leather seats. We cruised Hollywood Boulevard, belting out the lyrics to "Rock Lobster" with his B-52s tape and whooping at the leather-clad boys who strolled hand-in-hand through the rainbow-flagged streets of West Hollywood.

"Faggots!" Artie yelled.

I socked him in the arm. "Hey! My mother is gay!"

He sneered with Judd Nelson's world-weary derision. "It's different for lesbians, *chica*."

"What is?" I demanded.

Instead of answering, Artie headed the BMW toward the narrow, curving roads in the Palos Verdes hills. He pulled off to the side of the road and smiled at me. "Let's drive with the headlights off."

"No!" I cried. "That's way too dangerous."

He leaned over and kissed my lips. A sudden lust dizzied me. John Hughes be damned, I thought. I could be Kim Basinger's character, if that's who Artie needed me to be. "Okay," I murmured. "Whatever you want."

He raced through the hills, and I held my breath, prepared to die. Once, a car appeared in the opposite direction. The driver, seeing our BMW in front of him, swerved toward the mountain. I stared out the back window. His car recovered, the horn echoing against the rocks. Artie grinned, white teeth flashing in the darkness. "That was close."

We ended up at Del Aire Park. He toted blankets and a boom box up to the covered top of a children's double slide. I followed him, shivering in the cold mist off the ocean. "Lie down," he told me, and I stretched out obediently on the wool blanket from his bed. He slipped his *9 1/2 Weeks* cassette into the boom box and began to kiss me. His hands on my back awoke a desire I'd never felt for Mike on those sticky Arizona nights, but they never moved below my waist or to my breasts.

"Are they too small?" I whispered, drenched and swooning in the scent of Brut cologne.

He shook his head. "Be quiet," he ordered and closed his eyes to kiss me.

A few weeks later, Artie managed to graduate. "Redondo Beach Theatre's putting on *My Fair Lady*," he told me. "Let's audition."

He picked me up in front of my father's house, and I wore the outfit he'd given me. The director cast me in dual parts as "Cockney Chorus Girl" and "Maidservant Number Two." "I get to sing the counterpart to 'I Could Have Danced All Night!'" I told Artie.

He shrugged. "I get to be 'Bum Number One' and sing backup to 'Get Me to the Church on Time.' Can you believe that shit? Didn't they know I've had the lead in every Drama Club production since freshman year?"

The director, balking at the idea that the distinguished academic Henry Higgins could be played by a stout, asthmatic Latino, had offered the role to a handsome Redondo Beach pediatrician. "The guy's got the charisma of a rat," Artie scoffed.

The director tapped a red-haired community college actor named Stefan to play "Bum Number Two." He was to dance and sing with Artie in the "Get Me to the Church" number.

"Sorry, ol' girl, but I 'ave to stay late." My boyfriend broke the news to me one evening after regular rehearsals had ended. "Me mate Stefan and I 'ave a special re'earsal. From now on, I can tike you to the thea'er, but you 'afta find your own way 'ome."

"Loverly," I said and shuffled off to call my stepmother.

Artie and Stefan became inseparable at rehearsals. They acquired twin black leather jackets and walked with their arms around each other, joking and whispering and slapping each other on the bloomin' arse. I listened long past midnight for the BMW's horn outside my bedroom window, but it never came.

Still, Artie picked me up for rehearsals. "Your house is on the way," he reasoned. "But make sure you're outside on time. I don't want to have to get out and knock on your door."

The evening of the dress rehearsal, I stood out on my father's lawn half an hour before Artie was due to pick me up. I thought of the scene in *The Breakfast Club* when Molly Ringwald undoes one of her diamond earrings and places it in Judd Nelson's hand after they kiss. The exchange seemed so poignant, so indicative of the type of relationship Artie and I might share after the play ended.

But an hour later, the white BMW hadn't appeared. And an hour after that, I had to admit—as I ripped the obsidian hearts from my ears and hurled them with their frayed pink bows into the gutter—that Artie couldn't be the character I needed him to be.

My senior year, I decided to audition for the school production of *Anything Goes*. I wanted to try out for Reno Sweeney, the brassy nightclub singer who entertained passengers on a cruise ship.

I saw Reno as a sort of 1930s Demi Moore from *St. Elmo's Fire*—a vivacious party girl whom all the men adore. But my drama teacher had different ideas.

"You should audition for Hope Harcourt." She flipped her golden hair extensions over one slender shoulder and looked down at me from her stiletto heels. "You're perfect for that part."

"I'm always the ingenue," I wailed to my friend Richard the next day. "Never the vamp or the vixen. Hope Harcourt is so boring. So . . . sweet."

"You're sweet," he said. We sat on the steps of Nyman Hall at lunch, drinking black coffee from the snack stand and sharing a bag of cheese popcorn. "You've got to toughen up if you want to land Reno."

I threw off my white cardigan in despair. "Teach me," I begged.

He pursed up his lips and folded his arms across his designer sweater. "It's going to be hard," he cautioned. "I'm not sure it's even possible."

Richard was a stocky, smartly dressed Filipino with black hair moussed and sprayed into a four-inch shelf atop his head. In him, I found a happy amalgamation of resourceful Ferris Bueller and the witty Duckie from *Pretty in Pink*. But Richard didn't need John Hughes to provide him with identity. He was Asian, and he regarded the man who had created the Japanese character Long Duk Dong in *Sixteen Candles* as a joke. "Stereotypes show a lack of imagination," he told me. "You've gotta keep people guessing."

Excluding me, all of Richard's friends were Asian, too. They occupied the roles of class president, cheerleading mascot, and captain of the Drill Team. Many of their parents had arrived in California in the 1970s from the Philippines, Thailand, and South Vietnam when their kids were in elementary school. They changed their names as quickly and deliberately as those who had passed through Ellis Island a century before. Thuy, Linh, and Jintana became Tiffany, Lynne, and Jenni. By twelfth grade, they presided over the highest social echelon with their New Wave haircuts, stylish clothes, and easy camaraderie that revealed nothing of turbulent pasts.

At Richard's suggestion, I began to ditch my math class, driving him in my gold Chevy Nova to the local hamburger joint, where we communed over French fries with his friends. They largely ignored me as they planned pep rallies in suave alto voices.

Just once, they invited me to help with a Student Council fundraiser. "You can grill the *satay*," Jenni offered magnanimously. "It's my mother's recipe."

I stood over a hibachi for four hours one afternoon, endlessly grilling and marinating pork kabobs. During a lull, Jenni approached me. She appraised my white tennis shoes, covered with peanut sauce, and wrinkled her nose. "So are you Richard's girlfriend, or what?" she demanded.

How I longed to say yes, and thus become an honorary member of the popular crowd, but Richard excited none of the lust in me that Artie had inspired. Still, I wasn't about to reveal this to Jenni.

What would Reno Sweeney say? I thought quickly. "Life's too short to be tied down to one boy," I said in as sultry a voice as I could manage.

Jenni shook her head and turned away. "By the way," she called over her shoulder, "your basting brush is on fire."

Richard and I began to hang out every Saturday to rehearse for the audition. He hoped to land the part of the gangster, Moonface Martin. At first, he taught me dance moves on the lawn outside Nyman Hall. But one day, he pointed to a two-by-three-foot window. "Hey, let's break into the school theater," he said. "You're small. I'll boost you up, and you can climb in and open the door."

I peered at the window halfway up the stucco building. We appeared to be the only people on campus that day, but I was three months from graduating with a 3.75 GPA and a dorm room waiting for me at UC Santa Cruz. "I don't know," I told Richard. "If we get caught . . ."

He frowned. "I thought you wanted to toughen up." He bent down and wove his fingers into a step. "Here's your chance."

I stepped up and hoisted myself through the window. Inside the theater, we took turns playing the piano and mimicking our unfortunate weekday accompanist—a prissy retired choir director who sang so enthusiastically as she played that her wattle wobbled. On the dimly lit stage, Richard taught me to dance a wild Charleston for Reno's signature song, "Blow, Gabriel, Blow."

"You can't give a shit about your throat," he said. "You've gotta belt out the lyrics."

When my voice gave out, he sat cross-legged beside me on the stage and gave me further instruction. His countenance hardened, and his dark eyes glittered with challenge. "Do you like your balls attached to your body?" he snarled.

"What?" I shrank back against the heavy velvet curtain.

"Say it," he commanded. "And act it."

I tried, but by the time I reached the testicular portion of the threat, my voice shook with laughter. He scowled. "If you want the part of Reno Sweeney, you've got to sound merciless. Let's hear it again."

"Do you . . . " I began dutifully. "Do you like your . . . your . . . your *balls!*"

He threw up his hands. "I give up," he said.

We lay back on the stage and gazed up at the lights. "We should rent a house in Hollywood and audition together for movies next year," Richard told me.

"In four years," I reminded him. "After I graduate from college."

He sat up. "Honestly, Melissa, why would you waste all that money? Actors don't need a degree."

Like Molly Ringwald's character in *Pretty in Pink*, Richard lived on the wrong side of the tracks with a father who struggled to pay the bills. "There's no way I can afford college," he told me.

"But you always have nice clothes," I said. "And no job. What's up with that?"

He studied me under the stage lights. "Can you keep a secret?"

I nodded.

"All right," he said. "But you take this to your grave."

Richard explained that Schick had introduced a fifty-dollar razor, small enough to slip unnoticed into an inside coat pocket. His process was simple. He'd pilfer a razor from the local Nordstrom, then return it a week later in a box he'd carefully mauled around the edges.

"I'm so sorry." He mimicked himself gazing plaintively at the department store cashier as he pleaded his case. "I gave this razor to my mother for her birthday, and she didn't like it. She's from the Philippines, and she didn't realize she had to keep the receipt. We don't have much money . . ."

He trailed off, shaking his head over his mother's endearing ignorance. "Then the cashier counts five ten-dollar bills into my hand," he told me, "and I go buy a new sweater."

"That's sticking it to the man," I said hoarsely. "I'd love to see you in action."

"Not a chance. You'd blow my cover for sure."

"I wouldn't," I protested.

Then Richard leaned over and kissed my cheek. "You're too sweet," he said. "Trust me, baby, you're nobody's moll."

At home that night, I put a hand to my cheek and tried to feel a thrill, as I had when Artie kissed me. Nothing. But I resolved to become Richard's partner in crime, if only to prove to him and my drama teacher that I was tough enough to play Reno Sweeney.

I watched *Ferris Bueller's Day Off*, studying Mia Sara's serene demeanor as she deceived her high school principal. I scrutinized Ally Sheedy as she nabbed Judd Nelson's knife and revealed that she'd stolen Anthony Michael Hall's wallet in *The Breakfast Club*. I practiced Richard's phrase until it rolled off my tongue.

"I'm going shoplifting with you," I announced to him one Saturday. "I can keep my cool. You'll see."

He peered at me. "Let's hear it."

Swiftly, I composed my face into a cold, hard sneer. "Do you like your balls attached to your body?" I growled.

He nodded thoughtfully. "Very nice. Let's go."

I drove him to Nordstrom, and we sauntered into the women's department. I wandered among the clothing racks, as he'd had instructed. "Don't watch me, in case the cameras are watching you," he said. But I couldn't help peeking over the coat racks, heart pounding, as he approached a center table laden with boxed razors and elegantly slipped one under his black trench coat.

"Miss, is there a problem?"

The salesman took me by such surprise that I spun around and sputtered the first words that came to mind. "Do you like your balls attached to your body?" I squeaked.

"Excuse me?"

The man glared down at me. Trapped, my inner ingenue took over. She simpered and widened her guileless blue eyes. "Tennis balls," she trilled. "I'm looking for tennis balls."

The salesman shook his head. "Downstairs and to the left. That's funny," he said, grinning suddenly. "For a moment, I thought you said . . ."

I didn't give him a chance to finish. I turned to join Richard, but he'd melted into the mall crowd and disappeared, leaving me alone.

"Where'd you go?" I asked him at the audition the next Monday.

He shrugged. "I can't afford to go to jail."

Our drama teacher called his name then, and he headed for the stage to execute his song and dance. For my own audition, I pulled on the tight pants and off-the-shoulder pink shirt that Artie had given me. I smeared on red lipstick and vamped and vixened for all I was worth. My teacher wrote something down on her notepad and smiled broadly. "Your volume is fantastic," she said after my song. "But doesn't your throat hurt?"

"Not at all," I croaked and went to take my seat as a big-bosomed blond girl in gold sequins walked up onstage.

"Blow, Gabriel, blow!" she sang out in a tremendous, vibrating alto. My heart sank.

In high school, I discovered who I was by learning who I wasn't. I wasn't Ally Sheedy, Molly Ringwald, or Mia Sara. I wasn't Demi Moore, and as it turned out, I wasn't Reno Sweeney. The morning after the audition, the Drama Club kids gathered early on the steps of Nyman Hall to look at the cast list taped to the window. "Moonface Martin!" Richard raised his fist in triumph.

"I got Reno!" the big blond girl cried.

"Who are you playing?" one of the younger thespians asked me from the bottom step.

I knew without looking. "The ingenue," I said and walked away from the theater.

STUDENT COUNCIL SATAY

First, cut your hair in an asymmetrical New
Wave bob. Put on your drill team skirt and
sweater, and get out a shallow pan. In it,
mix half a cup of soy sauce with half a cup
of water. Whisk in a tablespoon of peanut
butter and a teaspoon of chili powder, two
cloves of minced garlic, and a tablespoon of
brown sugar.

If you're not too exhausted from fending
off the amorous advances of your romantic
partner, grate a teaspoon of fresh ginger, and
squeeze a tablespoon of lime juice into the
pan. Otherwise, just use a quarter teaspoon
of powdered ginger and a tablespoon of
white vinegar.

Cut up a pound of pork tenderloin into
thin slices. Place it in a fresh Ziploc Baggie with
the marinade. While the meat marinates—
preferably overnight—recite over and over,

"Do you like your balls attached to your body?" When you've perfected your sneer and you no longer giggle, fire up your hibachi.

Thread the marinated pork pieces on the skewers, and grill for five to eight minutes— just long enough to sing "I Could've Danced All Night" from *My Fair Lady*—lead and maidservants' parts. While the pork is cooking, put the marinade in a saucepan, and bring it to a boil. You can now use it as a dipping sauce for your *satay* without fear of food poisoning—but do make an effort not to spill it on your white tennis shoes.

11 .

No Va

My junior year, I signed up for Driver's Education at my high school. The teacher looked and sounded like Paul Lynde, the actor who'd cracked my great-grandmother up nightly on reruns of *The Hollywood Squares* and voiced the character Templeton the rat in *Charlotte's Web*. Packed into the school theater with a hundred other kids, I closed my eyes and tried to pretend I was listening to an animated rodent. But instead of delivering acerbic observations on a spider that could write epithets such as SOME PIG in web-floss, my teacher focused on the litany of disasters that would befall us if we didn't keep our eyes on the road and three seconds of space between our car and the one in front of us.

"After a crash, your insurance goes sky-high," he sneered into a microphone on the school stage. "You may suffer broken bones, whiplash, or head trauma. You may be responsible for another person's death. *You may die. What is a car, class?"*

One hundred teenagers whispered in terrified unison, "A car is a machine."

To emphasize his point, the teacher pulled down a screen, dimmed the lights, and showed us clips from the iconic driver's education series, *Red Asphalt.* I closed my eyes and shoved my fingers into my ears to drown out the sirens and the screams. I thought of my friend Kim, a senior on the yearbook staff who drove with her left foot casually stuck out the driver's side window of her red Toyota. Over the past year, she'd hit three parked armored vehicles. "A fluke," she'd said and tossed her head. "Driving's a snap," she assured me. "You'll love the freedom."

I hoped so. I finished the class and got my learner's permit. "I'll teach you to drive," my mother said. "I've taught several people."

We practiced one afternoon in Monterey, in the shady parking lot at the community college. I traded seats with her in the VW bus and attempted to wrestle the long, skinny stick shift into first. "I'm afraid it'll break!" I wailed.

Beside me, my mother white-knuckled her seat. "It's stronger than it looks," she managed to sing out cheerfully, as if her oldest wasn't currently endangering her life by attempting to hurtle over a speed bump in fourth gear.

The bus stalled, and I glared at her. "What now?" I muttered.

"Put in the clutch and give it some gas," she instructed.

"Which is the gas, and which is the clutch?" I asked for the fourth time. My white Keds did a desperate tap dance on the pedals. My mother sucked in a ragged breath.

"That's the brake," she said faintly.

After an hour, I burst into tears. "I cannot drive this thing!" I leaped down from the seat to the asphalt and kicked one tire. My beloved childhood vehicle—this bus in which I'd cruised Saviers Boulevard and ridden up and down Pacific Coast Highway hundreds of times—had betrayed me.

"Don't worry." My mother climbed back into the driver's seat with palpable relief. "It's hard to learn on a manual. You should ask your father for lessons. His Buick practically drives itself."

My father turned out to be a surprisingly clear and patient instructor. In his office parking lot, he coached me into guiding the plush Buick in slow circles. This car had no baffling clutch to maneuver. I appreciated the simplicity of two pedals—accelerator and brake. Most of the time, I didn't get them mixed up.

"Let's take it out on the freeway," he said after our second lesson.

I winced. "Are you sure?"

"Why not?" He grinned. "What's the worst that could happen?"

I closed my mind to the macabre images from *Red Asphalt* and pulled the car into the turn lane for the 405. The grille of someone's 4x4 leered in my rear-view mirror. As the light turned green, I held my breath and accelerated toward the freeway.

Cars and trucks rushed by me at seventy miles an hour. The truck behind me sped up and passed me, its driver honking. I braked and checked my mirrors. Cautiously, I inched into the slow lane as people swerved around me. I got behind a dump truck full of gravel and counted out three seconds between the back of it and the front of the Buick.

Triumphantly, I smiled at my father. He sat pressed against the seat. His grimace looked sideswiped. "Never!" he yelled. With difficulty, he lowered his voice and continued the lesson. "Never brake as you merge."

Eventually, I could enter the 405 like a pro, all the while popping my Police tape into the player, putting on lipstick, and rummaging through my backpack for a pen and notebook. Proudly, I demonstrated my multitasking abilities for my DMV instructor. He ignored them, but my parallel parking job nearly undid him.

"You can't hit the bumpers of the cars in front of you and behind you!" he sputtered. "I could flunk you for that."

"But that's how my father parallel parks," I said.

Confronted with my innocence, the man turned a light shade of purple. "I'll pass you," he said, "but God forbid you drive in my neighborhood."

That night, I drove my father, stepmother, and younger siblings to Farrell's Ice Cream Parlour. The following day, however, the truth hit me.

Summer vacation beckoned two weeks away, and I had no car.

My father drove his car to work. My stepmother needed hers for trips to the grocery store and to aerobics classes. "Plus, I take your brother to appointments and the cat to the vet," she reminded me. "You can borrow my car on weekends."

This was fine, but I knew Elsa would never let me drive her car up to Oxnard to visit my mother. More and more, I'd been skipping my twice-monthly visits with her because of yearbook obligations and plans with my friends. She drove Katie and Tim back early on Sundays, and took me out to dinner, but I longed to see her whenever I wanted.

"My mom makes me crazy," Rose muttered in the movie theater one Saturday. "You're lucky to live far away from yours so she can't nag you incessantly."

But I didn't feel lucky. I felt deprived.

I thought I'd get to see her more often once summer began, but right before the end of school, I landed a job as an intern at a local newspaper. My yearbook adviser knew the editor and persuaded him that I'd work hard for no money. "Mom!" I shrieked into a pay phone in the school hallway. "I'm going to be a journalist like you!"

"That's wonderful, honey," she said. "At the *L.A. Times?*"

Her faith in me was touching, but I had to take her down a peg, noting that the paper was a small biweekly based in Culver City, across from the MGM studios and a good twenty miles by car from my father's house.

"Can you drive me to work?" I asked Elsa at home that night.

She shook her head. "That's an hour twice a day in rush hour traffic," she observed. "Didn't you tell me that Rose just got a job at Pizza Hut? Maybe they're still hiring."

Insulted at the prospect of throwing dough and slicing olives instead of contributing to the journalistic body of belles lettres, I turned and stomped out the back door with my backpack. "I'll take the bus," I muttered.

I stalked to the bus stop a half mile from the house and sat there in a huff until it arrived. I'd brought *In Cold Blood* to read, but instead I gazed out the grimy window at the houses and businesses—all of them thrown suddenly into a half-romantic, half-tawdry light from my perspective in the city bus.

I had to transfer midway through my commute, and so I found myself waiting for the next line at a stop in the middle of an industrial street, attempting to read as cars and trucks rushed by. I clutched my backpack as homeless people rolled their carts up to me and demanded spare change. I tried to comfort myself with the fantasy that my adventures on public transportation might make for a great three-part series in the newspaper.

Half an hour later, I found myself in a bustling office punctuated by the clack and ding of electronic typewriters and the urgent pealing of a dozen telephones.

"You'll write headlines and edit the calendar," the editor told me. He had white curly hair matched by a close-cropped beard and wore a rumpled Hunt Club polo and jeans. He deposited me in a back corner with a stack of typed articles and pointed out the dictionary, thesaurus, and empty frozen orange juice container full of pencils. "Headlines are short," he said, "and put some conflict in them. Remember, if it bleeds, it leads."

He walked off, leaving me to chew on my pencil eraser. Newspaper journalism bore no resemblance to the stories I'd been writing for yearbook on football stars and math club fundraisers. I peered over my sheaf of papers at the reporters populating the newsroom. Most of them were middle-aged men, hunched over their typewriters with cigarettes permanently affixed to their lips. I saw only one woman—a frowning brunet with her hair in a ponytail—pacing her cubicle. Next to her jeans and USC sweatshirt, my selection of a brown-and-black-striped dress and black velvet flats felt ridiculous.

She looked up, caught my eye, and walked over. "I'm Katherine," she said. "So you're the new intern? Well, it's good to have some estrogen in the room." She jerked her head at the men behind her. "They're a kettle of vultures, so if you need anything, come to me. We women have to stick together."

"I will," I said gratefully.

I found out in the next few weeks that "stick together" meant writing her headlines, slipping in her last-minute calendar items, making her fact-checking phone calls, and fielding messages from readers furious at being misquoted, misrepresented, and otherwise maligned.

My third week as an intern, Katherine disappeared. "Gone to get a Master's in Feminist Theory." The editor lit a Marlboro and shook his head. "What a waste. She was shaping up to be a fine reporter. I don't know who we're gonna get to fill her place."

I raised my hand and piped up timidly. "I'd like to write a profile for the paper," I told him.

He raised his white eyebrows. "Who on?"

Resisting the urge to correct his grammar, I told him about a press release I'd received. "There's a man in Hermosa Beach who calls himself a sea vampire. I think he'd make a fascinating story."

My editor took a deep pull on his cigarette. He nodded into his smoke. "Sea vampire, huh? I don't know what the hell that is, but Katherine left us up shit creek, and we've got a big hole in Wednesday's edition. Go for it, kiddo."

I went for it. I rode my bicycle out to Hermosa and interviewed an eccentric middle-aged gentleman who got his jollies climbing out of the ocean in a black seaweed-strewn cape to scare the crap out of little kids. The piece appeared that week. My editor, impressed with my having interviewed the man both in the ocean and in his Dracula-themed kitchen, decided I should write another profile. "You know what a Ziegfeld Girl is?" he asked.

I looked up from my typewriter. At last, my great-grandmother's showbiz stories were paying off. "The Ziegfeld Follies was a sort of vaudeville show," I said. "Scantily clad girls in feathers and sequins, plus stand-up comedians like Fanny Bryce. The girls must be in their eighties now, right?"

He nodded and tossed a press release on my desk. "Yup. Got this from one of 'em. She's still alive and kicking—giving a performance at the community theater in Manhattan Beach this weekend. Get on it, kiddo."

I threw down my pencil and picked up the phone. "I'm on it, sir," I said and dialed the woman's phone number.

She turned out to be a genteel, petite little old lady with silver hair and sugar cookies that she'd cut to look like cats. We sat at her living room table, and she poured me a pink china cup of mint tea. "The peppermint is from my garden," she informed me musically.

I looked around at the black-and-white stills of showgirls on the wall and wondered which one was she. Over the woman's shoulder, I studied what appeared to be a shrine to Ziegfeld himself—his framed photograph overlooked a shelf upon which sat a vase of roses and a flickering candle. I took out my notebook.

"I know you're giving a one-woman show this weekend," I said. "And a lot of it involves tap-dancing. How have you kept in shape?"

"Swimming." She sipped her tea primly and replaced the cup on its thin saucer. "And I dance every day. My glutes are still as firm as they were when I was seventeen."

I frowned over my notebook, attempting to write legibly. My subject must have suspected doubt about her physique because suddenly she stood up and presented her behind in lavender polyester pants for my inspection. "Honey," she said, "feel my butt."

I stared up at her. "Excuse me?"

She shifted her hip so that one cheek protruded, inches from my hand. "Feel my butt."

I'd spent months immersed in books by Gay Talese and Truman Capote. I knew Tom Wolfe would stop at nothing to get a good story. But my mother had trained me to be a lady. Always hold the door open for people, never ask a woman her age, refer to people older than myself as Mr. or Mrs., and never feel up a grande dame's ass. "That's all right," I stammered. "I believe you."

But my subject would not be deterred. "Feel it!" she commanded. "You'll be shocked."

At last, I reached out and tapped her behind, blushing furiously. "It's very firm," I said.

"Told you." She sat back down and passed me the plate of cookies. "Another kitty cat?" she asked.

That summer, I conducted all of my interviews on my bicycle. Sans helmet, I pedaled my red Schwinn all over town, my notebook and pencil tucked into a fanny pack. Surreptitiously, in front of the Redondo Beach mayor's house, I scrubbed at my pits with Handi Wipes and prayed I looked like a hip young journalist instead of a pathetic carless amateur. My subjects treated me with respect, and if I smelled of sweat and naivete, they hid their dismay.

My mother picked me up at the bus stop near the office one Friday afternoon. "I'm scared to death for you, sitting alone in the middle of Los Angeles and biking all over town to work for free," she said, easing the VW into traffic. "Is this how your editor treats his interns? What if something horrible happens?"

I looked out the side window at the MGM lion roaring from its sign above the studio. "Then I'll write about it," I said. "Anyhow, I can outrun the bad guys."

My father and I had taken to running six miles together every other Saturday morning. We headed out at eight and ran past Holly Glen Park to streets more opulent than ours, their mammoth houses shaded by purple-blossoming jacaranda trees. We ran our last mile back in our own, less flowery neighborhood. It was on one of these runs, on a Saturday in August, when I spotted my perfect car in the turquoise-painted driveway of a run-down pink house.

It was a 1967 Chevy Nova. More gold than brown, it matched the sparkly eye shadow I'd pilfered from my great-grandmother's bathroom drawer in Monterey.

It wasn't a car, ordinarily, that might cause me to shorten my stride and pause in my run, except for one critical detail—the red and white For Sale sign in the back window.

"A thousand dollars," I murmured. Such a sum seemed unattainable. For a year I'd been giving my father the money I earned from baby-sitting to put into my savings account. "How much do I have?" I asked him.

"I'll look up the total when we get home," he promised.

Up in his office, he studied my savings book. "Three hundred and twenty-four," he said. "I'll tell you what. I'll front you the money, and you can buy this car. But I want you to help Elsa with errands and drive Katie to high school in September. I trust you don't mind being seen with your little sister?"

I shook my head. "Of course not!" I cried. "It's a deal! Can we go buy the Nova right now?"

My father took out his checkbook. "Why not?"

We walked the few blocks to the car and approached the pink house. The owner of the Nova turned out to be an elderly man in slippers who spoke in what I thought might be a Russian accent. "Hello?" he said.

"I'd like to buy your car!" I squeaked on the doorstep.

He stepped back, overcome by my high-decibel demand. "Really?" he said.

My father cut in. "For nine hundred dollars," he said.

The man's half-moon brown eyes went from Dad's face to mine. He wrinkled up his face in thought. "Okay," he said. "You come in. I have contract. You sign."

My father wrote a check on the spot, but as I drove my new car home, he delivered his terms from the passenger seat. "You have to get a job to pay this back."

I nodded. Suddenly, my internship at the newspaper office paled in comparison to the magnificent responsibility I felt as a car owner. "They're hiring at Miller's Outpost in the Manhattan Village," I said. "I'll drive over and apply today."

"Nova. *No va*," Rose repeated when I drove the gold Chevy over to her house for inspection. "*No va* means 'no go' in Spanish."

"It goes just fine." I patted the seat, its jagged rips giving way to crumbling yellow foam. "Get in," I said. "We're going to Venice Beach!"

Driving through late summer and into fall, I fell in love with Los Angeles. I lacked money for gas, so I traveled to its beaches and parks and farmers markets and museums on fumes. As a junior with wheels, I sauntered into my Honors English class and approached Mr. Sloane. "I read the first section of *Beowulf* last night," I told him, "and I really loved the part where he rips off Grendel's arm with his bare hands, but I have to miss class to go report on a story for yearbook," I lied smoothly.

My teacher nodded, his good-natured smile unsuspecting. "Write a two-page paper on the pagan elements in *Beowulf* for tomorrow," he said.

"Of course," I replied and sashayed to the parking lot, where I climbed into my Chevy. I cranked up "Synchronicity II" on the cassette tape player and headed for the beach.

Armed with a notebook and pen, I trudged through the damp sand and climbed an empty lifeguard stand to sit with my back against the aqua fiberglass. Alternately scribbling and staring out at the surf, I composed a short story in which Beowulf met Ronald Reagan and debated about whether a cowboy-actor turned president could be considered a hero. I threw in a few references to monsters and enchanted swords and Hawk antiaircraft missiles and called it an essay, then turned my attention to composing a rhyming ode to my Chevy Nova.

I began to excuse myself from math class regularly as well. Lunch fell between English and Trigonometry, so under cover of official yearbook business, I used the three-hour block of time to visit Exposition Park.

"You're ditching school so you can go to a museum?" Rose balked in the hallway. "Why not go to the Galleria?"

But shopping held no interest for me. I parked near USC and paid the five-dollar fee, then headed for the tableaux of taxidermied mountain lions and elephants at the Natural History Museum. My mother and I had wandered through the museums at Exposition Park when I was younger. We'd ordered Chicken McNuggets and fries at the McDonald's at the Museum of Science and Industry and eaten in the enormous rose garden. The same tall, thin African American man always rollerbladed the cement walkways around the flowers, dancing to tunes on his Walkman.

He was there now, as I left the history museum and strolled around the rose garden. He circled me once, grinned, and waved. I wondered if he recognized me as a grown-up version of the girl who used to sit on a park bench sharing French fries dipped in barbeque sauce with her mother.

For a moment, my stomach ached with missing her, and I wished she were beside me as I walked to the science museum. Between her work and my school, we'd barely seen each other that year. But now, with my own car, I could make it to Oxnard in an hour and a half. If I ditched History class, I'd have an hour to visit with her before driving back down Pacific Coast Highway.

Cheered, I headed downstairs to investigate the gyroscope and the camera lucida until the lure of the simulated earthquake proved too powerful. I could hear its rumbling and the mixture of gasps and nervous laughter in the next room, and I hurried in.

The display itself looked like someone's middle-class living room. You stood on a platform and looked over the railing at an easy chair and a television, which flickered to life when you pushed a button. A newscaster appeared on the screen to deliver the evening news. All appeared tranquil and nondescript until the ground beneath you began to tremble. Suddenly, the entire platform shook with the living room. Pictures on the walls tipped, and the TV news turned to static. The rainbow stripes of the emergency broadcast system appeared on the screen, replaced by another grim-faced newscaster reporting from a pile of rubble in what used to be downtown Los Angeles.

The simulated earthquake distracted me from thoughts of my mother, and I pushed the button again. Earthquakes didn't bother me. They offered, once or twice a year, an alternative to sedentary suburbia. For me at seventeen, constant motion was nonnegotiable.

My Nova had different ideas, though. That winter, I baby-sat to earn gas money, but I drove the car far beyond empty. I chauffeured my high school friends to the movies with the understanding that they'd contribute—both to the peanut butter jar of spare change in the back seat and to pushing the Nova to the gas station if it ran out of fuel.

"I can't come up this weekend because I have an all-day baby-sitting job this Sunday," I told my mother on the phone in February. "But don't worry. I'll have money for gas, so I can ditch school and drive up to see you in Oxnard on Monday!"

She paused before answering. "I have meetings at work all day," she said at last, "but meet me at the house, and we'll have lunch together."

That Monday morning, I filled the Nova with gas, bought a bottle of Coke and a pack of red licorice, and drove through Westchester to the Pacific Coast Highway. From my position behind the wheel, the scenery I'd been passing for eight years looked vastly different. The Malibu beaches, the seafood restaurants, Pepperdine University, even the strip mall with the petting zoo where my father and mother would exchange us after a weekend—all felt fraught with tender nostalgia.

I passed the Air Force base at Port Hueneme and navigated downtown Oxnard. Mariachi players in short black coats with silver trim strolled the streets with their trumpets. Women pushed babies in strollers. I parked outside my mother's house and turned off the ignition.

She hugged me at the door in her black work blazer and pants. A turquoise necklace hung around her neck, and matching earrings dangled from her lobes. "I've got an hour before I have to get back to the office," she said.

I walked into the living room. Ordinarily, it was immaculate and cozily shabby. Now, Annie's entertainment magazines lay splayed open on the coffee table. My mother's laundry took over the couch. I felt suddenly and uncomfortably like a visitor.

She'd made tofu tacos, along with pinto beans from a can, which she served on two plates with microwaved flour tortillas. We sat at the table to eat. "So how's the college search?" she asked me.

"I've settled on UC Santa Cruz," I told her. "That way, I'll live just an hour from Grandma and Grandmary, and I can see them on the weekends. Maybe you could drive up, too, sometimes?"

"Of course." She gazed out the window into the back yard. "It's a five-hour drive. You'll be so far away . . ."

I finished my tacos and reached for the plastic bear on the table to drizzle honey on my tortilla. "I know, but I want to live up north for a while. I'm tired of Southern California."

She nodded and stood up to carry the dishes to the sink. I helped her wash them, looking out the back window at the fuzzy purple trumpets of Mexican sage. The neighbors were quiet on either side of us. I wondered where Kenny, my old baby sitter, had ended up. Was he in Hollywood making movies?

I thought about how he had told me that style was everything, and I wished I could show him my Chevy Nova. "It's definitely unique," my mother said as she walked me to the car. "But it looks like it's about to fall to pieces."

"Mom." I rolled my eyes. "You drive a VW bus."

"Good point." She glanced at her watch. "I've got to get back to work, honey. You can stay here if you'd like."

I stood uncertainly on the lawn. Without Katie and Tim there, without Annie and my mother cooking and playing music, the house felt unfamiliar and cold. "No," I said at last. "I'll head back. I want to stop at Venice Beach for a while."

We hugged good-bye, and I climbed into the Chevy. My mother got into her VW bus and pulled away. I drove behind her, keeping the requisite three seconds of space between us. At the Saviers intersection, she turned left and I turned right. I cranked up my Police tape and sang along with "Wrapped Around Your Finger" to keep from crying.

My mother called me at my father's house that night. "I've decided to rent an apartment down by you," she said.

"Really?" I yelped. "Where? Why?"

"You're growing up so fast," she said. "I want to be closer to you. I can work four days a week in Oxnard and spend three days there with you."

Long ago, a judge had ruled that she could only see me four days a month. But if she lived in the same town, my father couldn't possibly keep me from visiting her—especially now that I had a car. "That's awesome!" I said. "I'll help you move in."

My mother found a stark but clean apartment a few blocks from my high school—a one-bedroom with a view of a parking lot and frenetic El Segundo Boulevard. "I didn't get it for the view," she said and closed the nicotine-stained curtains. "We'll put a fold-out sofa in the living room, so you can spend the night whenever you want. For now, I brought sleeping bags."

"That's great," I said. Legally, my mother had to tell my father she'd taken an apartment in his town. But unsure of how flexible he might be regarding the custody arrangements from long ago, I resolved not to tell him if I spent the night at my mother's place. Half the time, I got home from school when he and Elsa were already in bed and left again before they got up. They'd never know.

"And if they find out," I told my mother, "well, it's better to ask forgiveness than to ask permission."

Someone knocked on the door—my friend Tuan. "Hi, Mom." He greeted my mother with a kiss on her cheek. "I'm here to help you hook up your TV."

My friend Richard walked up behind him, followed by Rose, who bore two bags of Doritos and a six-pack of Coke. She stuck out her hand to shake my mother's. "It's so good to meet you at last," she said.

"I hope you don't mind that I told my friends where you live," I said. "I thought we could have a housewarming party."

My mother went to the kitchen and pulled out a bag of tortilla chips and a container of salsa. "I'm thrilled," she said with tears shining in her eyes.

We sat on the living room carpet and ate and talked. My mother wanted to know all about our yearbook class and Honors English and Drama Club and who was dating whom.

"Your mom's so cool," Tuan said as he and Richard left.

Rose hugged her. "Thanks for a great party," she said. "See you soon."

My mother waved at my friends, then closed the door. "They're wonderful," she said. "I'm so glad I get to share this with you."

She walked into her new bedroom to unpack her suitcase. She'd brought a wooden milk crate to use as a nightstand; I watched her place a clock on top of it and unroll her sleeping bag in one corner of the bare, chilly room. Without my friends there, the apartment felt empty and sad. I thought of Annie alone in their bedroom in Oxnard, and guilt overwhelmed me.

But my mother appeared to be fine. "Let's go to Pizza Hut for dinner," she suggested. "I called Katie and asked if she wanted to join us, but she's got Drill Team practice. I wish we could pick up Tim, but I'm still figuring out the legalities of my living here part-time."

I nodded, glad to have her to myself. "I've got to go to school at six thirty tomorrow morning," I told her over pizza, "but I'll be back from play rehearsal by nine at night, and then you and I can have dinner together again."

"I didn't realize you'd be gone all day," she said. "Well, I brought my typewriter, so I can work from the apartment tomorrow."

That night I slept on her living room carpet to the sound of traffic and the unsettling feeling that something wasn't right. My mother woke up at six to make me peanut butter toast and hot cocoa. "Have a good day," she said and hugged me. I walked to my Chevy with my breakfast and looked back at her, standing alone in the doorway of the apartment. For so many years, I'd been used to leaving her for ten days at a time. I didn't know how to feel about this new arrangement.

That week, I felt guilty if I left early for school and worse if I stayed late working on the yearbook or rehearsing a play. Another week went by, and I tried to divide my time between my father's house and her apartment, school, and friends. "It's crazy," I told Rose. "All these years, I've wanted her in the same town. And now that she's here, I don't have time to see her."

My mother must have realized this. Three weeks after she moved in, she gave notice on the rental. "I can't handle the expense of a house and an apartment right now," she told me as she carried her typewriter to the VW. "I miss Annie. I barely see you. I'm so sorry, honey, but the apartment's a no go."

It was a Saturday morning, early. I had to take the SAT in Palos Verdes at nine. I loaded the milk crate into the bus and tossed in the rolled-up sleeping bags. "Well, at least we tried," I said.

She embraced me, her face stoic. "I'm sorry," she said again and climbed into the front seat.

For a moment, I hated her for being too late. I watched her pull out of the parking lot with my fists clenched at my sides. Then I climbed into the Nova and pushed in my Police tape. I stopped for an Egg McMuffin and an orange juice, then headed up to Palos Verdes to take my test. Looking out at the winding stretch of road in front of me, I glimpsed my future in the fog. I would get a high score on the SAT. I'd get into UC Santa Cruz.

I would go.

SHOWGIRL COOKIES

Begin by watching *The Great Ziegfeld*, and pause to pay your respects to Leo the Lion before the film begins. Practice your high kicks as you cream together half a cup of softened butter and three-fourths of a cup of light brown sugar. Add two beaten eggs and a teaspoon of vanilla, plus a half a teaspoon of lemon rind. Beat mixture for five minutes, which should give you plenty of time to compose a journalistic lead that bleeds appropriately.

Sift together two cups of white flour with two teaspoons of baking powder and a quarter teaspoon of salt. Add this to the butter-sugar mixture and stir well. While the dough is chilling for an hour, immerse yourself in Truman Capote's *In Cold Blood*, noting that he may have spent time in prison, but he never had to feel up a grande dame's derriere.

Preheat your oven to 375 degrees. Roll your dough on a floured board to a quarter-inch thick and cut into kitty cat shapes, of course. Bake on a lightly greased tray for eleven minutes, or until nicely browned. Remove from tray, cool cookies slightly, and serve to a wide-eyed rookie journalist with tea.

12 •

CREAM OF THE CROP

STUDENT COUNCIL, A FIRST-PERIOD ELECTIVE, REPRESENTED POP-ularity, privilege, and prestige—which is why I lasted only two months. Near the end of my senior year, I sat among miniskirted and mascara-laden cheerleaders and gelled and Old Spiced valedictorians who shot disparaging looks at my fishnet stockings and gold thrift store skirt with black polka dots.

Mr. Morello, our faculty adviser, delivered a version of his 7:00 AM motivational lecture every morning. "You are the cream of the crop," he'd say, trapping us all in the tractor beam of his hypnotic gaze. "The best that the school has to offer." He touched his fingertips together as if hoping to ignite sparks. "Now say it along with me."

Then, twenty-nine students sat up straight at their desks and intoned the chant like zombies from an Ed Wood movie. "We are the cream of the crop. The best that the school has to offer."

Mr. Morello was missing half of his right ring and middle finger. "Accident in 'Nam," he'd say when questioned. "Some commie pinko's probably using my digits as earplugs."

I'd watch, at first mesmerized, as two fingertips of his left hand prodded the stumps of two knuckles on his right.

Student Council smacked of elitism. *We* were the best that our school had to offer? What about the art students who sculpted and sketched potential masterpieces twelve hours a day and worked night jobs at Pizza Hut to earn summer study in Rome? What about the yearbook photographers inhaling volatile chemicals in the school darkroom as they labored to document our high school years? What about the sprinters and shot-putters who woke up at 4:00 AM for Saturday invitationals a hundred miles away while the cream of the crop slept off their hangovers from the post-basketball-game kegger? What made them lesser beings than the Council kids whose primary contributions lay in spray-painting posters for the Sadie Hawkins dance and organizing ice cream socials?

My friend Richard had been on Student Council since his freshman year. "It gives me an excuse to get out of Math and English class," he reasoned to me as we blew up pink and green balloons for the Spring Formal. "In fact, we're ditching next period. Come with us!"

When I should have been in Physics, I instead found myself sitting with him and our class president, our secretary, and our valedictorian in a French bakery, eating crème brûlée and drinking espresso from tiny white cups. The Council members smoked clove cigarettes and fumed over the upcoming graduation festivities.

Apparently, a student had complained that Grad Night, which involved an all-hours party in a pricey hotel near Disneyland, was restrictive. It excluded those without money to pay for a room or thirty-dollar admission to the amusement park. Why not just have a dance in the gym, some teachers had suggested.

"The thing is," said the president, cracking into the brûlée's burned sugar topping with her spoon, "most students are stupid. They'll accept whatever we tell them. So I say let's party at Disneyland, and the plebeians can drink Coors in the park."

The other kids laughed and clinked their Coke glasses together, toasting their good fortune. The president touched her clean fingertips together as if to ignite sparks. She didn't have to say the words. We all knew them. In just half a semester, I'd memorized their inflection, their fervent, hypnotic tone.

If Mr. Morello—seemingly hell-bent on creating semester after semester of separatist snobs—was the best my school had to offer, I wanted out. In April, I quit Student Council and immersed myself in the Drama Club, where at least people admitted to playing a part.

Politics was not my bag. The subject was too unwieldy, dictated by rules I couldn't comprehend. In Government class, the teacher tried repeatedly to explain the electoral college until I groaned in despair. "So you're telling us we're supposed to register to vote, show up at the polling place on Election Day, and mark a ballot, but our vote doesn't really count?" I sputtered.

"That's correct," he replied.

"But that's totally bogus!"

From him, I learned about Lord Acton, the nineteenth-century historian who devoted his life to the study of political liberty. "Power tends to corrupt," he observed famously, "and absolute power corrupts absolutely."

This was 1988, the year that Oliver North was indicted on sixteen felony counts involving the sale of weapons to Iran and the diversion of funds to Nicaraguan contra rebels, who busily conducted guerrilla warfare against their left-wing Sandinista government. My stepmother spent her afternoons gazing at the Colonel's earnest brow and puppy dog countenance on her kitchen television. "I don't care what he's done," she said, vehemently chopping carrots. "He looks so handsome in that uniform."

That was patriarchy for you. A pair of soulful eyes and a little charm trumped all sorts of bothersome deceptions. A politician could get away with murder, and a volatile father could take his children away from their lesbian mother.

Having turned eighteen in March, I no longer felt helpless. I believed I could counteract the elitism and the corruption. The summer between my high school graduation and college, I took a job registering Democrats to vote.

A handsome college junior named Dan—a poli-sci major on summer break from Sacramento State—interviewed me for the position in a windowless office in Redondo Beach. With his curly hair and chiseled jaw, he looked like a dead ringer for the bust of Thomas Jefferson in my Government teacher's classroom. "Oh, no, Melissa. *This* is how you give a handshake." He clasped my limp palm warmly in his. I gazed into his brown eyes and hung on every word delivered in his stirring tenor voice.

"This election marks a defining moment in our nation," he told me. "For eight years, Ronald Reagan has waved a flag of injustice over all except his own allies. We must return power to our tired, our poor, our huddled masses. It's time for minorities to take a stand."

By minorities, he meant Michael Dukakis, whom I knew because of his cousin Olympia, who had stared in *Moonstruck* with Cher. I suffered a moment of doubt that we could indeed land our Greek in the White House, no matter how assertive our collective handshake. But I was sick to death of dominating patriarchs, and Dan, with his prodigious intelligence and biceps bulging from his short-sleeved dress shirt, struck me as boyfriend material.

I saw us married after college, exchanging political letters like John and Abigail Adams, and immortalized in musical theater.

"Count me in!" I cried and shook his hand with renewed idealism.

My job duties consisted of meeting him and five other recruits each morning for a twenty-minute pep talk in a chilly office building. Then we each shouldered an ironing board and headed to a supermarket of our choice.

"Why an *ironing board?*" I demanded the first morning. My stepmother ironed my father's dress shirts—five every Sunday night—religiously. I wanted nothing to do with such oppression.

"It doubles as a table," Dan explained. "You can tape your sign to it. Here." He handed me a red, white, and blue cardboard placard that commanded simply, VOTE! "You can adjust the board so people don't have to bend over when they're filling out their registration forms."

"Brilliant!" The other recruits murmured their admiration. I studied them: a young African American man with a shaved head, an aging gentleman in tie-dye, a woman with curly white hair and a peace sign on a silver chain, and a ponytailed blond girl with blue fingernails to match her snug Smith College T-shirt. Dan explained that we would earn two dollars for every Democrat we registered to vote. By law, we had to offer registration cards to Republicans and people from other parties as well, but we wouldn't get paid for them.

"So the key is," he continued, "to debate with unregistered voters, and even Republicans, until you persuade them to come over to our side."

"Even *Republicans?*" I scowled, but again, my coworkers exclaimed over Dan's political savvy.

"That's incredibly astute," the blond observed. "We've got to build rapport with the opposing party, and then nail them with statistics on Republican corruption."

I raised my hand. "What if they know more about politics than I do?"

I'd passed Government mostly because my teacher showed film footage of World War II all semester, then offered an open-book exam from a tome that concluded with Richard Nixon. "What if I lose the debate?"

Dan glanced at my clinging red dress, which I'd paired with the fishnets. "You'll do fine, Melissa."

The next Monday, I donned my red dress and hoisted my stepmother's ironing board into my Chevy Nova. "Where are you going?" My father peered at me from the doorway.

I squared my shoulders and looked challengingly over the board. "I'm going to register Democrats to vote."

My conservative father went as white as his starched collar. Up until that moment, he'd maintained an undisputed position as Speaker of the House with a firm "don't ask, don't tell" policy. Now, all at once, his constituency had grown up—and she was pissed.

But he regained his composure and smiled with the bemusement afforded to those who know they have the winning candidate. "Shouldn't you be wearing blue?" he asked.

"Jeez, Dad. It doesn't matter what I wear!" I drove off in a huff.

That first day, I set up my ironing board in front of a Vons supermarket in the trendy section of Redondo Beach. This was no tepid warehouse redolent with fish odors and Barry Manilow Muzak. No, the manager of this store piped Offenbach through the speakers and made sure his employees waxed each apple individually.

Under the purple jacaranda trees, I taped my sign to the ironing board at a jaunty angle and affixed an American flag to the end of my ballpoint pen. A tan woman in running shorts and a tank top approached the door. I took a deep, bracing breath of the salty ocean air. "Excuse me, ma'am. Are you registered to vote?"

She turned to me, manicured eyebrows arched. "I'm on the city council."

"Oh! Sorry."

She delivered a parting shot from the sliding glass door, radiantin a blast of air-conditioning. "I certainly hope you're not one of those *Democrats*."

An elderly man shuffled toward me, clutching a cane. "Excuse me, sir?" I approached him with my clipboard. "Are you registered to vote?"

"Which side are you on?" His rheumy eyes peered into mine.

"I have to register everyone," I chirped, "but I'm particularly interested in Democrats."

At once, the cane flew in my face. "You commie liberal!" he shouted. "If you had your way, you'd take what little social security I've got and we'd all be speaking Russian. Or Japanese. Or German!"

I had no idea how to address this barrage of accusations, and so I turned my back on him and approached my next potential client, a young woman my age pushing a baby in a stroller. "Hey, you registered to vote?"

She waved me away. "I did your job last month," she said. "I can make more money baby-sitting."

That first day in front of the supermarket, I observed several distinct political demographics. Most of the women I approached went out of their way to avoid speaking to me, pretending fascination with the outdoor display of cantaloupes or crossing over to the other door as soon as I made eye contact, as if democracy might be contagious. Most of the men rushed past, too, with an occasional grunt or "I'm in a hurry." Elderly gentlemen stopped by my board consistently, all of them spoiling for debate.

A retirement home stood nearby, and residents frequently walked over to the market for exercise and onion bagels. They knew their politics.

"I remember that Republican, Herbert Hoover," spat a man as he filled out my first registration form. "A chicken in every pot, my ass! What do *you* think?" he demanded, signing his name with a flourish.

"About what?" I stepped backward, in case his walker turned weapon.

"About the Democrats! Think we got enough spunk to win this election? That Jimmy Carter was more trouble than he was worth—good foreign policy, but no spunk. We need someone with spunk, see?"

The one memory I had of Jimmy Carter was more a recollection of my little sister, Katie. At four, she'd perched on top of a table in the polling place and duly recited the words our father had taught her as our mother filled in her ballot. "Carter is a peanut!" she shrieked, so that voters in their curtained alcoves alternately gasped in horror or smothered appreciative laughter.

"Dukakis has spunk," I stammered, uncomfortably aware that I didn't know a thing about my Democratic nominee.

I was saved from admitting my ignorance because a man my father's age stepped out of the market wielding a giant Toblerone bar.

I ducked as he thrust the Swiss chocolate toward me. "*Thank you* for your patriotism," he murmured in the mellifluous tones of a radio commentator. "We're lucky to have women like you in this country."

I embraced the half-kilo candy bar, glowing with all the pride of an Elizabeth Cady Stanton receiving her first ballot. The man beamed at me from under libidinous eyebrows. "I've just moved to a beachside condo with an incredible view from the master bedroom."

He paused to let the implication sink in, but my sensibilities stayed solely focused on the chocolate. "And I need to update my voter registration," he finished sullenly.

That evening in the office building, Dan passed around Cokes and tallied up the day's registrations. "Marco: twelve Democrats, one Republican, two Libertarians. Sandra: fourteen Democrats, two Republicans, one Peace and Freedom. Way to go, Sandra!"

Around the table, we whooped and applauded. Sandra flipped her blond ponytail and shrugged modestly.

"Melissa: two Democrats, two Green Party, *ten* Republicans?"

I hadn't bothered to check my forms for party affiliation as people handed them back, too intent on offering an earnest handshake and a sincere "Thank you for preserving democracy!" Now, I shrank in my seat. "Oops," I whispered.

Dan asked me to remain after the rest of our cadre had departed. Momentarily, I allowed myself the fantasy that this gorgeous, impassioned man might also gift me with a bar of imported chocolate and wax poetic about his beachside boudoir. Instead, he lowered himself into a chair across the table, his soulful eyes sober, and laid a warm hand on my arm. "I'm mainly concerned with your financial well-being," he said gently. "You earned four dollars for eight hours of work."

Under his hand, goose bumps stung my flesh. Dan really cared about me. He was so much older, so much wiser than I was. I'd forgotten that I didn't get paid for registering Republicans, much less those tenacious third-party defenders.

The trouble lay in my choice of venue, I decided. Redondo Beach, with its crisp ocean breezes and crispier residents, would blaze red on any election map.

"I'll do better tomorrow," I told him and placed my hand over his. "Tomorrow, I'll go to where *our* people shop. Hey, there's a bar around the corner. Wanna go grab a Sam Adams?"

He pulled his hand out from under mine. "Whoa, there. We need to maintain a professional relationship. No dating allowed."

Mortification washed over me, and my cheeks flushed red as my dress. "I'm sorry!"

"No worries." Dan turned back to his paperwork, then looked up. "And Melissa, one more thing."

I paused in the doorway. Was he reconsidering my offer?

Dan frowned. "You might want to lose the red dress and the fishnets. The manager from the Redondo Beach Vons called. She thought you were a hooker."

The next morning, I pulled on a pair of overalls and knotted a blue kerchief around my head, fancying myself a modern-day Rosie the Riveter. I drove off, ignoring the stuffed elephant my father had placed on the dashboard of my Chevy, and headed for the proletariat part of my hometown. The Green Apple Market was a modest, lukewarm center of commerce with window signs advertising six-packs of Budweiser for $2.50 and generic cartons of cigarettes. I cranked up my ironing board on pavement that reeked of stale beer and approached a man in coveralls.

"*Con permiso, señor.*" I struggled to recall my high school Spanish. "Register to vote . . . uh . . . *votar?*"

He squinted at my clipboard and shook his head, shrugging an apology. "I sorry. *No comprendo.*"

"No, *I'm* sorry." Chagrined, I looked down at the registration forms, all in English. Did we offer them in Spanish? I had no idea.

A woman stepped off a city bus, trailing toddlers. "Are you registered to vote?" I asked as one child clambered onto the mechanical horse beside the soda machine and an older, chunkier kid clambered onto his brother.

The woman rolled her eyes and plucked her offspring from the horse. "Do I look like I have *time* to vote?"

A trio of ragged men shuffled up, clutching forty-ouncers. I assessed their grimy hands and toothless leers, then proffered my flag-tipped pen. Democrats embraced all people, regardless of gender, age, or blood alcohol level. "Are you registered to vote?" I asked.

One man, obviously the diplomat of the bunch, staggered up to me. "You're in our spot," he said and promptly collapsed under my ironing board.

"My apologies." I carted the board to the other door. Today, I would disappoint neither Dan nor Michael Dukakis. But upon reviewing my forms that afternoon, I found that I had registered only three voters.

One Democrat, one Libertarian, and one person who'd filled in the blank under POLITICAL AFFILIATION with the words BEER PARTY, DUDE!

The people I approached at the Green Apple also avoided my eyes, gazing instead at the food stamps in their hands or scanning the parking lot for pennies before bolting past me into the market. The presidential election appeared to be of little concern to them. "Reaganomics got me a room in a halfway house—crack addict on one side of me and a pimp on the other," one man snarled. "I ain't votin' never again."

As I carried my ironing board past the panhandlers toward my car, one of them called to the other. "Hey, Vern. How much you make today?"

"Twelve bucks!" The other man jingled pockets full of change.

The irony sent my spirits plummeting. Twelve bucks. I had made two, without even a chocolate bar to show for my efforts.

The next morning, I returned to the upscale Vons. "You've got to exercise savoir faire," Dan coached me. He placed his hands on my shoulders and kneaded them expertly. "Think like a politician. Use charm and rhetoric to persuade the Republicans to switch sides, to join the party that celebrates competence instead of ideology."

"Competence instead of ideology!" I repeated, attempting to emulate his rousing tone.

"You got it, comrade!"

Dan ceased his massage and high-fived me. I marched out of his office. Two minutes later, I marched back in.

"Um . . . Dan? What exactly does 'competence instead of ideology' mean?"

He looked up from smoothing a Dukakis/Bentsen sticker across his leather briefcase. "Didn't your application say you earned a 3.75 GPA?"

"Sure. I got all As in Drama, Yearbook, and Creative Writing."

I could see from his expression—a mixture of panic and nausea—that Dan was despairing over what our country had not done for me in terms of basic high school education. He explained that our party embraced action instead of empty talk, and I headed off determined, with tenacity worthy of a Kennedy, to do something for my country.

Back in Redondo Beach, the retirees set upon my political ignorance like vultures.

"Reagan got our hostages out of Iran. How do you like them apples, missy?"

"Do you *want* to pay higher taxes, child? Are you *crazy?*"

"I have a boat docked in Marina del Rey. I'd love to take you for a ride."

This last comment came from a stunning gentleman in shorts and a T-shirt. He introduced himself as George Papadelis, Esquire. He looked to be in his thirties, with black curling hair and teeth so white I squinted. "I need to register to vote," he said, "but it looks pretty complicated."

"It's easy!" I cried.

"I'll be right back," he assured me. "I'm visiting my mother, who lives in the home near here, and I promised I'd buy her some strawberries."

Strawberries for his mother! Swiftly, I assessed the situation. Dan was obviously too preoccupied with the upcoming election to even think about dating me. But this man was even more handsome than my boss, and he was flirting with me. Papadelis. That was a Greek name. Greek, like Dukakis!

I murmured thanks to Athena and wrote down my phone number on the back of a registration form. *For the good of the party*, I thought.

George Papadelis, Esquire, walked out of the market and presented me with a large, perfectly ripe strawberry and a fluted aluminum cup of crème brûlée. "What say I whisk you away from all this asphalt and we sail to Catalina?"

"Catalina!"

As he filled out his registration form, I considered the brown sugar crust on the brûlée along with the possibility of a union. There on the island, I could frolic blissfully unaware of presidential tracking polls, battleground states, and teeming political rallies. *Yes!* I thought. But the word stopped short of my lips, thwarted by a sudden memory of Olympia Dukakis telling John Mahoney's professor in *Moonstruck* to stop dating his students.

"Don't shit where you eat," she said.

Sorrowfully, I relinquished the dessert. "I need to maintain a professional relationship with my clients," I murmured. "No dating allowed."

"Suit yourself." George Papadelis handed me his completed registration form, sunlight gleaming off the silver ring on the third finger of his left hand.

"You're *married?*" I cried.

He shrugged. "Seven-year itch."

I looked down at his registration form as he rocketed out of the parking lot in his Ferrari.

Republican.

I packed up my ironing board late that evening—determined to earn at least enough money for gas—and returned to the darkened office. I longed for Dan's optimistic political coaching. I thought we might trade neck massages. But I opened the door to find him holding hands with my ponytailed coworker in her Smith T-shirt. He was bending to kiss her when I walked in.

He snapped upright. "Just teaching Sandra to give a proper handshake," he said.

I slapped my stack of registration forms down on the table. "Six Republicans, two Democrats," I said before he could examine them. "I quit."

He stared at me, open-mouthed.

"You're the cream of the crop, Dan, really." I paused in the doorway. "But just one piece of advice . . . don't shit where you eat."

Disgusted, I stumbled to my Chevy and sped out of the parking lot. The tail end of Lord Acton's most famous quote rang in my ears.

"Great men are almost always bad men."

CREAM OF THE CROP BRÛLÉE

Channel your inner elitist, and spring for a vanilla bean, so much more refined than a bottle of vanilla extract. Split the bean in half. Scrape the seeds into a saucepan along with two and a half cups of light cream, and throw the bean pod in there, too. Warm cream mixture until it's as steamy as Ollie North's sex appeal, then turn off the heat. Let the mixture sit for ten minutes.

Preheat the oven to three hundred degrees. In a bowl, beat together six egg yolks and half a cup of white sugar until thick. Add the cream to the yolk mixture, stirring constantly. Make sure to remove the vanilla bean or you'll piss off your constituency.

We live in a democracy, and so you have a choice. You can either make one enormous brûlée in a one-quart ovenproof dish for the plebeians or pour the custard into four individual ramekins to bestow upon the elite. Set your elected vessel or vessels in a baking pan, and add hot water up to one inch from the top of the dish or ramekin. Bake twenty-five to thirty minutes, until the mixture has just set. Note that it should tremble just a little, like a charismatic colonel on trial for illegal activities.

Cool your brûlée, then cover it with plastic wrap, and chill in the refrigerator. When you're ready to serve it, place a rack as close as possible to your oven broiler, and preheat. Sprinkle the top of the brûlée with a half a cup of white sugar. Stick it in the oven, and broil it until the sugar browns.

Alternately, wield your personal blowtorch like Lady Liberty, and heat the sprinkled sugar until it bubbles, golden and crisp. Serve atop an ironing board, adorned with perfectly ripe strawberries.

13.

6.9

"MELISSA, YOU'RE NOT USING YOUR COLOR PROPERLY."

Across the big table, the white-bearded creative writing professor shook my rolled-up manuscript in his fist as one might grip the neck of a doomed chicken. "Every college freshman has her wise bum story." The man sighed mightily and lowered himself into his padded leather chair, apparently overcome by my clichéd prose. "And 99 percent of these stories take place on the mall downtown."

He removed his wire spectacles and surveyed the fourteen other students sitting around the table. They leaned forward, pens poised to catch his next words. "If you want to write fiction, you've got to immerse yourself in color."

Brightening, the professor turned to the young man next to me. Jason wore his hair in tiny dreadlocks that resembled fuzzy black caterpillars.

A pot leaf dominated his black T-shirt, and his pants were baggy, woven from hemp. "Now Jason here knows how to use color." The professor smoothed out a wrinkled, fragrant manuscript and beamed. "His story about being the only Jamaican man on an Alaskan cruise ship crackles with vibrancy."

While our teacher waxed poetic about Jason's memories of lavish Inside Passage buffets at which passengers consistently mistook him for a waiter, I crumpled my own story surreptitiously into my backpack. Color was apparently synonymous with legitimacy. And I was colorless, so pale I was practically transparent at UC Santa Cruz, which teemed with eccentric, exuberant hippies. What story could I possibly tell to prove my worth?

I reached for my pen. In black, I wrote two words on the white flesh of my palm: Switch majors.

As an opera student, I studied with a ferocious blind teacher who strode the halls of the music building brandishing a cane and her golden retriever, Verdi. "Stop smiling," she commanded at my first lesson in her high-ceilinged studio. "Gabriel Fauré is a serious composer. If you want to giggle, go study musical theater."

Mystified, I sought out my classmate, June. "How'd she know I was smiling?" I demanded.

June was Filipina and a year ahead of me. Tiny and dark with a rich mezzo-soprano, she explained, "She can hear it in your voice when you sing. Smiling tightens the vocal chords and fades color from your tone, you know?"

I didn't know, but I nodded and changed the subject. "Are you going to audition for the opera?"

Our teacher Patricia planned to mount an enormous production of Mozart's *The Marriage of Figaro*. In a cast of lords and ladies—each with a demanding vocal score—the only role that seemed attainable to a novice freshman singer was that of Cherubino, the adolescent servant boy who flits about the stage trilling about his sexual awakening.

In the tiny practice room, I listened over and over to Margaret Price singing "Non So Piu." I practiced her inflections until I could imitate them and then sat cross-legged atop the piano, meditating on the mind-set of a horny thirteen-year-old boy.

"I can't give you a good explanation," I sang soberly in my audition, "of this new and confusing sensation . . ."

I did not smile. I did not giggle. Patricia cocked her head toward me, one hand absently petting Verdi's golden neck. "Again," she demanded. "This time, with color."

That word again. I stifled a sigh of despair. I had not yet experienced a sexual awakening, having dated little in high school. Still, I tightened my diaphragm and made taffy-pulling motions with my hands in front of my mouth as my teacher had taught me, to better conjure up tone.

But I was a no go.

"Cherubino's a short Italian kid." My dreadlocked friend Jason consoled me with a walk through the redwoods and a hit off his bong. "June looks the part."

"But my teacher is blind!" I wailed.

"So ask her what you could've done better."

At my next practice, I ventured timidly to inquire about my failed audition. "Is it because I didn't sing with color?"

My teacher scowled, her sightless eyes fierce. "Cherubino must be played by a legitimate mezzo-soprano," she snapped. "Furthermore, 'Non So Piu' should be sung with great joy. And you weren't smiling."

I changed my major to Social Psychology. If no group would have me as a member, I could at least study them. The Zimbardo Prison Experiment, the Kitty Genovese case, Jane Elliott's bewildered blue- and brown-eyed third graders—all of these studies fascinated me.

"I need to move in with mom and her girlfriend in Oxnard this summer," I told my father after my freshman year.

"Then I need to stop paying for your college education," he retorted.

I took the loss. In my mother's house, I studied the interactions of a lesbian couple from the perspective of a budding social psychologist. But all I could ascertain, after careful consideration, was that Mom and Annie ate breakfast, went to work, had dinner, and watched a little nighttime TV just as my father and stepmother had always done.

Desperate for color, I began to scour the local paper for cultural events. "I'm off to a Greek festival," I told my mother one Saturday, before driving to the Orthodox church to drink ouzo and folk dance with a bunch of white-bloused men clutching sweaty handkerchiefs.

"It's Japanese Obon," I said a few weeks later, as I headed out for the Buddhist temple in Oxnard, where I shuffled to the beat of *taiko* drums and ate pickled eel and rice crackers. When Ziggy Marley and the Wailers played at the Ventura Theater, I pulled on my favorite skirt—black cotton with turquoise figures grinding corn and leading pink burros by the nose—and hopped into the white Honda Civic that had replaced my beloved Nova when it died.

The ticket taker at the theater stamped my wrist and held it under the fluorescent purple light. "Mon, look at dis girlie!" he called to the bouncer. "She so white."

A predictably large man waddled over. "Ja, mon, she look like a ghost."

I pulled my arm away and drifted into the theater. All around me, dark-skinned people bobbed and swayed to the beat of reggae drums. I made my way to a corner by one speaker and gazed enviously up at the "I-Three" backup singers dancing in synch in their red and yellow skirts and green headscarves.

I'd brought a pocket notebook and a pen. I extracted them now from my purse and tried, as a legitimate psychologist might, to take notes on people dancing, drinking, and sucking on joints behind enormous speakers. *What am I doing here?* my pen wrote instead. *I feel like an intruder.*

I looked up to find a man watching me. He was tall and broad-chested, with brown eyes and shoulder-length black hair. When he moved closer, I could see fine wrinkles around his eyes. Something about the way his lower lip stuck out over crooked teeth reminded me of a snapping turtle.

"My name's Tony Canché." The man held out his hand. "It's nice to meet you."

"Canché." I studied his hairless brown arms. *"Buenas noches. ¿Eres mexicano?"*

"Hunh?"

"Are you Mexican?" I repeated in English.

He shrugged. "My family's Mayan, from the Yucatán Peninsula."

"Oh." I put my notebook in my purse and fingered the cool tube of my lipstick. I removed the top, but wasn't sure how to put it on without being obvious. To cover my confusion, I said, "Shall we get a drink?"

At the bar, Tony bought me a Coke and swallowed down half a Redhook in one gulp.

"You're old enough to drink?" I reached into my purse again for my lipstick, this time rubbing my index finger over it and then onto my lips. Tony's eyes followed my finger across my bottom lip. He laughed.

"I'm twenty-five," he said. "How old are you?"

"Old enough," I said, blushing. "But I've had enough beer for one night."

For a while, we talked over the band, leaning in close to one another. "I'm a writer," I told him. "I mean, an opera singer. Well, actually, I'm a psychology major. I'm living with my mom and her girlfriend, Annie, this summer."

I divulged this last bit of information as a dare. Tony met it with a shrug. "That's cool," he said. His mocha eyes lingered a moment longer on my mouth. "I'm a writer, too," he said. "I'm at the community college."

His gaze ignited a new and confusing sensation within me. Heat suffused my body. I turned away to face the stage, where Ziggy and the others danced and sang. I moved my black Mary Janes to the beat of the drums. Tony's hot breath caressed my right ear. "You've got to move your hips to the music, beauty."

Fueled by the pot smoke drifting sensuously under strobe lights, I looked him in the eye. "Show me," I said.

He stood behind me and put his hands on my hips, kneading them in time with the beat. "Relax."

I smelled beer on his breath. I tried to let go, to will my hips to undulate like those of the women onstage. I bobbed my head from side to side and let my hair fall into my eyes.

"Much better." When the song ended, Tony turned me so I faced him and made a little bow. "I like your skirt. Can I give you a ride home?"

"That'd be great," I said wistfully, "but I've got my Honda in the lot."

He nodded. His neck gleamed with sweat below the frayed collar of his Bob Marley T-shirt, and his biceps swelled. "I'm on my bike," he said.

"Oh! You have a Harley?"

At once, I could feel the wind sharp and cold against my face, hear the roar of the muffler on the freeway as we sped toward the midnight lights of Santa Monica.

"No." Tony's lips stretched into a crooked smile. "It's a Schwinn."

Outside, he shoved his bicycle into my car and directed me until we reached a quiet neighborhood street. "My older cousin lives here." Tony pointed to a suburban tract home under the dim glow of a streetlamp. "I rent a room in his garage."

Having just moved away from a place where eighteen-year-old boys lived two to a minuscule dorm room, I found Tony's living arrangement to be terribly sophisticated. "That's so cool!" I cried.

He leaned across the stick shift and kissed me. "It is," he breathed. "You'll have to see the place sometime when my cousin's kids aren't home."

I took a deep, emboldening breath. "Why wait?"

He shrugged. "It's in the rental agreement. No girls unless the family's on vacation."

The family vacationed often that summer. In a chilly six-by-six-foot makeshift room, I shivered with sexual awakening. Tony and I made love two and three times a day, breaking for hash browns, which he fried up on his cousin's stove. "Can you make enchiladas?" I asked him once. "Or tamales?"

He snorted. "You kidding? I never eat that stuff unless my mom forces me to go to a family reunion." He searched his cousin's cupboards and pulled out a blue and white box. "How about a Twinkie in bed?"

As the girlfriend of a Mexican American man, I achieved cultural legitimacy at last. For nineteen years, I'd suffered the lowly misfortune of being born into the body of a white girl. But now I rode high on Tony's cultural coattails.

One August afternoon, we lay on his garage cot smoking a joint. Naked, half-covered by a red and black Mexican blanket, I gazed at my lover's crate full of reggae cassettes. "Where're all your books?" I wondered lazily. "I mean . . . what exactly do you study at the community college?"

Tony shrugged and took a long hit off his joint. "I'm a janitor there." Smoke snaked from his nostrils. "It's my job to keep the gyms and the cafeteria clean."

I struggled to sit up. "A janitor? But at the Wailers' concert, you said . . ."

Tony rolled over and linked his hand with mine, pulling me down beside him. Brown and white, the pattern of our fingers reminded me of an M. C. Escher painting of geese, or maybe fish.

He unlaced his fingers and slipped one hand beneath the blanket. At once, Mozart's lyrics rushed back to me. I nuzzled into the pillow and sang them in Tony's ear. "I can't give you a good explanation / for this new and confusing sensation . . ."

Tony reached across me and snubbed out his joint on the top of a Coke can. "And what sensation is that?" he breathed.

Lust, I wanted to say.

Instead, I looked into his eyes and whispered, "Love."

My boyfriend took the train up to visit me at the university in mid-October. I drove to the station in San Jose and hurried right past him in the crowded lobby, not recognizing him in what he believed to be his dapper best—a black trench coat over black sweatpants, a snug red sweatshirt, and a cowboy hat. "Nice skirt," he whispered in my ear.

I whirled around, heart pounding, to face him. "I missed your burros," he said by way of hello.

Formality froze me. "It's nice to see you." I stuck out my hand and shook his. Suddenly, Tony seemed unfamiliar and middle-aged as he walked to my car toting his belongings in a paper grocery bag. How could I possibly take him to my dorm room, to the college cafeteria? What did we really have in common besides a healthy regard for hash browns, Bob Marley, and sex?

Beside me in the Honda, Tony slipped a tape into the player. With the first drum beat, the magic of the Wailers' concert flooded back. "Let's go get cheeseburgers at Wendy's," he suggested. "My treat."

In the parking lot, he did a puppet show with his burger, turning the bun into lips that synched Marley's "Three Little Birds." "Don't worry . . . about a thing," Tony and the burger crooned with the tape. "'Cause every little thing is gonna be all right."

"Oh my god!" I squealed. "That is so funny!" I laid my head on his shoulder, limp with relief. On our way home, Tony leaned over to kiss me at a red light. I savored the secondhand taste of pickles and ketchup until the drivers behind us honked their horns.

That week, I ditched all my psychology classes. Tony rented a motel room on the beach, and I drove over to meet him, stopping on the way to replace my white cotton underwear with a pink padded bra and a matching satin thong.

"Ooh. Who's the lucky guy?" the Sears cashier smirked.

"*Mi novio,*" I said proudly.

When Tony and I wearied of making love on the stiff bleached sheets, we ate pizza in bed and watched TV, or pulled on jeans and T-shirts and wandered the Boardwalk. We rode the giant rickety roller coaster and dropped quarters into a machine that promised to tell us whether or not our astrological signs were compatible.

"Oh, no!" I wailed, studying the long printout. "Pisces like me are ambitious and artsy, loyal and sensitive, while Geminis are restless and drifting, eccentric and impossible to pin down."

Tony exchanged his giant pink pod of cotton candy for the printout. "'This is not a match made in heaven,'" he read. "'In fact, this couple is doomed to failure.' What the hell?" He crumpled the paper and arced it in a trash can. "I though those machines were s'posed to tell you what you want to hear!"

"It's all bogus anyway," I giggled and bit into the cotton candy. Fall leaves glowed red and yellow on the hillsides. The ocean shone bluer than I'd ever seen it. Pink spun sugar melted sweet against my tongue. I nestled into Tony's brown neck and breathed in the aroma of marijuana and Head & Shoulders. "Let's get our picture taken!" I cried.

We crowded into a photo booth and squandered more quarters, eyes wide in the glare of the flashing bulb. When the four-frame strip slid from the machine, we howled. The camera had burned Tony to a dark black and faded me into a pale facsimile of myself.

"I'll put this in my office." He stuck the photo in his wallet and his tongue into my mouth. "Mmm. I'm feeling restless and eccentric, Pisces. Let's go back to the motel, and you can try to pin me down."

Tony piggybacked me up the steps to the second-floor room and closed the curtains. I posed like the underwear model from the Sears package, vamping on the cheap gold bedspread. He jumped on me and yanked down my pink thong with his teeth. "Let's get it on!" he growled. But suddenly, the room began to tremble.

"What the hell is that?" I yelped as the TV skittered across the pressboard dresser and crashed to the floor.

"Earthquake!" Tony leaped from the bed. "Put your underwear on!"

I grabbed my thong and yanked it on backward. In unbuttoned jeans and T-shirts, we raced out to the balcony. A couple from the room next to us clutched each other with wide, wild eyes. Below us in the parking lot, two little kids screamed beneath a woman who covered them with her body. White pebbles plummeted off the motel's roof and bounced around them.

"Look!" Tony pointed at the swimming pool. Water slopped over the sides. Across the street, telephone poles swayed. The rickety roller coaster rocked back and forth as if made from matchsticks. I heard glass shatter somewhere downtown. Bricks crumbled. Over the remaining buildings, a fine mist of mortar rose into the wavering air.

I clung to Tony. *I'm going to die*, I thought. And then, *But if I don't, I'm going to stay with this man forever.*

In December, undone by two months of nearly daily aftershocks, I packed up my Honda and quit college. "But you were a straight-A student!" my mother wailed. She'd taken me out to our favorite coffeehouse after I moved my futon and disco ball and Jim Morrison posters into her spare room. Now she fixed penetrating eyes on me, fueled by a double shot of espresso. "You were going to be a psychologist. What's your plan now?"

"Have sex" was not an acceptable career goal, and so I found part-time work as a gofer for the local newspaper and spent the spring of what should have been my sophomore year in college alternately pouring coffee for editors and traveling with Tony. We biked and camped all over Southern California, pausing to frequent his cousin's garage and my mother's house whenever the families were away. One day, Tony showed me how to drop my bike into its lowest gear and pedal the mountain road to his parents' ranch north of Oxnard.

"They're living in a trailer until the county lets them build a house," he explained about the twenty-four-foot trailer nestled among oak trees and fields of tall pink flowers. "Those are naked ladies," he said of the lilies. "My parents won't be home for another four hours," he added.

"Their trailer's so . . . authentic!" In my yellow bike jersey and padded shorts, I peered through the door at a tiny living room. A Mexican flag hung thumbtacked over one window. A basket held rounds of pink and brown *pan dulce* on the narrow table.

Tony walked to the edge of a cliff and peered down to the valley below, listening. Then he lifted a potted ficus from its position next to the trailer's metal steps and extracted a key. He unlocked the door and pulled me inside. "Let's get some grub!" He opened the refrigerator and pulled out Tupperware containers. "Rice, beans, enchiladas. Man, we scored. My mom made *nopalitos* and killer salsa!"

"What's *nopalitos?*" I asked.

"Cactus and cheese. They kick ass."

I slid onto the bench seat behind the table. Once, I would have worried about stealing someone else's dinner. Now, all I could see was Tony, all I could smell was a spoonful of piquant cactus topped with fiery salsa. "Not that Ortega crap," Tony said as I chewed the savory bite he held out to me. "My mom makes hers homemade from three kinds of chilies."

He fed me bits of *nopalitos* rolled up in pieces of warm flour tortilla. I studied the framed photos on the walls. "Who're that man and woman?" I asked of two people who shared Tony's lopsided smile and high cheekbones.

"My brother and sister," he said.

"Where's your picture?"

He shrugged. "My dad and I don't get along. He's a Republican, I'm a Democrat, you know? My mother probably burned any pictures they actually took of me."

My heart ached with sympathy for Tony. I turned away from his siblings' photos and peered up the steps leading to a dark, low-ceilinged bedroom. "Hey, don't you have that same Mexican blanket?" I asked, recognizing the red and black design from his garage cot.

"Yeah. I think it was on sale at Kmart. My mom bought an extra one and gave it to me." He crammed half an enchilada into his mouth. The lines around his eyes deepened as he chewed, and his brows lowered in sudden, inexplicable rage.

"So how's your writing going?" I chirped, knitting my fingers together under the table.

Tony shrugged again. "It's going." He reached into his backpack and tossed me a pocket notebook. I opened it and studied a crude sketch of a sun and moon, with letters slanted and deliberate as a child's.

"'I said to the moon, why do you leave when the son is high,'" I read out loud. "'And the moon said, when your high, I have no home.'"

"I wrote that when I was homeless," Tony told me. "My parents kicked me out last year. I didn't have a job, so I slept on the street."

"That's so sad," I whispered. I told him about the man I'd met downtown my freshman year. My stepmother had sent me ten dollars, so I tucked the bill into my pocket, intent on buying the new 10,000 Maniacs CD. A bearded guy not much older than I was sat at the bus station playing a battered guitar while a pit bull looked on. "Hey, gorgeous," he'd called to me.

Flattered, I'd stopped, and we talked about politics and the freedom of homelessness. "No job, no rent, no worries," he said.

I looked at the man's gaunt cheeks. "No food?"

He laughed. "My dog's pretty hungry."

The pit bull wore a green ribbon with a makeshift cardboard tag that read THOREAU. Recognizing a fellow transcendentalist, I gave the man my ten-dollar bill. "Thanks, gorgeous," he said and offered me a swig off a paper-bagged bottle.

"Am I beautiful?" I asked Tony now.

My boyfriend stood at his mother's sink, meticulously washing and drying Tupperware, replacing it in cabinets. "Actually," he said over the faucet, "I was kind of surprised when we first started dating. Oh, don't get me wrong. You're above average. But I usually go for pretty . . . uh . . . for Mexican chicks."

I stared out the window, trying to catch a reflection of my face. The glare of sunshine rendered me invisible. *Looks don't matter*, I told myself. Tony's and my relationship transcended mere appearance. We united on a deeper level.

I cranked open the window. A breeze blew, and the limbs of the oak trees swayed gently. All around the trailer, naked ladies released their pink perfume. I breathed in their scent and looked at Tony's brown neck above the ragged collar of his Bob Marley T-shirt. Here was color, mine for the taking.

I pulled off my yellow bike jersey and took it.

Killer Salsa

Prepare the cooking space by making sure its owners are not home. Listen for the warning rumble of tires. Hearing none, look in the refrigerator for chilies. Find two serranos, two jalapeños, and two yellow chilies.

Locate a griddle, and toast the chilies until their skins are the glossy black of Rastafarian dreadlocks. Peel the chilies, being careful not to touch the sensitive areas of your body, as chili oil burns like the discovery of a dishonest lover.

Place chilies in a borrowed blender with one tablespoon each of oregano, cumin, and minced garlic. Add a fourth of a cup of water from the filtered pitcher in the refrigerator, and toss in a teaspoon of salt. Pray that there's a twenty-eight-ounce can of whole tomatoes in your mother's cupboard. Add them to the blender, and mix slightly, but do not puree. Salsa should be chunky.

Serve with tortilla chips. Explain to your girlfriend that the endorphins in hot salsa are a guaranteed aphrodisiac. Put your clothes back on, then wash your dishes well, and replace in exactly the same spot where you found them. Make sure that the kitchen is spotless, and pack out any trash in your bike pannier.

14 •

Trials and Tribulations of Trailer Trash

Disappointed with life as a college dropout, I transferred to UC Santa Barbara to study literature at the College of Creative Studies. Its exuberant musicians and angst-ridden poets resembled characters from the movie *Fame*. It wasn't unusual for students to break into an impromptu aria from *Dido and Aeneas* or a stanza of Ginsberg's "Howl" in the tiny student lounge, and I felt that I had found my people.

Tony and I lived in Isla Vista, the beer-saturated town abutting the university, during my junior year. But we grew weary of our dingy urban apartment, tucked as it was between frat houses, and resolved to get back to nature in a two-room mountain cabin in the hills above Santa Barbara. A few dozen hippies and societal dropouts resided in the colony of Painted Cave, named for the fenced and faded petroglyphs just down the road from our cabin. Our middle-aged landlady lived in the big log house below ours. Weekends, she liked to sunbathe nude in her back yard, on full display, as I gardened on our shared brick patio.

Tony decorated the mantel above the wood-burning stove with his collection of *Star Wars* figures, and I climbed fifteen feet up the round blue water tower behind our home to write poetry. From there, I could keep an eye on Daniel, our long-haired gray cat, as he hunted moles in the dandelions. But the twenty-minute drive to town curved in a series of hairpin turns, and I lived in fear of a head-on collision in my new Honda.

For a time, I biked eight miles down to the university, but my chain and my knees gave out enough times on the ride home—straight up—that I decided it was time to move.

"I'd love to live closer to my mother and Annie," I told Tony after a few months.

He thought about this. "Good idea," he said. "They cook great grub, and they have cable, right?" So we packed up and moved into a blue stucco studio festooned with purple morning glories, five miles from their house. Once again, the landlord lived on the premises. From my kitchen window, I could peer through his open front door to the bed in his living room, where he often entertained female visitors. He looked to be seventy, and his stamina never failed to impress me.

The blue studio possessed a loft bedroom. I, along with Daniel, grew adept at springing up the ladder and leaping down to the cement floor. I loved studying under the oaks that dotted the property with a mug of tea steeped from the peppermint leaves that grew in the garden. Tony enjoyed the free cable. But our landlord believed in communal living and thought nothing of strolling into our studio whenever he needed something from his enormous metal file cabinet that doubled as our coffee table. When he woke us at midnight, nailing a bedsheet to the outside of our home for a late-night Fellini film festival, we knew it was time—again—to move on.

"I'm so tired of throwing away five hundred dollars a month on rent," I told Tony. "We should try to save money and buy our own house."

He looked up at me from the futon, where he was attempting to repair a plastic replica of the Millennium Falcon that Daniel had knocked off the file cabinet. "We could move to the ranch," he suggested.

Tony was referring to his parents' acreage, ten miles from my mother's house. They lived in a tiny trailer at the top of the property. They'd been waiting ten years for the city to grant them permission to erect a modular home. At fiestas, I'd often stood in their front yard of hard-packed dirt and gazed below at the flower fields and fruit trees.

"Will they let us live there?" I studied my boyfriend. "I know you haven't always gotten along with them."

"Things are different now," he said. "I've got a job and a girlfriend. They'll be fine, and they won't make us pay rent."

"It's an idea," I said slowly, "but how? Where?"

Tony reached for the newspaper and tapped a finger on the section that read VEHICLE SALES. "Here's a forty-two-foot fifth-wheel for five thousand dollars," he said. "We'll pull a car loan, buy this trailer, haul it down to the bottom of the ranch, and it's home, sweet home."

I winced. "A trailer?" Those were for poor people, and for ignoramuses who spit tobacco and played endless games of solitaire in the middle of the day while Jerry Springer shrieked from the TV. "I don't think I could live in a trailer," I said.

Tony shot me a disgusted look, disparaging my elitist attitude. "Didn't your great-grandfather live in one?"

I'd forgotten that. After they retired from their show business career, my great-grandparents had purchased a house in Monterey and towed a small Airstream into their back yard. Rumor had it my great-grandfather had promptly set up camp there, declaring an inability to live in the same house with Grandmary because she drove him nuts.

After his death, the Airstream remained. A silver cocoon under the redwoods, it shone like a beacon of simplicity with its bed and stove and refrigerator. I crept into it as a child and closed the door behind me, noting with awe that everything I needed in order to live—even the tiny toilet tucked into a narrow closet—was right there, at arm's length.

"All right." I sat down beside Tony and studied the newspaper ad. I had no idea what a fifth-wheel was, but the price was right. "Let's go look at this trailer."

We stepped out of my Honda and onto the gravel road winding through a trailer park near Santa Paula. Trailers loomed all around us. Would ours turn out to be one of the shiny blue oblong ones decorated with herds of stampeding horses? Or would it be more venerable, perhaps the classic Airstream gleaming beside the magnolia tree across the park?

I turned toward the familiar silver trailer. Suddenly, three white toy poodles raced into my path and nipped at my ankles.

"Faith! Hope! Charity! Goddamn it, get in here!"

I turned at the sound of a woman's gravelly voice and stepped back, genuinely frightened. She stood in front of one of the large blue trailers, all of four foot five, brown as an almond with biceps that bulged from her lavender tank top. "I'm Mrs. Madison. You the kids that called about the fifth-wheel?" she demanded.

Tony and I nodded in unison. She jerked a thumb in the direction of the Airstream. "Well, that's no fifth-wheel," she told me and burst into hoarse laughter. "I've got two trailers—Big Blue here, and that one in back of it."

She walked and put an arm around my shoulders, guiding me behind the blue monstrosity. "That there's your girl."

It sat partially hidden behind hers. I blinked at the faded white metal box striped midway down with brown plastic trim. "She's old,"

Mrs. Madison informed us, "but she can still put out. Well, don't you want to see her?".

I looked at Tony. He shrugged. "Why not? It's got a pop-out." He pointed to the three-by-five-foot protrusion jutting from one side. A pop-out was desirable. It offered the trailer owner more room, more space for windows. In this case, it offered a dusty nook for a brown corduroy couch that reeked of cigarettes.

Flanked by the poodles, I examined the tiny living room. One end had shelves for a television and books. Someone had tacked up a mirror on the sloping ceiling above the couch. "To make the room look bigger," Mrs. Madison told me, then winked broadly at Tony. "But you can use it in whatever way that suits you."

I walked up three carpeted steps to the bedroom. A queen-size mattress and built-in nightstands filled the room. The ceiling hung so low that I couldn't stand up, but windows lined three sides of the room, and I thought of how I'd wake up to birdsong every morning at the ranch.

I turned and stepped down into the kitchen. It boasted a decent-size refrigerator and stove, plus an oven that could accommodate a whole chicken or a pork roast, if required. "You're gonna love the bathroom," Mrs. Madison told me. "You don't see them like this anymore." Her three poodles yipped and scampered in front of me.

Mired in 1970s brown and orange daisies, the bathroom offered room enough for a sink, a vanity, and a yellow bathtub alongside the toilet. In the mirror, I studied my reflection. Could I live in a trailer?

I'd resided happily, two weekends a month, in my mother's bohemian apartment with its mattresses on the floor and the milk crate furniture. She and Annie wouldn't disparage the fifth-wheel. But what would my father and Elsa think, from the comfort of their crystal and Asian-print parlor? Would they view me as "trailer trash"?

I thought of my college classmates, and what they would say from their hip urban apartments on the beach. I wouldn't invite them to visit.

Mrs. Madison appeared at my elbow and smiled. I saw that she was missing several teeth. "You've got to see the back room," she said. "It's the piece of resistance, so to speak."

I walked through the bathroom to the room at the rear of the trailer. Tall closets took up one end, with long windows at both sides. A back door opened out onto the trailer park. One end of the room supported a built-in pine desk in beautiful condition.

Tony looked over my shoulder. "You could write short stories at the desk," he said. "We'll put the trailer next to the creek, so you can open the door and listen as you work."

Suddenly, I saw myself sitting at that desk, a young, ambitious writer like Thoreau, composing my tales as chipmunks and fawns looked on. On the weekends, we'd join Tony's family for cookouts. My mother and Annie would drive over, and we'd all bask in the glories of the ranch and familial camaraderie. "You're sure your parents won't mind if we move onto their property?" I asked Tony.

He shook his head. "We can live there for free as long as we chip in and help on the ranch," he assured me.

"Well, I . . ." I looked at Mrs. Madison. Her tiny brown eyes twinkled. "I guess we'll take it."

"Thatta girl!" She clapped her hands and gathered her poodles to her ample chest. We retired to her lush blue trailer to draw up the paperwork on a dining table littered with cigarette butts and wet rings from her Mr. Pibb can. "You got a bank loan." She nodded approvingly. "Good thing. Last week, I thought I'd sold the fifth-wheel to a man for cash, but he forgot to pay me."

She balled up one liver-spotted fist. "Good thing he didn't come back. He was this close to meeting Mrs. Thumb and her four fingers."

A dusty, rutted road snaked from the top of Tony's parents' ranch down to a valley. Flowers took over most of the land, along with an enormous greenhouse. Off in one corner, in a clearing beside a creek, lay a flat patch of dirt—perfect, we thought, for our new home. "We can put the trailer near the mountainside." Tony pointed up the steep wall of dirt and canyon sunflowers to the road a quarter mile above us. "To protect it from the wind."

I had to be in class on moving day, so I didn't get to watch Bill's Towing navigate the fifth-wheel down the narrow, winding road. Tony's father sat with us at the picnic table outside his own trailer that evening and described it in hushed tones usually reserved for recounting the NBA playoffs. "That motherfucker was hanging off the edge," his father said reverently. "I was sure it was a goner, but Bill backed up his truck, gave it a little gas, and hauled that bitch all the way down to the bottom."

Tony's mother called out the window above the stove, where she stood warming tortillas. "I've never seen anything like it," she told me. "Tony, I hope you tipped that driver well."

Tony shrugged. "Mom, he charged us three hundred dollars."

"Well, he earned every penny. That trailer could've crushed him."

She brought out bowls of Spanish rice and beans and green chili and cheese enchiladas. We scooped up bits in pieces of flour tortilla. The sweet scent of naked lady lilies rode the Indian summer breeze, and a raven cawed from an oak near us. I did a swift calculation in my head. Tony and I were used to paying five hundred dollars a month in rent. In two years, we could save twelve thousand dollars—plenty of money for a down payment on a house.

His father finished his dinner and put on his wide straw hat. "Kids," he said and wiped his bushy black mustache, "I don't mind you living here for free, but you've gotta be prepared for hard work on the weekends."

I nodded vigorously. "Don't worry. We're happy to pitch in and do our share."

Tony's father glanced at me. "You're in school," he said. "Your job's to get As and graduate. Tony's no stranger to hard work. He knows what he's in for."

Beside me, my boyfriend sighed, just audibly. "Well, I guess it's time to go home," he said. We bid his parents good-bye and walked hand in hand down the dirt road. Lizards bobbed and skittered on the path in front of us. A vulture swirled lazily in the distance, sniffing for one last meal. We paused beside the little creek for a moment and gazed at the oaks and groves of stinging nettles all around us. "That creek's just a trickle now," Tony told me, "but in the winter, it gets pretty big."

A barn owl screeched overhead as we neared the trailer. The fifth-wheel looked almost idyllic, stretched out against the bank of scrubby sunflowers and sage. "We're home!" I cried and pulled Tony up the two metal steps to the living room.

He'd cranked all the windows open, and some of the cigarette stench had dissipated. Still, I tore down the curtains. "I'll sew new ones this weekend," I promised.

For light, we had two glass kerosene lamps that we could carry from room to room. Propane powered our stove and refrigerator and ten-gallon water heater. Tony stretched out on the couch and opened his mouth wide, examining his molars in the overhead mirror. "We should get a generator so we can watch TV and play video games," he said. "They're only a thousand dollars."

I shook my head. "We're supposed to be saving money—not spending it. Besides, they're so loud."

Outside our screen door, crickets sang. Coyotes started up their mournful yips and howls in the mountains around us. Tony gazed forlornly at his Nintendo on the bookshelf. "Well," he said, "I guess I'll go read." He got up from the couch and climbed the stairs to duck into the bedroom with a back issue of *National Geographic*.

"I'll be up in a while," I told him. "I want to write a little before bed."

I sat at the pine desk with the back door open, alternately turning to gaze out at the stars and contemplating my notebook and pen in the glow of the kerosene lamp. I felt like a transcendentalist, embracing voluntary simplicity in a life grown suddenly tranquil and happy.

A week later, the sewer line broke.

"I think it's just a matter of gluing new PVC pipes together, kind of like Tinkertoys," Tony called from under the trailer. I held my breath against the noxious odor emanating from the plastic holding tank.

"Maybe we should call someone?" I gasped.

"Too expensive." My boyfriend extracted himself and emerged, covered with dirt and bits of detritus better left unexamined. "I'll run up and get my dad."

His father rattled down the road in an ancient black truck and stopped at our front door. "Crawl under the trailer and cut out the leaking part." He thrust a hacksaw toward Tony. Then he handed me a piece of plastic pipe and two small jars. "One of these is primer. You paint the inside of one pipe and the outside of the other," he explained. "The other jar is glue. When the primer's dry, do the same thing with this stuff."

I nodded, flattered that he trusted me to help. "Then what?"

He shook his head at my ignorance. "Stick them together. Jesus Christ, what a stench. I'm out of here, kids."

I watched his truck head back up the road, then dutifully painted the pipe. The primer shone bright purple, while the glue glowed blue. I breathed in their fumes and felt high on the responsibility of home ownership.

Tony slid back under the trailer and glued the new pipe to the old sewer pipe underneath. "Just like Tinkertoys!" he reiterated. Back in the bathroom, he flushed the toilet as I stood outside scouting for drips. "Nothing!" I called triumphantly.

My boyfriend pulled off his shirt and turned on the shower. "I think that fixed it," he said as I ran back inside. "But I wouldn't flush anything down the toilet. Not even toilet paper."

"No problem," I sang out, thrilled that we'd successfully navigated our first potential disaster. "We'll get a trash can with a lid."

For a while, we lived a carefree life. Tony and I planted a garden of fall lettuce and chard. Our cat spent lazy days stretched out on top of the trailer, absorbing the autumn heat. Tony's father had no work for us, and so I spent weekend afternoons writing in the back doorway, keeping one eye on the yellow butterflies that flitted about the oaks.

Monday through Friday, we drove into Santa Barbara. I dropped Tony off at work and continued on to the university. We reconvened at five for the drive home. Sometimes we had dinner with his parents, and sometimes with my mother and Annie. A few times, we invited my mother and Annie to the trailer, and we all sat outside eating pizza on our makeshift patio with the trailer as a backdrop.

"This isn't so bad," Annie said as she opened a beer and reclined in a chair alongside the creek.

"It reminds me of your great-grandfather's Airstream," my mother observed kindly as she brushed a bee off her pizza.

But then came the problem of winter. Nighttime temperatures began to drop into the twenties. Gone were the airy days of open windows and doors. Now, Tony and I sat shut up in a metal box every evening, staring at each other in the dim light of our kerosene lamps.

"The smell of that shit gives me a headache," Tony complained of the fuel.

I had to agree. My temples pounded and my stomach soured at the noxious scent of burning kerosene. "Maybe we *should* get a generator," I allowed. "But let's run it only a couple of hours a night. Those things eat gasoline, and we're supposed to be saving money."

We drove to Sears and purchased a red and black behemoth so heavy that it took four men to wheel it up a makeshift plywood ramp into the Honda. Immediately, the car sank toward the ground. "Now we'll have lights and heaters to take the chill off," Tony reasoned. "And we can watch movies on the VCR."

We built the generator a ramshackle shed at the end of the trailer, to keep the rain out. Now, twice a night, one of us walked with a flashlight to the back of the trailer to turn the thing on or off. Its roar was deafening, and the smell of burning gas and oil sickened me more than the kerosene.

"Feel free to go write," Tony said the first night, plugging in his Nintendo. But I couldn't write, not at the pine desk with the generator ringing in my ears.

I moved to the bedroom and lay on my stomach on the mattress, trying to compose a short story, but the beeps and burbles from Tony's video game distracted me. At last, I threw down my pen. "Let's watch a movie." I stepped into the living room and pushed *RoboCop* into the VCR, then collapsed on the couch.

Winter finally passed, and in the spring, Tony's father had a job for us. "Gotta chop down the weeds," he said, referring to the chaparral that grew up along the sides of the road. "Otherwise the fire department fines us thousands of dollars."

Now, every weekend, Tony and I awoke at six and put on hats and jeans and long-sleeved shirts in preparation for the day's hard labor. We bought goggles and earplugs and thick leather gloves. We pulled bandanas over our mouths to keep out the dust and wielded two gas-powered Weedwackers.

After the first morning, grass and leaves covered my clothes and face. We stopped for lunch and headed up the road to Tony's parents' trailer, where his mother had set out cold cuts, bread, and cheese. I gobbled down two sandwiches, and she stared at me. "I didn't realize you were such a hard worker," she said.

I shrugged. Pain ricocheted across my shoulders and down my arms. Sweat burned my arms and reeked at my armpits. I couldn't fathom another four hours spent cutting weeds.

Tony's father walked in and slapped together a sandwich. He gave me a sidelong glance, taking in my stringy hair under a Dodgers hat and my filthy, sunburned neck. "Don't you have homework?" he muttered.

I nodded. "I'll do it tonight." I wasn't going to disappoint this man who had so generously let us live on his property.

I downed a can of Coke and grabbed my goggles. "Tony," I cried. "Let's go whack some weeds!"

We spent three weeks clearing weeds from the land along the main highway, as well as the sides of the road leading from the top of the ranch to the bottom. Tony's father drove his truck past us a dozen times a day on various errands, always staring straight ahead with his mouth set inscrutably under his mustache.

When the weeds had been sufficiently whacked, we turned our attention to picking flowers. Tony showed me how to pluck them near their base and plunge them in a bucket of water. Three Mexican immigrants worked in the next field. The men raised their heads as we walked over from our trailer.

"¡Hola!" I called. "*Con mucho gusto.*"

They shook their heads and bent over their work. But I heard one say to the others, "*Ay, que gringa,*" and indignation festered in my chest.

My frustration intensified as Tony's father drove up in his truck. He stared at me in my tank top, shorts, and hiking boots. "Good morning," I said and smiled uncertainly under my flowered sunhat.

It was a beautiful day for picking flowers. The sun had just begun to rise over the mountains, and the sky glowed pink and gold. But Tony's father scowled. He glanced at his workers in the next field, then motioned his son over and spoke to him in a low voice. I caught only one phrase.

"Can't you tell her to go bake a cake?"

Tony shook his head and resumed working, his head bowed over the plants. "I know you want to help," he told me when his father had driven off, "but feel free to go study."

"Bake a cake?" I fumed to his mother later, as I sat on her narrow couch and ate the burrito she'd made me. "Why would I want to bake a cake?"

She looked out the window. Tony and his father stood in the driveway, attempting to fix a chainsaw. "In our family," she said carefully, pausing to stir the rice browning in a saucepan with diced onions, "there's a division of labor. Men do the physical work, while women cook and clean and care for the children."

I knew this. I'd witnessed this separation at their family gatherings, but I couldn't see how such an archaic lifestyle applied to me. I'd grown up watching my mother fix a broken fan belt in the VW bus with a pair of panty hose. Annie built furniture and did oil changes on her Miata. Even my grandmother, divorced from my grandfather long before I was born, mowed her own lawn and cleaned the gutters each fall.

"I can't bake a cake," I said. "And anyhow, I'd rather work outside next to Tony."

If his mother questioned my choice, she said nothing. She simply poured a can of tomato sauce into her pot and rubbed oregano between her hands, sprinkling it on the rice. I sat for another moment, marveling at how her trailer—half the size of ours—looked so cozy and tidy. I glimpsed how invaluable her cooking skills must be to her husband, famished from his days of labor. But I'd promised to work on the land in lieu of paying rent. That didn't mean flour and sugar—it meant blood and sweat.

The tears came later. Our second winter on the ranch defied every myth about sunny Southern California. Rain poured down for days on end, and the land, unprepared for the deluge, began to collapse. One evening, my Honda wimped out at the side of the narrow dirt road turned six inches of mud. Rivulets rushed down on either side. When the car began to slide sideways, I yanked up the brake and Tony pushed it to what would become its permanent parking spot beside his dad's truck.

We hiked down the road by flashlight, sliding in our shoes, arriving at the trailer door shivering and covered in mud. "This rain's supposed to go on for weeks," Tony said. "We'd better buy some decent boots and coats. Eddie Bauer's having a sale. I'll go this weekend."

That Monday at seven o'clock, we hiked up the muddy half mile in new thigh-length waterproof raincoats and knee-high fleece-lined rubber boots. My Honda had developed a leak. Now, two inches of water met my feet as I slid into the driver's seat. I arrived at the university dirty and soaking and changed awkwardly in the parking lot. I missed the early morning bike ride from our off-campus apartment to school. And as the rain continued, I even began to miss the cement that had surrounded us.

One evening, on a walk back to the trailer after classes, I slid and fell in the soupy mud. Short stories tumbled out of my arms, along with my copy of *Paradise Lost*. I recovered my schoolwork and burst into tears. "Don't worry." Tony attempted a cheerful grin and launched the sodden book into the air. "You never liked Milton, anyway."

The rain continued. The highway flooded with water, cracked in two a mile past the ranch. Now, a ten-minute trip to visit my mother took an hour. "We have to drive in the opposite direction down the mountain, turn south, and travel east to get to your house!" I told her over dinner.

"You've got to get a phone." She packed up leftover casserole and bread to send home with us. "I'm worried sick about you out there in the wilderness."

"There's no phone line down to the bottom of the ranch," I reminded her. "To get one, we'd have to dig a trench for a conduit a quarter mile up the mountain to the pole alongside the highway. In the mud, that's just not going to happen."

"So get a mobile phone," my mother demanded.

At that time, cell phones were shoe-size and heavy. Tony and I reluctantly agreed to purchase one. "You pay as you call," the salesman told us.

He neglected to mention that calls were a dollar a minute. Our first bill came to three hundred dollars, most of it nightly missives to my mother to assure her that we and our trailer hadn't floated away.

In the storms, our trickling creek had become a rushing river. One Saturday morning, I peered outside and watched it carry the neighbors' trash along my front yard, down to the next property over. "There goes a broken lawn chair," I told Tony. He had his head in the closet, attempting to fix our broken heaters. "And there goes a Canada goose statue."

My boyfriend threw down his flashlight and screwdriver. "Unless we want to pay someone to come out and fix this damned thing, we'll just have to wear our hats and coats inside."

I shivered. "It's so cold in this trailer," I wailed. "I think we should call someone."

He cast a malevolent glare at the mobile phone on the couch. "It can wait until I get to work on Monday," he said. "In the meantime, put on some gloves."

That night, our generator stopped working as well. Our propane tank was empty, since no driver would attempt to navigate his truck down our road. We ate apples and graham crackers by the light of the kerosene lamp and gazed at each other in dismay.

"The Eddie Bauer bill came yesterday," I said. "We owe seven hundred dollars."

Tony nodded. "And we missed a payment on the trailer. The bank fined us forty bucks, the assholes."

I knew without looking that the total in my savings account was zero. "We've been here a year, and we haven't saved a penny," I said. "How will we ever buy a house?"

"I guess we'll just have to stay here a couple more years." He tossed his apple core into the sink, and Daniel leaped up from the couch in alarm. Suddenly, something hit the side of the trailer with a thud. The cat hissed and flew into the bedroom.

"What the hell was that?" I yelped.

Tony grabbed a flashlight and ran outside. In a moment, he reappeared, his face grim. "The mountain's coming down behind us," he said. "That was the sound of a big-ass boulder hitting the side of the trailer."

Again, we heard a thud as rocks and dirt struck the pop-out. "We've got to get out of here!" I cried. "Or we'll be buried alive! Can we go up to your parents?"

Tony tossed me the phone. "There's no room in their trailer," he said. "Call your mom, but make it quick."

In less than a minute, with the sound of thudding mud and rocks punctuating my sobs, I managed to convey the desperation of our situation.

"I want you over here in an hour," my mother commanded. "Bring enough clothes for a week. You're staying until the storms end."

We stuffed clothes into backpacks and put on our rain gear. "How'll we get Daniel up the hill?" I cried. "We don't have a pet carrier."

Tony yanked the blue flannel case off his pillow. "Put him in here," he said.

Somehow, we managed to get the cat in the bag. With bloodied hands,

I slung the pillowcase over my shoulder as Daniel yowled. I stepped out of the trailer, wondering if I'd ever see it again. In the beam from the flashlight, I could see muddy rivulets flowing down off the mountainside, and three boulders mired in the mud behind the pop-out.

We slogged up the road, slipping and falling in the rain as we struggled to hold on to our backpacks. I collapsed in the driver's seat of the Honda, and my feet splashed into the puddle below the accelerator. "Take Daniel," I said and thrust the pillowcase at Tony. "Don't let him out until we're inside my mother's house."

We arrived at midnight, soaked and filthy. My hair hung in my eyes. I pulled off my boots on the back porch and wrung out my socks. Tony let Daniel out of the pillowcase in the living room, and the cat ran to hide under the couch.

"Who wants chili?" Annie asked from the kitchen.

"Yes, please," Tony said, shedding his wet jacket and hat.

Annie surveyed him. "But first, let's get you a shot of brandy."

My mother waited long enough for me to take a shower and blow-dry my hair, but once I was safely ensconced upon her barstool and wrapped in a flannel robe with a bowl of Annie's chili, she approached me. "You have to move," she said. "You can't live like this."

I shook my head. "And throw away more money on rent? That's ridiculous."

"No." She sat down on another barstool and indicated the pile of muddy wet clothes on the kitchen floor as my unseen cat howled with ire. "*This* is ridiculous."

We lasted one more spring on the ranch. One afternoon, I heard a sound that was completely foreign to me—like someone shaking dried beans inside a cardboard tube. I stepped out onto the patio to find my cat face to face with a rattlesnake.

"Daniel!" I screamed. In one swift move, I grabbed him by his tail and flung him backward, then leaped into the trailer as the snake slid away.

"Should've chopped the fucker's head off with a shovel," Tony's father said that night. "I don't need him biting my workers."

"But the rattlesnake is native," Tony protested. "This is his home. We invaded it."

I blushed, thinking of how those words might apply to my boyfriend's father, as well. For months now, he'd barely looked at me, and he never spoke directly to me anymore. I'd been studying too much—I knew it—reading novels and writing short stories on the weekends, in preparation for my college graduation. I resolved to work harder on the land, to earn my keep. Sure, he would've preferred that I stay inside cooking and cleaning, but I wanted to prove to him that I—a woman—could do everything that his son could do to be of help on the ranch.

That year, the county finally agreed to let Tony's parents put a modular home on their property, provided they built a concrete driveway. His father rented a jackhammer one weekend to break up the hard-packed dirt.

"Fun!" I exclaimed that Saturday morning as the machine's staccato motor echoed across the valley. I pulled on jeans and hiking boots. "Do you think he'll let me use it?"

"It's pretty heavy." Tony stood at the door, studying the river that had diminished at last so that it no longer acted as a conduit for the neighbors' trash. Remnants of plastic and metal littered our yard. "I'll pick it up tonight," I said. "Right now, we'd better get up to the top of the ranch and get to work."

All of Tony's brothers and sisters gathered that morning. The men got to work with the jackhammer and shovels, while the women gathered in his mother's tiny trailer to cook. Unsure of where to be of use, I watched the little nieces and nephews as they bounced balls and rode tricycles around the trailer. But soon, I grew restless and approached the men. "Can I give it a try?" I yelled to Tony above the jackhammer's racket.

He shook his head. "Not right now. Maybe at lunch."

I returned to the children and waited patiently until noon, when all the men washed their hands at the garden hose and then filed up to the porch to fill their plates. I grabbed Tony's arm. "Now can I try it?" I said. "Please?"

He glanced in the direction of the trailer, and then at my wide, pleading eyes. "All right," he sighed. "You've got to step up on one pedal like this, then turn it on and jump onto the other pedal. It's got a strong kick, and it's really loud." He handed me a pair of earplugs. "Go for it."

It felt a lot like I imagined riding a bucking bronco would feel. I fell off once, twice, and at last managed to keep my balance while clutching the handles. The dirt below me broke into satisfying chunks. "This is fun!" I squealed.

I looked up as a shadow fell across the dirt in front of me. The look on Tony's father's face caused me to jump off the jackhammer and turn off the motor. His dark eyes flashed with rage under his straw hat, and his mouth made a hard line under his mustache. He opened it long enough to spit out two words. "That's enough," he said, and his fury propelled me back to the trailer, where I played with the children, head bent with shame, for the rest of the afternoon.

"Why is he so mad at me?" I asked Tony that night as we sat outside the fifth-wheel.

My boyfriend sighed and turned away from me. "He thinks you're not fulfilling your role," he muttered. "Maybe you should stay out of sight for a while."

I walked around to face him and bent to look into his eyes. "Do you think I should go bake a cake?" I asked him.

He shrugged. "Do whatever you want," he said. "I'm going in to play Tetris."

I took on one last project before I surrendered. The hill behind our trailer had firmed up in spring sunshine, and I decided to dig a trench for the conduit that would cover a telephone line leading from the highway-side pole to the trailer. "This way, we can get rid of the mobile phone," I reasoned to Tony one Saturday morning. "Let's get digging!"

But he stayed where he was, sitting on the couch and reading the newspaper. "In a while," he said.

It was brutal work. I perched sideways on the mountain, struggling for a foothold as I dug past soft shale into hard-packed dirt. The telephone pole beckoned a quarter mile up, but by noon I'd only dug about twenty feet. "Aren't you going to help?" I asked Tony at lunch as I slapped together a peanut butter and jelly sandwich.

He shook his head. "No, my dad needs me this afternoon. Anyhow, I don't use the phone. This is your deal."

His apathy stung. I swigged a Coke and ascended the hill once more. My blistered hands gripped the wooden shovel, and I swore under my breath as the metal edge hit rock. Sweat ran into my eyes, and they burned with salt and dirt as I worked. By late afternoon, I'd dug another twenty feet. My legs and arms were covered with dirt. My hair had come out of its braids—now it hung limp and dusty in my face.

I paused to gaze at the sun setting over the mountains and breathed in the cool evening air. Below me, I heard voices. I peered down to the patio of the trailer. Tony and his brothers and his father sat drinking beer and looking up at me, laughing.

"Hey, you guys," I called down. "Want to come up and help?"

All but Tony shook their heads. He just looked carefully away from me. Even from where I stood, I recognized his humiliation—not because

I worked alone up on the mountainside with no help from the men, but because I was up there working at all.

I continued digging in the waning light until they'd gone. Tony started the generator, and I dragged myself into the living room to find him playing video games. I kicked off my hiking boots and called for my cat. "Have you seen Daniel?" I asked.

He shook his head. His face, usually amiable, gathered in hard, wrathful lines.

I located the cat on the top of the trailer and brought him inside. Quietly, I fed him. I glanced at Tony, who stared unblinking at the television screen. "Dinner?" I asked him.

"There's no food in the house," he muttered.

"There are eggs," I whispered, "and carrots . . ."

In the tiny trailer kitchen, I took out a bowl and my electric mixer. I grated four carrots and sifted flour and cinnamon. Contrite, I greased and floured pans, then poured the batter in to bake for an hour while I showered in the yellow tub.

Under the warm water, under cover of the generator's mighty roar, I wept.

CONTRITION CARROT CAKE

Put on goggles and thick leather gloves in preparation for hard labor. Preheat your oven to 350 degrees, and grease and flour two nine-inch round cake pans, or one nine-by-thirteen-inch pan. Channel your frustration at rigid gender roles into beating three cups of grated carrots with two cups of sugar, four eggs, a cup and a half of canola oil, and an eight-ounce package of softened cream cheese.

Pause to fix your leaking sewer pipes and separate your cat from an alarmed rattlesnake, then sift two cups of white flour with two teaspoons of baking soda and a teaspoon each of salt and cinnamon. Stir into the carrot mixture, and add a teaspoon of vanilla. Mix well and pour batter into prepared pans. You do own cake pans, don't you?

Bake for fifty-five minutes, and resist the urge to whack weeds or dig trenches during that time. Instead, take a shower, and note that the toothpick you insert into the finished cake should emerge as clean as your delicate limbs. While the cake is cooling, fire up the generator, and watch *RoboCop* for an additional dose of patriarchy.

The men will expect frosting, so cream together another eight-ounce block of cream cheese with a quarter cup of butter. Sift a pound of powdered sugar into the bowl, resisting the urge to pound your head against the wall, and add two tablespoons of milk and a teaspoon of vanilla. Beat until the frosting's smooth as mud.

15.

O, Christmas Tree

"LISTEN TO THIS." LONG BEFORE WE MOVED INTO THE TRAILER, I'D looked up from my Existential Literature reader and highlighted Albert Camus's words as I recited them to my boyfriend. "Without culture and the relative freedom it implies, society, even when perfect, is but a jungle."

"Oh yeah? Then I must be Tarzan." Tony sunk lower onto the futon in our university apartment and fixed his eyes on his video game. In it, zombies ate their way through a suburban neighborhood. The postal carrier walked past our door. Seeing us at home, he slipped a stack of mail through the window left screenless for our cat. I glimpsed a red envelope between the bills, addressed to Tony.

"Oh god." He paused his game and tore open the envelope to reveal a card printed with a red-nosed reindeer taking a dump in a serene conifer forest. "It's time for the Nana Canché Annual fucking fiesta."

He read the invitation in a strained falsetto. "Bring a dish to share, and come in holiday wear."

I slapped my reader shut and bounded across the room to snatch up the card. "It's addressed to Tony Canché and guest!" I crowed. "I get to meet your family. We're going, right?"

"One hundred and fifty of my relatives crammed into a rental hall?" Tony laughed, unamused. "No way."

"It sounds wonderful!" I flew to my closet and flipped through my dresses, searching for holiday wear. "I'll make my mom's Tortilla Flats," I called. "Your family'll love them!" I danced back into the living room in a long black dress festooned with enormous pink and red roses. "¡Perfecto! ¿Sí, mi amor?"

Tony killed two zombies and wrenched the joystick to the left, pursuing a third. "Why d'you want to meet my family?" he grumbled. "We're a bunch of high school dropouts. My mom had three kids when she was your age." He jerked his chin at my literature reader on the table. "She called me the other day. She's worried that you're . . . "

"White." I sighed, scowling at the reader's beige cover.

"Overeducated. I mean, Existential Literature? Come on."

Tony shot the last zombie and thrust his fist up into the air in triumph. "My family doesn't think a lot about life," he said. "We just . . . exist."

"No way am I missing a real Mexican fiesta," I retorted. "You come to all my family gatherings."

Tony rolled his eyes. "There're eight of you. We play poker with your great-grandma and your disabled kid brother. We watch John Waters movies with your moms and your grandmother. It's fun."

He looked at my downcast face and sighed. "All right. We'll go."

The last Sunday in November, we parked in a sun-drenched lot outside a rental hall in Camarillo. A tumbleweed snowman stood near a plastic crèche on the withered grass. Guitar music drifted from an open door. Children shrieked. Voices sang in harmony. I sucked in the warm corn smell of masa. "Someone's making fresh corn tortillas!" I told Tony and smoothed down my black dress.

From the passenger's seat, he handed me my blue platter, heavy with cheesy triangles topped with chopped olives that resembled little insects.

"¡Ándale!" I tried to flick the olives off the tortillas with my fingernail. "The Flats are getting cold!"

Tony climbed out of the car in torn Levi's and his ancient Bob Marley T-shirt. He sauntered around to the trunk and extracted a bottle of Redhook. "Relax." He cracked open the bottle and downed half the beer in one gulp. "I've gotta prepare."

I tapped one black velvet shoe against the hot asphalt. "No pot today. Please?"

Tony's hand froze on its way to the small pocket of his backpack—a zippered receptacle I knew to function as his own personal head shop. "How d'you expect me to survive the next two hours?" he grumbled, but he stomped after me to the hall.

Red and green streamers twisted across the vast room. At one end stood a twenty-foot buffet table, its red plastic tablecloth crowded with platters and Crock-Pots and bowls. At the other end, dozens of people circled a man who strummed a nylon-stringed guitar.

From the doorway, I gazed out upon the unfamiliar scene. Old *abuelos* reclined on metal folding chairs in faded denim and ironed cowboy shirts. They nursed Budweisers as the older women buzzed around the buffet table in their red and green pantsuits and orthopedic shoes. Little girls in red velvet dresses and gleaming Mary Janes skittered across the polished hall floor with boys in tiny suits. As I watched, this last demographic loped over to the dessert end of the buffet and fixed predatory eyes on the dishes of flan and fudge and gingerbread men.

"Oh, Jesus," Tony muttered. "Cousin Chico's playing 'De Colores.'"

"What's 'De Colores'?" I whispered.

"Some Mexican traditional crap."

"I've gotta learn it!" From where I stood, I saw sheet music making the rounds. But my platter stymied me. The cheddar cheese, which had previously oozed from golden flour tortillas, now congealed into shiny strips of orange rubber.

"Tony!" A flock of middle-aged women caught sight of my boyfriend and rushed over. "We haven't seen you in years. Who's this?"

Their eyes widened at me. I looked back at the women in their knitted reindeer and snowman sweaters, their brightly colored earrings shaped like Christmas tree lightbulbs, and shook hands all around. "*¡Hola!*" I cried. "*¡Buenos días! ¡Con mucho gusto!*"

"It's nice to meet you too, honey." Tony's four-foot-nine mother patted my hand and peered up into my face. "I don't know why you put up with my son, but we're glad you could be here."

"Nice to see you too, Mom." Tony stalked across the hall to join a group of men gathered like elk around the watering hole of a giant silver keg.

The other women regarded me warily. "So how long have you been dating Tony?" one asked.

"Where's your family?" questioned another.

"A year," I replied to the first woman. The second question I let go, unsure of the reception my mother and her girlfriend, my disabled brother, and my oversexed great-grandmother might receive from this crowd.

"So you're Tony's homegirl." A man walked up to me, looking like an older version of my boyfriend with his red eyes and lopsided smile. I recognized him from the framed photo in his parents' trailer. He shook my hand and grinned down at my wrist peeking out from under my buttoned black sleeve. "Damn, *chica*. You're white."

The men trailing him erupted with laughter. The women hid smiles behind genteel hands. Red-faced, I focused on the man's T-shirt. It read, I'M THE REASON SANTA HAS A NAUGHTY LIST.

"No offense." The guy socked me in the shoulder. "I'm Tony's big brother."

The laughter trickled off as a tall young woman walked up. "I'm Laura." She shoved the man out of the way. "It's good to meet you." She took the platter from my hands. "These look delicious. Let's put them on the buffet."

I followed her through a throng of family members, who parted respectfully. Laura wore tight Gloria Vanderbilt jeans and a knit sweater in a blue and white snowflake pattern. Her light brown hair fell across her shoulders in a gentle, perfumed perm. None of this by itself struck me as remarkable. But as she set my platter between dishes of homemade enchiladas and tamales, I stared at her.

Laura was white.

"Are you . . . are you a member of the family?" I stammered.

She rolled her eyes and nodded at Tony's brother across the room. "That *tonto*'s my boyfriend for the last ten years."

She lifted a framed photo of a sober, fat-faced woman from an overturned ramekin in the center of a nine-by-thirteen-inch pan of tamales. "Welcome to the Nana Canché clan. Nana died five years ago, but *ay dios*, her spirit lives on. Her favorite food was tamales." Laura lowered her voice. "Better learn to make 'em in a hurry."

I peered into Nana Canché's grim eyes and vowed to be worthy of her family. All that afternoon, I watched Laura as an anthropologist might study a particularly self-assured native. Her skin was as pale as mine, her foundation at least a shade lighter, and yet she chatted with Tony's elderly uncle in flawless Spanish and copied a recipe for what I learned was her famed chicken mole onto a napkin for one of the aunts. She leaned in close to the woman, who listened intently. "The secret's in buying the best dark chocolate you can afford," she revealed.

"Do Laura and your son have children?" I asked Tony's mother as she heaped food onto my plate.

"They've got two little boys." She pointed at a couple of youngsters who'd shed their coats and were busy covering mouths and starched white shirts with taquitos in red sauce.

No more information forthcoming from Tony's mother, I plied his aunts and girl cousins with questions about Laura. I learned that the women gathered at her house each Christmas Eve to make roast beef tamales because she knew which *panaderías* sold the fluffiest masa and where to find the widest corn husks.

"She can down a Tecate in less than a minute." Tony's sister gazed at Laura with admiration. "And she knows the words to every Santana song."

That afternoon, Laura became my role model and my nemesis. She'd bushwhacked her way through the jungle of her own unfortunate ethnicity and emerged into cultural clarity. I wanted to be just like her.

After the reunion, we washed dishes in the kitchen and put away leftovers. My Tortilla Flats had plastered themselves to my platter. Laura chipped them off with a spatula and moved toward the garbage can, then caught my eye. "Hey, mind if I wrap these up for my boys?" she asked. "They'll love them for lunch with guacamole."

Tony drifted in and popped a piece of fudge into my mouth. "Man, that keg's *history!*" he said.

Laura threw him a towel and pushed him toward the dish rack. "You two should come with us to the Rose Parade," she told him. "We're driving down with your parents and sister. Your cousins are meeting us there."

"The Pasadena Tournament of Roses Parade?" I cried.

"What else?"

"We'd love to! Wouldn't we, Tony?"

My boyfriend swayed slightly. He dipped an enormous wooden

spoon into a pot of his mother's Texas Hash and stuck it in his mouth. "Not really," he mumbled.

I rolled my eyes at Laura. "Of course we'll go. ¡Qué maravilloso!"

Her green lightbulb earrings swayed as she scrubbed the blue platter. "Well, I don't know how marvelous it'll be, but it's a good party."

People who merely observe the Rose Parade from the comfort of their living rooms on New Year's morning don't realize the magnitude of live-spectator preparations. On December 29, while participants busily paste petals on larger-than-life depictions of Winnie the Pooh and Abraham Lincoln, onlookers from all over the country roll up in their family Suburbans and rental RVs and shell out hundreds of dollars for parking spaces near the parade route. Armed with blankets and lawn chairs and coolers of beer, they duct tape twenty feet of prime real estate on the sidewalk lining Colorado Boulevard.

At least one member from each family remains in the designated spot at all times over the next three days, guarding against claim jumpers. The rest of the tribe hangs out in the parking lot and plays poker or drinks or ingests their drug of choice. Whole families gossip and window-shop and otherwise piss away the seventy-two hours before the parade begins.

Tony and I parked my Honda, blasting my new Santana tape, behind the RV his parents had rented. "This is gonna be so much fun!" I bounced from the car and gazed at the forest of vehicles surrounding us.

"Three solid days of hell," he muttered. But his eyebrows leaped to attention as Cousin Chico spotted him and jogged over.

"Dude, I scored some killer blow from a guy camping out in an ice cream truck," he hissed. "You gotta check this shit out. Oh. Hi, Michelle. Didn't see you."

I surveyed Chico's wild eyes and disheveled hair. "It's Melissa," I said.

"Oh. Yeah." He corralled Tony around to the back of my car. I listened to their frantic whisperings and watched three little girls kneeling in a corner of the parking lot chalking out a hopscotch court.

"My daughters." Chico strutted over to me. "You be good, *niñas*. Daddy's going shopping." He winked at Tony. "See ya in a few, *hombre*."

"Tony!" I grabbed my boyfriend's arm and peered into his face. "You're doing cocaine?"

"Shhh!" He met my eyes with the expression that would come to define our relationship—a bewildered, censorious stare to remind me that while I might possess the ability to quote Camus and Kafka at will, he'd earned an A+ in Life Skills. "It's Chico's night to guard our parade space," Tony said. "How else is he gonna stay awake?"

The door to the RV opened. Laura peered out, resplendent in a knit sweater patterned with multicolored confettilike squiggles, and large gold hoop earrings. "You made it!" she cried. Her husband pushed past her and nodded at Tony.

"You coming?"

Tony sniffed the garlic-rich air. "Mom's cooking up grub in the RV," he told me. "Why don't you hang with the women. And don't worry." He kissed me quickly. "I won't do a line. My bro's got some primo bud."

I watched the men scurry behind a Payless shoe store. RVs towered around me, wires dangling vinelike between them. Televisions squawked from open windows, and children skittered and howled in the parking lot. I gazed at them, not sure whether they were nieces and nephews or strangers.

For just a moment, I longed to be back at my mother's house, where she and her girlfriend would flip through back issues of *Bon Appetit*, tearing out recipes for every starchy side dish they could find in preparation for their prodigious New Year's meal. My grandmother and great-grandmother would select the evening's music—a conglomeration of Frank Sinatra, Neil Diamond, and John

Denver and the Muppets. Devoid of culture, my poor younger brother and sister would shovel in our mother's famous sourdough stuffing while Kermit the Frog crooned sappy ballads. My yearning for them turned abruptly to pity.

I navigated a path to Tony's parents' RV and scaled the metal steps to the door. "*¡Buenos días!*" I chirped.

Tony's mother stood at the stove frying rice. Laura, Tony's sister, and two aunts crowded around a table with a Thermos of coffee and a giant bottle of Kahlúa. "Want some?" Laura held out the tall brown bottle. I shook my head.

"Liquor in the morning puts me to sleep. But I'll take a cup of coffee."

She poured me a mug, and the aunts heaved themselves over to make room for me on the cushioned bench. "So when are you and Tony gonna have a baby?" One of the aunts leaned her dimpled arms on the sticky table and smiled at me.

I flushed. "Um . . . we're not really in a hurry."

Tony's sister nodded sagely. "I'm thirty-one, and my kid just started high school. You're getting pretty old to have children."

I studied the brown and yellow Kahlúa bottle. "Well . . . first I have to finish my master's degree," I explained.

The women exchanged a blank look. "Why?"

"So I can teach college."

"What for?" Tony's sister demanded.

Her husband worked in a warehouse. Laura's husband worked in construction. They themselves presided over receptionists' desks in medical offices five days a week, off at three to pick the kids up from school.

Suddenly, my career goal sounded silly and presumptuous. But I was saved from further humiliation by the appearance of Laura's two little boys in the doorway. "Mom, we wanna go see how they make the floats," the older one cried.

"Not without an adult," Laura said. "This is a big city. Lots of drugged-out weirdos wandering around."

"And drunks." Tony's sister uncapped the Kahlúa bottle and sloshed a dollop into Laura's coffee. "Your mom's busy right now, kids," she chuckled. "She tries to get down those stairs, she'll fall on her ass."

"Aw, Mom. Please?"

Laura looked at me. Tony's sister looked at me. The aunts looked at me. Even Tony's mom glanced sideways as she sprinkled cumin and oregano into her rice. All at once, my role in the family became clear. I saw that I could redeem my unfortunate ethnicity, my lack of culture, even my overeducation with one sentence. I stood up and took each little boy by the hand.

"Let's go see some floats."

The Rose Parade provided Tony's family with an excuse for a three-day party—a kickoff to ordinary Saturday afternoon fiestas, during which, twenty of them might congregate to drink beer and eat "'que"—thin slivers of marinated tri-tip that his brother grilled outside his apartment. "I want to go," I told my boyfriend the first time Laura called and invited us.

"You won't like it," Tony told me. "My culture's way different from yours."

I kissed him with pleading eyes and whispered in his ear. "*Tu cultura es mi cultura.*"

But within the first five minutes of our arrival at his brother's house, I began to doubt my words. At my mothers' and grandmothers' parties, men and women mingled together all over the house and yard. Male tap dancers debated Reaganomics with lesbian librarians. Hotel concierges and theater costumers played Clue and Skittles with my octogenarian great-grandmother, and so on. But at Tony's family fiestas, men and women stayed segregated.

"I want to play horseshoes," I told him one Saturday. His brother and male cousins gathered in the side yard, at either end of a long sandy court.

Tony grimaced. "The girls're in the kitchen," he said. "Maybe you could help cook."

He lobbed a horseshoe toward the iron stake. It bounced on the lawn and came to rest by my sneaker. I picked it up and hefted it wistfully. "Laura's kitchen is so small," I said. "She and your aunts are crammed in there making salsa and drinking strawberry wine coolers."

Tony glanced at his father who stood near the barbeque and watched me grimly from under his straw hat. "Tell you what." He took the horseshoe from me and tossed it across the lawn to his brother. "I'll come in and hang out with the women. I'll even drink wine coolers."

I shook his hands off my shoulders. "I'll be fine," I said, aware of what it would look like to enter the culinary sanctuary on the arm of a male escort. "Laura's waiting for me to help with the guacamole, anyway."

"Good girl." Tony swatted my butt as I shuffled into the house, shoulders hunched under my lie.

The truth was that Laura never asked me to cook. None of the women in his family did. Upon hearing my request to bring a dish to a party, they'd say vaguely, "Oh, just bring a bag of tortilla chips."

Still, I approached the kitchen and stuck my head in between the aunts. "Can I help make salsa?"

Laura appraised me. "Ever chop jalapeños? It's tricky. You can't touch your mouth or eyes for days. Anyhow," she pointed to a heaping bowl of tomatoes, peppers, and onions on the table, "the salsa's made."

I gazed at the bowls of rice, beans, salad, the bag of tortilla chips I'd brought. "I could warm tortillas on the *comal* . . ."

If Laura and the aunts were impressed by my intimacy with the flat metal disc that fit over a stove-burner, they didn't reveal their admiration. "Done already." Tony's sister nodded at the napkin-covered basket on the counter. "Want a wine cooler?" she asked. "Make yourself comfortable. There's a *Los Angeles Times* in the living room."

I took the bottle she handed me, but left it unopened on a coaster beside the newspaper. I studied the walls of family photos, then wandered into the little boys' room.

"Aunt Melissa!" The kids looked up from their toy-littered carpet. "Wanna play Lincoln Logs?" I sighed. "Why not?"

We moved to the ranch. After two years there, I gained the wisdom to stay in the trailer and clean and bake cakes. I became a model aunt, making homemade birthday cards, tutoring math, and baby-sitting gratis. I thought of the children—the sweet, feisty toddlers and first-graders, the grinning, spit-chinned babies—when I opened the enormous package I'd requested from my grandmother and dressed for my second Nana Canché Annual Holiday Reunion.

"Don't forget the casserole dish!" I called to Tony as I hoisted myself awkwardly out of the passenger's seat the last Sunday in November. I cocked one ear toward the rental hall. "They're singing 'De Colores.' Hurry!"

I waddled toward the door. Inside, 150 family members in cowboy shirts and pantsuits and velvet dresses and witty T-shirts gathered around Cousin Chico's guitar to sing. "¡Y por eso los grandes amores de muchos colores me gustan a mí!"

But the message of love for all colors of the world apparently did not extend to green. As the song lilted from my lips in the vibrato I'd picked up during my brief stint as an opera major, 150 pairs of eyes swiveled toward me and widened in shock. Chico's fingers froze on the guitar strings. Tony's father glared. Beside him, Laura glanced at Tony's mother and slowly shook her head.

At last, his brother broke the spell. "¡Ora pues! She's dressed like a freakin' Christmas tree!"

A giant cone of green fake fur swathed me from head to toe. Plastic gold tinsel crisscrossed up my sides to accessorize with the gold cardboard star that I'd glued to Tony's bike beanie and now balanced on my head. Miniature red and white candy canes dangled from tiny green loops of thread I'd painstakingly sewed onto the fur. I'd hoped my costume would add levity to the reunion, confirming my place as the family jokester. But nobody laughed.

"Hey, will you take this?" Tony thrust the casserole dish into my hand and made a beeline for the keg at the back of the room as Laura's oldest son leaped up from his chair.

"Aunt Melissa's got candy!" he cried. A crowd of children rushed toward me, their fingers opening and closing like the pinchers on tiny crabs. I stood rigid as they ripped the candy canes from my fur.

"Look at you," Laura said stiffly as she ministered to her squalling younger son, who hadn't been fast enough to reap the benefit of my branches. "You're gonna upstage Santa."

Dismayed, I gazed at her white sweater embroidered with tiny holly leaves and berries. "Did I do something wrong?" I asked.

"The family thinks you're making fun of their party," she whispered. "Holiday wear doesn't extend to silly costumes."

I held out my casserole in defense. "Tamale Pie," I said. "*Sunset* magazine says it's out of this world!"

"Put it on the buffet," Laura said shortly and walked back to the circle of relatives.

I lumbered over to the table and placed my casserole beside the pan of tamales. Nana Canché glared at my offering from the confines of her framed photo atop the ramekin. I reached up to touch my gold star. It tumbled into a Crock-Pot of beans. "Shit," I muttered.

Tony appeared at my side. "The grub looks good this year."

"You always say that." I fished my star out of the pot and tossed it into the trash can. "I'm dying in this stupid costume," I groaned. "It's a hundred degrees in here."

He grabbed a plate and scooped up two of Laura's tamales. "So take it off."

But I couldn't deforest, as it were. I'd forgotten my jeans and sweater at home. "I'm naked except for my underwear," I hissed. Not just naked, but painted. In an effort to depict tree limbs, I'd slathered my arms and bare feet with brown tempera. My face glowed brown, as well. The chemical smell of paint curdled my stomach and burned my eyes.

Tony shrugged. "Looks like you're screwed."

He's right, I thought. On the other side of the hall, his family sang and gossiped and cast bewildered glances in my direction. The children hovered around a vacant red throne, awaiting Santa's arrival. Out a side door, I saw Tony's brother getting suited up and stoned in preparation for his jolly entrance. Cousin Chico walked past me, guitar strapped to his chest.

"*¡Hola!*" I touched his arm. "I did an English translation of 'De Colores,' and I want to run it by you," I told him.

Chico turned away from me and loaded his plate with tamales. "Sorry, Michelle, but I can't take you seriously in that getup."

I fled to the kitchen and attempted to redeem myself by washing dishes. Laura reached across me for a towel, and her jingle-bell bracelet caught on my fur. "*Ay dios*," she muttered, bending to extract herself from me. "Maybe you should go help Santa pass out presents."

I returned to the main hall to find a tangle of children surrounding Tony's brother and his bag of plastic dolls and water guns. Their parents gathered close, exclaiming over the gifts. My boyfriend, meanwhile, had slipped out the side door. When I caught sight of him, his fingers were already unzipping the small pocket of his backpack.

Stomach churning, I made my way to the hall's tiny bathroom and locked the door. At the sink, I thrust a giant wad of paper towels under hot water. Then, avoiding my bloodshot eyes in the mirror, I scrubbed the brown paint from my face.

TAMALES

Locate the *panadería* that carries the fluffiest masa. Buy a pound. Ask the owner—in Spanish, *ay dios*—where to buy the widest cornhusks. Pick up a package of at least twenty-four husks, and while you're at it, grab a pound of roast beef.

Back home, crank up Santana on your sound system and tie an apron over your snowflake-patterned sweater. Boil the roast beef in water until you can shred it with a fork. Pour a thirty-six-ounce can of red enchilada sauce into a soup pot. Radiate confidence as you add a tablespoon each of chili powder, cumin, and oregano, two teaspoons of salt, and a bay leaf. Heat to a simmer and shred beef into this mixture. Keep heat on low.

Pour a shot of Kahlúa into your coffee, and place cornhusks in a sink of warm water to soak. When they are pliable, choose the widest, and lay it out on a plate. Spread about two tablespoons of masa on the husk, leaving an inch-wide space all around and two inches of space at the bottom. (Surreptitiously ask someone which end is the bottom.)

Drop a generous tablespoon of the roast beef mixture from a slotted spoon onto the center of the spread masa, and top with a black olive. Add a few cubes of cheese. Now it's time to wrap the tamales. Knowing that your entire reputation hinges on how well you can perform this task, begin by folding the two long edges toward one another. Fold the bottom edge up. Your goal is to create a neat three- to four-inch-wide package. Secure it with a quarter-inch-wide strip of corn husk, tying it around the tamale with a festive little bow.

When you have finished assembling the tamales, stack them vertically in a steamer basket, in a large pot of boiling water. Savvy cooks know that to keep the masa moist, you must place a tea towel on top of the tamales and the lid on top of that. Steam them for the time it takes to learn the words to "De Colores," at least an hour, then check to see if the masa has thoroughly cooked. Lift one tamale from the pot, and cut off a small piece of masa. It should be fluffy and cooked through. Depending on the masa, you may need to put on another Santana CD and pour another cup of Kahlúa-laced coffee.

Serve with rice, beans, and Killer Salsa.

16 •

CITIZENS OF THE WORLD

UPON GRADUATING FROM COLLEGE AND SEPARATING FROM MY boyfriend, I almost went to Spain without my mother—an injustice that would have haunted me forever. At twenty-one, I longed to see the world and discover my place in it. Unsure of how to pay for travel with student loans due, I signed up for an all-expenses-paid week near Mexico City.

"All I have to do is take this new diarrhea medication they're testing," I told my mother, "and the researchers will cover my hotel and food and everything!"

She looked at me over her kitchen counter and put down her coffee cup. "You're not going down there to be someone's guinea pig," she told me. "What if the pills are poison?"

I stirred a packet of hot chocolate into a cup of her diesel fuel Yuban and shrugged. "Half the people in the group get a placebo. I'll probably get a free trip for taking a sugar pill."

My mother folded her arms and regarded me with the look she usually saved for my brother's petty coin theft and cursing transgressions. "You are not going to Mexico so some company can test its drug," she said.

"But I already bought a ticket," I wailed. "I've got to use it within a year. You know, Mother, I'm an adult now. If I want to travel, I'm going to travel."

My eye fell on the bookshelf behind her and settled on Cervantes. I recalled the Spanish classes we'd taken together when I was a little girl and thought of her love for Don Quixote. "I could change my ticket and go to Spain instead," I said, "and you could come with me."

At once, my mother's expression changed. She raised her eyebrows and smiled with delight. "Will we go on a tour?" she asked. The year before, she and Annie had trotted around Italy on a ten-day Trafalgar tour without a moment's consternation or autonomy.

I shook my head. "No tours. I want to assimilate into Spanish culture completely. People won't even know we're American."

She regarded my brown curls and blue eyes. "You're joking, right?"

I wasn't. I'd seen *Cinema Paradiso* three times, and so I knew that Spanish girls could be fair-skinned and blue-eyed. "I've got a good accent, thanks to Rose and her family," I told my mother. "We'll pass."

The next day, I produced a thick tome whose cover depicted an ancient clock tower over a charmingly narrow European street. "This is Rick Steves' *Europe through the Back Door*," I said to my mother. "He teaches readers to avoid tourist traps and experience the real country and its people. He'll show us how to blend in."

"Well, I don't know." She polished her espresso machine, purchased after her Italian adventure. "A tour is just fine with me. If you get lost or have a question, the guide is always there to help."

"We won't need one," I promised her. "We'll live for a week as if we're local to Madrid."

I couldn't be a lesbian, and I couldn't be a Mexican, but perhaps I could still be Spanish. I held the book aloft and thumped it with evangelical fervor. "*Mi madre*," I said, "We're going to be citizens of the world!"

As our Boeing 757 descended beneath the clouds and floated over wide fields of whirling white wind turbines, my mother and I squeezed each other's hands with tears in our eyes. We'd lived apart all the years of my adolescence, but now, as adults, we would share the trip of a lifetime, and it would be perfect.

"The Prado!" I breathed.

"Cervantes," she whispered.

"*Jamón serrano!*" I cried.

We got off the plane, and I successfully navigated the Spanish signs leading to the airport baggage claim. We shouldered our backpacks and walked outside. "The bus is supposed to pick people up right here." I pointed to a curb to the left of the glass doors. "But I don't see any signage."

"And I don't see any bus," my mother said after we'd stood for half an hour. "Let's just take a taxi."

I nodded and flagged down a cab. "Puerta del Sol," I told the driver. "*Por favor.*"

He stepped on the gas and sped us into downtown Madrid. My mother and I craned our necks to peer out the smudged windows at dirty office buildings and traffic-clogged streets. "This is Spain?" she said.

"*Sí, señora.*" Our driver left us and our backpacks on one of the crowded streets and pointed to a mirrored building. "Del Sol," he said.

I handed him several pesetas, and he pulled away. My mother and I looked around. "This doesn't seem like the town square," I said, "and I don't see the Hotel Europa anywhere."

We staggered a few blocks with our backpacks, searching for our hotel, and found ourselves in front of the mirrored building once more. Reluctantly, I pulled out my guidebook, hiding it from pedestrians with my arm lest they discover I wasn't a local. "I have no idea where we are," I confessed.

My mother headed for the office door. "I'm going to go ask someone," she said.

"No, don't do that!" I ran after her and burst into the building in time to hear a svelte dark-haired beauty behind a desk begin to laugh. "This is *Oficina* del Sol," she said in flawless English. "We produce light fixtures. You want to take the Metro downtown. The stop is three blocks west of here."

My mother nodded and shifted her feet in her thin-soled Payless sneakers. "Thank you," she said and mustered up a worried smile in my direction. "Looks like we're going for a hike."

"*Muchas gracias,*" I said loudly, mortified that the woman had spoken to us in English instead of her native tongue.

We found the Metro sign and descended the stairs, figured out which line we needed to take, and stood on the platform with dozens of other people to wait. Beside us, another couple hunched under the weight of their backpacks. I recognized the book in the woman's hand. *Europe through the Back Door.*

Smugly, I nudged my mother's arm. "Everyone'll know they're tourists," I whispered, proud that my guidebook remained in my backpack.

Our train rushed up, and a wave of people pushed toward the door. Suddenly, five ragged men leaped onto the platform, yelling and jostling each other. Two of them shouted and tore into my pack. Three others ransacked the bags of the couple beside us. My guidebook fell to the ground, and I snatched it up.

"What the . . . ?" My mother turned on them, teeth bared, and held her backpack to her chest. "Stop it right now!"

I yanked my mother off the train and flipped to the last pages of my book, then screamed the one word Rick Steves guaranteed would stop any thief.

"¡Policía!"

Instantly, the men vanished into the bowels of the Metro station. The train sped away, leaving my mother and me alone and trembling beside the track. "This doesn't bode well," she said in small voice, checking her pack's small pockets. "I think they got my toothbrush."

"They took my travel clothesline." I glowered at the men, who had already begun to reappear in doorways, watching us with predatory eyes. "I forgot that backpacks brand us as tourists," I explained, more confident than I felt. "Wear it in front, so you can keep an eye on it at all times, and we'll ditch the packs at the hotel. Don't worry about the *gitanos, Mamá.*" I swiveled my bag around to my chest. "They're just poor and desperate."

She struggled to balance her pack against her ample bosom, nearly toppling onto the track in the process. "I feel like a turtle with my shell on backward," she grumbled.

The alarm sounded the approach of the next train. I planted my sensible walking shoes into the cement and stared the men down, envisioning myself a steely Mafia wife. They left us alone this time, and we found ourselves safely on our way to Puerta del Sol.

As we rode the Metro, I reflected on the upcoming week. After my parents' divorce, I'd rarely spent seven consecutive days with my mother, and never in another country. Would we get along, or would we tire of each other and go off, as Rick Steves suggested, on separate expeditions?

We disembarked at the crowded square and found the Hotel Europa, stepping across its white tile floor and into a cavernous fluorescent-lit lobby. A Muzak rendition of Bizet's *Carmen* whined over the sound system. Three young men in pastel dress shirts stood behind the counter.

"*Hola,*" I said. "*Mi madre y yo tenemos reservas.*"

"That's cool," one of them told me.

Affronted, I pretended not to understand. "*No fumar, por favor*," I said and affected a broken English accent. "No . . . smoking . . . room."

He and the other men shot each other knowing looks. "Americans," he said.

The youngest of the men led us up the elevator to a tiny room with two beds, grinning at me the entire time. "Where are you from in America?" he asked carefully.

"Oxnard," I snapped. "*Gracias, señor*," I added and tipped him two pesetas.

"He likes you." My mother flopped down on one bed and smirked. "I'll bet he asks you out."

"Mother," I groaned. "He's way too short."

For a moment, I could've been any daughter who'd grown up with her mother, cheerfully fending off maternal attempts at matchmaking. I resisted the urge to throw a pillow at her and went to the mirror, smiling.

"What do the locals do for dinner?" she asked.

"A tapas crawl," I said over the blow-dryer as I straightened my bangs with a round brush. "We're supposed to wander through city bars, sampling house wines and local cheese and sausage."

My mother yawned, noticeably exhausted. "Tomorrow," she begged. "Tonight I just need a cup of coffee and some sleep."

"*Ay, Mamá*," I said. "It's only six o'clock. We'll sleep when we're dead."

She shot me a look, unamused. "Feel free to go do your tapas crawl without me," she said.

My need for authenticity battled my need for my mother's and my trip to be perfect. The latter won out. We ended up in Hotel Europa's outdoor café. An incessant parade of people strolled past the tables on their way to the square. "*Buenas noches*," I said to the black-coated waiter. "*Dos menús en español, para la cena.*"

"For *dinner?*" The man did a double-take, but brought us two Spanish menus and begrudgingly flicked a white cloth across our metal table.

"Coffee?" my mother asked.

He nodded curtly and stalked off.

"He's surprised we want dinner so early," I whispered to my mother. "Most people in Madrid don't eat until eleven or midnight."

The white cloth glowed incongruous in a sea of metal tables. I glanced sidelong at a woman and three children sharing hot chocolate and churros near us. They were slender, chic, beautifully dressed—unmistakably Spanish. They would never order dinner at such an uncouth hour. Embarrassment flamed my face. But my stomach growled audibly and I turned my attention to the unintelligible menu.

"I'll order for both of us," I assured my mother, who sat surveying her menu with a small, delighted smile.

"Yes, miss?" Our waiter clattered a cup of coffee onto the table and regarded me with his notepad poised. "What would you like?"

The woman and her children seemed to wait for my order, as well. From her table, she pursed her lips and appraised the red silk scarf I'd tied at a jaunty angle around the neck of my dark T-shirt.

The accessory, suggested by Rick Steves and so European in my home mirror, felt suddenly and inexplicably nooselike. What made me think I could be anything but a provincial white girl undone by the lack of tacos and chiles rellenos on a dinner menu?

I shrugged off my angst. *"Por favor,"* I said, rolling the *r* imperiously. *"Dos tintos, y dos mixtos."*

Our waiter shrugged and vanished into the kitchen. The woman smiled and turned back to her children and their churros.

"What are we getting?" My mother clasped her hands on the tablecloth, eyes shining. "Gazpacho? Paella? Sangria?"

I shook my head. I'd ordered the only two items on the menu whose ingredients I recognized, whose names I could pronounce. "We're getting two glasses of red wine," I told her. "And ham and cheese sandwiches."

Each morning, I woke up with the luxury of knowing that I'd get to be with my mother in Spain, but my inability to navigate language and landmarks in Madrid complicated our vacation. For three days, we wandered through crowds, searching for nonexistent signage and pulling over periodically to consult the guidebook I insisted on keeping hidden.

"How cheery." My mother lifted one foot and then the other in the manner of a beleaguered horse. We'd bolted espresso and ham and cheese—again—at Hotel Europa's café that morning and hurried out the door to avoid the tourist rush, but it took us an hour to find the Palacio Real. Now it loomed in front of us like a giant wedding cake. School children in yellow T-shirts flocked across its courtyard. Couples in sensible walking shoes—the women with bright scarves at their necks—consulted their guidebooks and aimed cameras at the palace.

My mother nudged me as we joined the long line of people waiting to go inside. "Lots of people have that Rick Steves book," she said.

"It's because he shows you how to see Europe through the back door!" I reminded her, but when we finally found ourselves herded down the narrow corridors of the palace—toe to heel with the crowd—and attempted to look out a door at ancient statuary tossed like refuse on the back lawn, a man in uniform barred the way with his hamlike forearms.

"*No entrar,*" he growled.

"*¿Por favor?*" I entreated, composing my face into an expression of cool Spanish nonchalance.

The guard scowled and jerked his chin toward the rest of the herd. "*No pueden entrar,*" he repeated. "*Son turistas, no?*"

"He's saying we're tourists. What does that even mean?" I grumbled and marched my mother past the gift shop at the end of the palace. "Citizens of the world don't need a bottle opener in the shape of King Philip."

She collapsed on a bench outside the palace and stared pointedly at a small restaurant. "What time do Spaniards eat lunch?"

"Locals like to pick up ingredients for a picnic at a little market and eat in the park." I pointed at a wide, treed space overrun with yellow T-shirts and their young inmates. "But we need to get to the Prado, and after that, Retiro Park. On our way back to the hotel, we'll pick up tickets to the opera and grab tapas at a bar. We missed sunrise at the Alcalá Gate. We'll have to see it tomorrow."

My mother raised a mild eyebrow. "What's Rick Steves say about taking time to enjoy a cup of espresso?"

"This isn't Italy." I stood up and helped her to her feet. "Spaniards just gulp it and go."

We stumbled upon the Prado after two hours of searching and hauled ourselves past El Grecos and Velázquezes, gazing blearily at Tintorettos on loan from Venice before setting out for Retiro Park. "*Retiro* means retreat!" I chirped to my mother. "We can sit in the shade and take a siesta, if we ever find the damned place."

"Coffee," she said faintly behind me, and then, "Maybe we should ask someone for directions."

"*Mother*. You know we can find it ourselves."

I saw then that we didn't really know each other. I'd underestimated her love of serene relaxation, and she'd underestimated my stubborn determination to see the entire city while masquerading as a native Spaniard as an abundance of youthful energy. Still, we plodded on.

At last, I spotted the magnificent iron gates and led her to a verdant expanse dotted with couples making out in soft-porn poses on benches and patches of sunny lawn. "This park features a statue of Alfonso the

Twelfth," I recited and marched toward a lake flanked by an imposing ancient structure composed of Roman columns surrounding a mammoth statue of a man on a horse.

We walked up the marble steps, trying to avoid looking at couples who necked beside the statuary. I thought of Tony, back in his Oxnard apartment, and wondered if he'd found himself a Latina girlfriend with whom he could smoke pot—a girlfriend his father adored.

I was saved from gloomy meditations on our breakup when a cat appeared—a calico blur that skittered across the stairs and vanished behind a bronze depiction of a nude woman astride a giant fish. "There's another one!" I pointed to a tiny white ball of fluff that popped out from behind a sculpture of a sulky loinclothed toddler riding a lion. "The guidebook didn't say anything about cats in Retiro Park."

A stern-faced, gray-haired *señora* stalked up, clutching a department store shopping bag. Suddenly, a dozen cats materialized and attached themselves to her support hose. She ignored them and headed for a statue of a toga-clad figure reading a book. I watched as she climbed the pedestal and braced her orthopedic shoes against the marble. One wrinkled hand plunged into the bag.

"What's she got?" I whispered to my mother, who shook her head.

"More cats?" she suggested wearily.

Felines leaped onto the statue's feet as the woman hauled up a fistful of bloody organ meat and slapped it onto the marble. At once, the cats set upon it, growling and whacking each other in the face with their paws.

The woman hopped down and moved to the lion statue to offer up more carnage. A cluster of cats plunged their muzzles into piles of livers and kidneys. A couple in tennis shoes and matching Museo del Jamón T-shirts consulted their guidebook, shot the woman a disgusted look, and moved on.

My mother gazed longingly across the lake at a brightly lit café, and so only I saw the old woman for what she really was—my back door entry into the real Spain.

I approached her. "*¿Los gatos tienen nombres, señora?*" I asked, pointing at the cats.

The woman flicked dark eyes in my direction. "Of course they have names," she snapped in English. "How else could I tell them apart?"

A gentle hand touched my arm. "An expatriate," my mother said. "You could be one of those, Lissa. Now, how about a café mocha?" Her eyes pleaded with mine. "I'll buy . . ."

"All right," I sighed and left the woman and her cats.

We stood at the stainless steel counter in one of Retiro Park's cafés and ordered. But café mocha did not appear on the menu. "*Un café exprés para mi mamá,*" I told the waitress, "*y un chocolate para mi.*"

My mother clucked her tongue against her teeth. "You know, honey," she said, "I can order for myself."

I shook my head. "You get better service if you speak Spanish. I don't mind ordering for both of us. Should we just stand up and drink like the locals do? We'll have to pay extra if we sit."

She moved to a small table and collapsed in a metal chair. "I'll pay the extra."

The waitress set a deep white mug of hot chocolate in front of me. A tiny silver spoon floated on the thick brown liquid. "It looks like pudding," my mother observed. "Not at all like the Ibarra chocolate I made for you when you were little."

For an instant, I longed for the relative simplicity of my childhood. I thought of how, on chilly weekend afternoons, my mother and I had sipped hot chocolate and practiced Spanish vocabulary with our flash cards.

But then I took a drink from the white mug in front of me and nearly swooned. How had I not discovered Spanish hot chocolate until this moment? "This . . ." I waved my spoon for emphasis, "is the drink of gods."

"The coffee's delicious, too." My mother savored a mouthful. "Do you think we might fit some more café stops like this into our itinerary? It feels like we're seeing the real Spain when we slow down for a few minutes."

"I'm not sure." I looked down at my notes and my guidebook. "We bought the three-museum pass. We've seen the Prado, but we've still got to see the Thyssen and go to the opera and do a tapas crawl. And we need to see the Alcalá Gate, and the Reina Sofía museum. Picasso's *Guernica* is there," I said in the tone she'd once used to bribe me with ice cream if I ate all my liver and onions.

She persisted. "But doesn't it feel good just to sit for a few minutes and enjoy a drink, sweetheart?"

"We don't have time!" I wailed.

This is how we'd always done things, packing movies and beach outings and trips to Monterey into a weekend. There was never enough time for my mother and me.

She sighed, drained her mug, and stood up. "Let's go."

But once again, we got lost. "I think we go this way." I peered down at my book. "Reina Sofía's right around here someplace."

My mother limped behind me on her tennis shoes. "Let's ask that couple walking toward us. They look nice."

"No need. My map says it's right around the corner. *Vámonos, Mamá.*"

We hurried past the man and woman and rounded the corner to find no museum—just a Dumpster, and beyond that a frenetic street devoid of any mention of the Reina Sofía.

Now my mother faced me. "What do you suggest we do now?" she asked, the words wrenched from her lips reluctantly, but firmly.

My feet ached. My head pounded. Frustration writhed in my chest. "I can't do this all myself!" I yelled.

My mother took a step backward. Shock constricted her face.

Incensed, I threw my guidebook down on the cement. "I need some help!" I cried. "I've been doing all the talking, all the navigating." I glared at her with sudden fury. "Can't you do anything?"

She surveyed me through inscrutable blue eyes. Then she walked swiftly down the street toward the couple. "*Por favor,*" I heard her say in an authentic Spanish accent. "*¿Dónde está la Reina Sofía?*"

She nodded at the couple's words and walked back to me. "It's across the street, just behind the Atocha train station. This way," she said and marched off.

Sullen, I slunk after her as she crossed the teeming street. "You could've told me you still know Spanish," I muttered.

She reached into her purse and produced the pack of cream-colored Spanish flash cards from our classes long ago. "It's okay." She patted my arm. "I knew you wanted to play tour guide. But honey . . ." She paused in the museum's courtyard to deliver her infuriating verdict. "We *are* tourists."

"We're not!" I said as we entered the museum. "We're citizens of the world."

I turned and began to walk. She pointed in the opposite direction. "Picasso's that way," she said.

I stomped after her to the crowded gallery. We stood at opposite ends of Pablo's apocryphal canvas *Guernica* and glared at each other across the heads of rapt art aficionados and dutifully awestruck tourists. "You need to stop trying to take care of me!" she hissed.

I bared my teeth like the rearing, wild-eyed stallion in the painting. I longed to be taken care of, but I'd forgotten how to be dependent, how to rely on anyone but myself. "You need me," I retorted. "You'll never get back to the hotel without this." I raised my guidebook in victory.

My mother plunged one hand into her day pack and produced a map. "Downtown Madrid." She paused to let her next words sink in. "I got it at the *Tourist* Information station."

That word. I cringed and looked around to see if the locals had noticed. The men and women clustering the floors of the Reina Sofía museum appeared oblivious, chatting and laughing in their Armani and Chanel and suede high-heeled boots. Only my mother registered my horror. She lifted her chin. "I'll meet you by Picasso's *Woman's Head* in an hour," she snapped.

"It's called *Cabeza de Mujer*," I shot back, but she'd turned on the heel of one sneaker and walked off.

Abandoned, I stared at the left corner of Picasso's "Guernica." A woman knelt—head stretched back and howling—over the body of her dead baby, victim of a Spanish Civil War bomb. I clutched my guidebook to my chest and closed my eyes.

When I was a child, my mother and I had learned to love Spanish culture together. We'd studied the language at the local library, our voices merging into one at the wide brown table. *La nariz*. The nose. *La boca*. The mouth. And my favorite, *la oreja*. The ear.

I knew now that my mother and I were foreign to one another. How could I truly know her, how could she know me, separated as we had been for so long?

I resolved to spend the rest of our vacation in any manner she chose, even if it meant sitting in a café all day. On our last morning, at her suggestion, we rode a double-decker tourist bus through the city streets. Headphones gave a running English commentary on the city's landmarks. When raindrops began to spatter our heads, the rest of the passengers retreated to the bus's lower level. But my mother unfurled her umbrella. "Isn't this fun!" she cried as a finger of lightning shot down to split the blue-black sky over the National Library. "I'll bet Rick Steves never sits atop a tour bus in an electrical storm!"

Thunder grumbled around us. I let the rain run down over my head and into my eyes. I had to admit that it *was* fun.

That afternoon, we filed onto another large air-conditioned bus with two dozen other tourists. Our guide quipped in English and told us what to expect from our trip to the Valley of the Fallen. "It's a memorial built for soldiers who died in the Spanish Civil War," he droned into his microphone, brushing back his glossy black hair. "A series of underground tombs that end in a chapel where General Francisco Franco lies buried."

Solemnly, we filed past the imposing white cross mounted on the hill beside the memorial before walking into a long, dimly lit corridor. I stumbled past tombs, berating myself silently. My mother and I had gone on the trip of a lifetime, and I'd nearly ruined it with my inability to hear her. Why hadn't I asked what she'd like to do and see? Why hadn't I stopped for espresso more often? Why had I been such a dictator?

I stopped at Franco's austere marble tomb and stared down at the memorial plaque. "Dude," I whispered, "you need to lighten up."

Our plane left Madrid at five the next morning. In the chilly predawn, I stuffed clothes into my backpack. With my box of marzipan and my T-shirt printed with Goya's fighting cats, I couldn't zip my pack. I looked down at the guidebook in my hand. Its pages were lovingly dog-eared, the front cover creased and dirty from when I'd hurled it onto the sidewalk. Resisting the urge to place a tender kiss on its cover, I dropped it into the bureau and closed the drawer.

My mother and I boarded the plane and slept most of the way back to Los Angeles. We took the shuttle to Oxnard and parted at her front door. Annie walked out and embraced us. "Welcome home!" she cried.

I wished that Oxnard felt like home. I thought of how Kenny, my baby sitter from long ago, had taught me the words *"Oxnard es mi hogar."* Once, before my father had taken me back, they might have been true. But I knew, as I watched my mother and Annie walk through their front door hand in hand, that in spite of my love for the town, I still hadn't found a place to call home.

Glumly, I drove north to the apartment I'd taken in Santa Barbara. My mother and I didn't talk for several weeks. Depression overwhelmed me. Our trip to Spain had been a disaster, and it was all my fault.

One afternoon following work, I got home to find a message on my answering machine. "Honey, I'm sorry I was so fatigued on our trip," my mother said tentatively. "The jet lag really got to me. I found a recipe for Spanish hot chocolate, and I thought you'd want it." She recited the ingredients quickly, before the tape ran out. I scribbled them down on the back of an envelope. Cocoa, sugar, milk, cornstarch.

"Cornstarch. So that's how they get it so thick," I murmured, stirring the mixture in my saucepan until it resembled pudding. I poured it into a white mug, sat at my kitchen table with my cat purring on my lap, and sipped the drink. All at once the memories of my mother's and my trip to Madrid flooded back.

It wasn't the vacation we'd hoped for, nothing close to ideal. Men stole from us. We lost our way so many times. We made mistakes and argued and misjudged and wept in frustration over how the most meticulously-planned itinerary can go awry.

But we traveled.

I reached for the phone and dialed my mother's number. "*Mamá*," I said when she picked up. "I just called to say . . . *muchas gracias*."

SPANISH HOT CHOCOLATE

Begin with a healthy dose of remorse. Add a quarter cup of unsweetened cocoa and half a cup of white sugar to a saucepan. In a small bowl, stir a tablespoon of cornstarch into a quarter cup of water until it dissolves with your fantasies of a perfect vacation in Madrid. Pour it into the saucepan, and stir until mixture is smooth.

Warm over medium-low heat. Slowly pour in two cups of milk, allowing yourself to reflect on deceased dictators as you gently whisk out lumps. Allow mixture to simmer for about ten minutes. The cocoa is ready when it resembles chocolate pudding. Serve with humility and a tiny silver spoon.

ABOUT THE AUTHOR

Melissa Hart teaches journalism at the University of Oregon and memoir writing for UC Berkeley's online extension program. Her essays have appeared in *The Washington Post*, *Los Angeles Times*, *The Advocate*, *Fourth Genre*, and *High Country News*. Hart is a contributing editor to *The Writer Magazine*. She lives in Oregon with her husband, photographer Jonathan B. Smith, and their daughter, Maia. www.melissahart.com.

Acknowledgments

This is my favorite part of this book—those pages on which I get to express, in print, my gratitude to all who inspired *Gringa* and brought it to fruition.

Many thanks to Michelle Andelman, formerly of Andrea Brown Literary Agency, who saw the potential of my story and helped me to shape it as narrative. I'm deeply grateful to Brooke Warner, my talented editor at Seal, for believing in this book and helping me to understand where it fits into the growing body of literature by children of LGBT parents. And to my publicist, Andie East, for her advice about blogging and Facebook. I also wish to thank the members of COLAGE, my fellow queerspawn, and in particular, Abigail Garner, whose work is much appreciated.

I could not have written the early drafts of these stories without the generous feedback I received from Kathryn Steadman and Amanda Smith-Hatch. I'm indebted to you for your honesty, your insight, and your willingness to meet at Full City for chocolate lattes and birthday cakes with that really annoying musical candle. I am grateful to the Center for the Study of Women in Society at the University of Oregon for a grant that allowed me to work on this book for a full summer.

The members of my family will inevitably remember parts of this story differently, but one thing we'll agree on—in spite of our challenges, we shared a great deal of love and a great deal of music in that VW bus.

My deepest gratitude goes to my husband, Jonathan. You are ever my inspiration, and ever my beloved. Thank you.

SELECTED TITLES FROM SEAL PRESS

The Chelsea Whistle: A Memoir, by Michelle Tea. $15.95, 1-58005-239-8. In this gritty, confessional memoir, Michelle Tea takes the reader back to the city of her childhood: Chelsea, Massachusetts—Boston's ugly, scrappy little sister and a place where time and hope are spent on things not getting any worse.

Bento Box In the Heartland: My Japanese Girlhood in Whitebread America, by Linda Furiya. $15.95, 1-58005-191-X. A uniquely American story about girlhood, identity, assimilation—and the love of homemade food.

Lesbian Couples: A Guide to Creating Healthy Relationships, by D. Merilee Clunis and G. Dorsey Green. $16.95, 1-58005-131-6. Drawing from a decade of research, this helpful and readable resource covers topics from conflict-resolution to commitment ceremonies, using a variety of examples and problem-solving techniques.

Real Girl Real World: A Guide to Finding Your True Self, by Heather M. Gray and Samantha Phillips. $15.95, 1-58005-133-2. In this fun and essential guide, real girls share their experiences, showing that there's no one "right" way to navigate the twisting road of adolescence.

Waking Up American: Coming of Age Biculturally, edited by Angela Jane Fountas. $15.95, 1-58005-136-7. Twenty-two original essays by first-generation women caught between two worlds. Countries of origin include the Philippines, Germany, India, Mexico, China, Iran, Nicaragua, Japan, Russia, and Panama.

Different Daughters: A History of the Daughters of Bilitis and the Birth of the Lesbian Civil Rights Movement, by Marcia M. Gallo. $15.99, 1-58005-252-5. The story of the world's first organization committed to lesbian visibility and empowerment, and the foundation of today's lesbian rights movement.